outlines

Medical-Surgical Nursing

Medical-Surgical Nursing

James Keogh, R.N.

Instructor, New York University

Schaum's Outline Series

New York   Chicago   San Francisco   Lisbon   London   Madrid
Mexico City   Milan   New Delhi   San Juan   Seoul
Singapore   Sydney   Toronto

JIM KEOGH is a registered nurse and has written *Schaum's Outline of Pharmacology, Schaum's Outline of Nursing Laboratory and Diagnostic Tests, Schaum's Outline of Medical Charting*, and co-authored *Schaum's Outline of ECG Interpretation*. His books can be found in leading university libraries including Yale University School of Medicine, University of Pennsylvania Biomedical Library, Columbia University, Brown University, University of Medicine and Dentistry of New Jersey, Cambridge University, and Oxford University. Jim Keogh, RN, AAS, MBA, is a former member of the faculty at Columbia University and is a member of the faculty of New York University.

Schaum's Outline of
Medical-Surgical Nursing

Copyright © 2012 by The McGraw-Hill Companies, Inc. All rights reserved. Printed in the United States of America. Except as permitted under the United States Copyright Act of 1976, no part of this publication may be reproduced or distributed in any form or by any means, or stored in a database or retrieval system, without the prior written permission of the publisher.

1 2 3 4 5 6 7 8 9 10 11 12 13 14 15   QDB/ QDB   1 9 8 7 6 5 4 3 2 1

ISBN   978-0-07-162505-0
MHID   0-07-162505-4

e-ISBN   978-0-07-162506-7
e-MHID   0-07-162506-2

Library of Congress Cataloging-in-Publication Data

Keogh, James Edward, 1948-
    Schaum's outline of medical surgical nursing / James Keogh.
        p. ; cm. — (Schaum's outlines)
    Outline of medical surgical nursing
    ISBN-13: 978-0-07-162505-0 (alk. paper)
    ISBN-10: 0-07-162505-4 (alk. paper)
    1. Surgical nursing—Outlines, syllabi, etc.   2. Nursing—Outlines, syllabi, etc. I. Title. II. Title: Outline of medical surgical nursing.
    [DNLM: 1. Perioperative Nursing—methods—Outlines.   2. Nursing Care—Outlines.
        3. Nursing Process—Outlines. WY 18.2]

    RD99.K45 2011
    617'.0231—dc22

                                                                                    2011005823

Trademarks: McGraw-Hill, the McGraw-Hill Publishing logo, Schaum's, and related trade dress are trademarks or registered trademarks of The McGraw-Hill Companies and/or its affiliates in the United States and other countries and may not be used without written permission. All other trademarks are the property of their respective owners. The McGraw-Hill Companies is not associated with any product or vendor mentioned in this book.

This book is dedicated to Anne, Sandy, Joanne, Amber-Leigh Christine, Shawn, Eric, and Amy, without whose help and support this book couldn't have been written.

James Keogh

Contents

CHAPTER 1   **Musculoskeletal System**   1

1.1 Definition 1.2 Carpal Tunnel Syndrome 1.3 Fractures 1.4 Gout 1.5 Osteoarthritis
1.6 Osteomyelitis 1.7 Osteoporosis

CHAPTER 2   **Immune System**   11

2.1 Definition 2.2 Acquired Immundeficiency Syndrome (AIDS) 2.3 Anaphylaxis
2.4 Ankylosing Spondylitis (AS) 2.5 Kaposi's Sarcoma (KS) 2.6 Lymphoma
2.7 Rheumatoid Arthritis 2.8 Scleroderma 2.9 Mononucleosis 2.10 Epstein-Barr
Virus/Chronic Fatigue Syndrome 2.11 Lyme Disease 2.12 Septic Shock
2.13 Systemic Lupus Erythematosus

CHAPTER 3   **Hematologic System**   26

3.1 Definition 3.2 Anemia 3.3 Aplastic Anemia (Pancytopenia) 3.4 Iron Deficiency
Anemia 3.5 Pernicious Anemia 3.6 Disseminated Intravascular Coagulation (DIC)
3.7 Hemophilia 3.8 Leukemia 3.9 Multiple Myeloma 3.10 Polycythemia Vera
3.11 Sickle Cell Anemia 3.12 Deep Vein Thrombosis 3.13 Idiopathic Thrombocytopenic
Purpura (ITP)

CHAPTER 4   **Cardiovascular System**   46

4.1 Definition 4.2 Aortic Aneurysm 4.3 Angina (Angina Pectoris) 4.4 Myocardial
Infarction (MI) 4.5 Coronary Artery Disease (CAD) 4.6 Peripheral Arterial Disease
4.7 Cardiac Tamponade 4.8 Cardiogenic Shock 4.9 Cardiomyopathy 4.10 Endocarditis
4.11 Congestive Heart Failure (CHF) 4.12 Hypertension 4.13 Hypovolemic Shock
4.14 Myocarditis 4.15 Pericarditis 4.16 Pulmonary Edema 4.17 Raynaud's Disease
4.18 Rheumatic Heart Disease 4.19 Thrombophlebitis 4.20 Atrial Fibrillation
4.21 Asystole 4.22 Ventricular Fibrillation 4.23 Ventricular Tachycardia 4.24 Aortic
Insufficiency (AI) 4.25 Mitral Insufficiency 4.26 Mitral Stenosis 4.27 Mitral Valve
Prolapse 4.28 Tricuspid Insufficiency

CHAPTER 5   **Respiratory System**   79

5.1 Definition 5.2 Acute Respiratory Distress Syndrome (ARDS) 5.3 Asbestosis
5.4 Asthma 5.5 Atelectasis 5.6 Bronchiectasis 5.7 Bronchitis 5.8 Cor Pulmonale
5.9 Emphysema 5.10 Lung Cancer 5.11 Pleural Effusion 5.12 Pneumonia
5.13 Pneumothorax 5.14 Respiratory Acidosis 5.15 Tuberculosis 5.16 Acute
Respiratory Failure 5.17 Pulmonary Embolism 5.18 Influenza

CHAPTER 6   Nervous System   103

6.1 Definition 6.2 Cerebral Hemorrhage 6.3 Amyotrophic Lateral Sclerosis (ALS)
6.4 Bell's Palsy 6.5 Brain Abscess 6.6 Brain Tumor 6.7 Cerebral Aneurysm
6.8 Encephalitis 6.9 Guillain-Barré Syndrome 6.10 Huntington's Disease (Chorea)
6.11 Meningitis 6.12 Multiple Sclerosis (MS) 6.13 Myasthenia Gravis
6.14 Parkinson's Disease 6.15 Spinal Cord Injury 6.16 Cerebrovascular
Accident (CVA) 6.17 Seizure Disorder

CHAPTER 7   Endocrine System   128

7.1 Definition 7.2 Hypothyroidism (Myxedema) 7.3 Hyperthyroidism (Graves'
Disease) 7.4 Simple Goiter 7.5 Hypopituitarism 7.6 Hyperpituitarism (Acromegaly
and Gigantism) 7.7 Hyperprolactinemia 7.8 Diabetes Insipidus 7.9 Syndrome of
Inappropriate Antidiuretic Hormone Secretion (SIADH) 7.10 Addison's Disease
7.11 Cushing's Syndrome 7.12 Primary Aldosteronism (Conn's Syndrome)
7.13 Pheochromocytoma 7.14 Hypoparathyroidism 7.15 Hyperparathyroidism
7.16 Diabetes Mellitus 7.17 Metabolic Syndrome (Syndrome X/Dysmetabolic
Syndrome)

CHAPTER 8   Gastrointestinal System   152

8.1 Definition 8.2 Appendicitis 8.3 Cholecystitis 8.4 Cirrhosis 8.5 Crohn's
Disease 8.6 Diverticulitis Disease 8.7 Gastroenteritis 8.8 Gastroesophageal Reflux
Disease (GERD) 8.9 Gastrointestinal Bleeding 8.10 Gastritis 8.11 Hepatitis
8.12 Hiatal Hernia (Diaphragmatic Hernia) 8.13 Intestinal Obstruction and
Paralytic Ileus 8.14 Pancreatitis 8.15 Peritonitis 8.16 Peptic Ulcer Disease (PUD)
8.17 Ulcerative Colitis

CHAPTER 9   OB-GYN   178

9.1 Definition 9.2 Breast Cancer 9.3 Cervical Cancer 9.4 Dysmenorrhea
9.5 Ectopic Pregnancy 9.6 Endometrial Cancer 9.7 Uterine Fibroids (Leiomyomas)
9.8 Infertility 9.9 Ovarian Cancer 9.10 Ovarian Cysts 9.11 Pelvic Inflammatory
Disease 9.12 Trophoblastic Disease 9.13 Rh Incompatibility 9.14 Preeclampsia and
Eclampsia

CHAPTER 10   Integumentary System   194

10.1 Definition 10.2 Burns 10.3 Dermatitis 10.4 Skin Cancers 10.5 Cellulitis
10.6 Pressure Ulcers 10.7 Wounds

CHAPTER 11   Genitourinary System   203

11.1 Definition 11.2 Benign Prostatic Hypertrophy (BPH) 11.3 Bladder Cancer
11.4 Acute Glomerulonephritis 11.5 Kidney Cancer 11.6 Kidney Stones 11.7 Prostate
Cancer 11.8 Pyelonephritis 11.9 Renal Failure 11.10 Testicular Cancer 11.11 Urinary
Tract Infection

CHAPTER 12   Fluids and Electrolytes   216

12.1 Definition 12.2 Hyponatremia 12.3 Hypernatremia 12.4 Hypocalcemia
12.5 Hypercalcemia 12.6 Hypokalemia 12.7 Hyperkalemia 12.8 Hypomagnesemia
12.9 Hypermagnesemia 12.10 Metabolic Acidosis 12.11 Metabolic Alkalosis
12.12 Hypophosphatemia 12.13 Hyperphosphatemia 12.14 Dehydration

CHAPTER 13   Perioperative Period   **233**

13.1 Definition **13.2** Preoperative Period **13.3** Intraoperative Period
13.4 Postoperative Period **13.5** Cardiovascular Complications **13.6** Respiratory
Complications **13.7** Infection **13.8** Gastrointestinal Complications

CHAPTER 14   Mental Health   **247**

14.1 Definition **14.2** Anxiety **14.3** Panic Disorder **14.4** Depressive Disorder
14.5 Bipolar Disorder **14.6** Schizophrenia **14.7** Anorexia Nervosa **14.8** Bulimia
Nervosa **14.9** Delirium

CHAPTER 15   Oncology   **259**

15.1 Definition **15.2** Normal Cell Proliferation **15.3** Causes of Cancer **15.4** Cell
Dysfunctions **15.5** Metastases **15.6** Cancer Classification **15.7** Stages of Cancer
15.8 Cancer Cells and the Immune System **15.9** Staging of Cancer **15.10** Cancer
Prevention and Detection **15.11** Biopsy **15.12** Treatment Goals **15.13** Surgical Therapy
15.14 Radiation Therapy **15.15** Chemotherapy **15.16** Biologic Therapy
15.17 Bone Marrow Transplant (BMT) **15.18** Complications from Cancer
15.19 Oncological Emergencies **15.20** Oncological Obstructive Emergencies
15.21 Oncological Metabolic Emergencies **5.22** Oncological Infiltrative Emergencies

INDEX   **285**

Medical-Surgical Nursing

CHAPTER 1

Musculoskeletal System

1.1   Definition

- The musculoskeletal system provides structure and function to the body.
- Skeleton division
    - Axial skeleton protects thoracic cavity and central nervous system
    - Appendicular skeleton consists of limbs
- Bone classification
    - Shape
        - Short bones in fingers and toes such as phalanges
        - Long bones in limbs such as humerus or femur
        - Irregular bones in joints and middle ear
        - Flat bone protects inner organs such as ribs or scapula
    - Composition
        - Outer layer: Cortex consists of dense compact tissue
            - Osteoblasts: Bone-building cells
            - Osteoclasts: Bone-resorbing cells
        - Haversian canals: Longitudinal canals in cortex supplies blood to bones
        - Inner layer: Spongy cancellous tissue filled with bone marrow
        - Bone marrow
            - Red bone marrow: Produces blood cells
            - Yellow bone marrow: Composed of fat cells
- Joints: Two or more bones join
    - Free moving (synovial joints), such as hip
        - Synovial joints
        - Lined with synovial membrane that secretes synovial fluid
        - Synovial fluid lubricates the joint and reabsorbs shocks

- Motion classification
  - Rotation: Circular motion
  - Circumduction: Combination of abduction, adduction, extension, and flexion
    - Flexion: Bending movement that decreases the angle
    - Extension: Bending movement that increases the angle
    - Abduction: Moving away from the body
    - Adduction: Moving toward the body
    - Supination: Facing up
    - Pronation: Facing down
    - Inversion: Inward
    - Eversion: Outward
- Partially movable, such as pelvic bone
- Immovable, such as suture lines in the skull

Muscles

- Muscle group
  - Sets of muscles create movement
    - Contraction: Reduces length of muscle
    - Relaxing: Lengthens muscle
    - Muscle tone: Small amount of constant contraction
- Muscle types
  - Voluntary (skeletal): Use for motion
  - Involuntary (smooth): Found in organ walls
  - Cardiac muscle: Found in the heart
- Connective tissues: Tissues that connect organs and other tissues
- Tendons: Attach muscles to bone
- Ligaments: Attach bones to bones
- Cartilage: Cushions weight-bearing joints to provide smooth surface
- Bursa: Fluid-filled sac provides cushion to friction points

Fracture Healing Process

- Hematoma: Bruise at fracture site resulting from bleeding
- Granulation tissue: Replaces blood clot at fracture site
- Callus: Nonbony union forms at fracture site
- Osteoblasts: Bone formation replaces callus

1.2 Carpal Tunnel Syndrome

Repetitive hand movement causes the median nerve in the anterior wrist to compress, causing pain and numbness to fingers. The median nerve passes through the carpal tunnel. This is more common in women.

Signs and Symptoms

- Weakness and pain in the hand
- Paresthesia in the hand
- Tingling in the hand
- Numbness in the hand

Medical Tests

- Electromyography (EMG) shows nerve dysfunction
- Magnetic resonance imaging (MRI) shows swelling of the median nerve
- Positive Tinel's sign in which tapping over the carpal tunnel area causes tingling, numbness, or pain in hand
- Inflating the blood pressure cuff on the upper arm causes pain, tingling, and burning sensation in the wrist and hand

Treatment

- Splint the wrist in a neutral or slightly extended position for 2 weeks to decrease compression
- Surgery to relieve pressure on the median nerve
- Administer:
  - Nonsteroidal anti-inflammatory drugs (NSAIDS) to decrease inflammation
    - Diclofenac, diflunisal, etodolac, fenoprofen, flurbiprofen, ibuprofen, indomethacin, ketoprofen, ketorolac, meloxicam, nabumetone, naproxen, oxaprozin, piroxicam, salsalate, sulindac, tolmetin
  - Corticosteroids to decrease inflammation
    - Hydrocortisone (cortisol), Decadron (dexamethasone), Medrol (methylprednisolone), prednisolone, prednisone

Intervention

- Check capillary refill, color, sensation of fingers following surgery
- Physical therapy
- Instruct the patient:
  - How to use wrist splints
  - How to use ergonomic devices to reduce the effects of repetitive motion
  - How to exercise the fingers after surgery

1.3   Fractures

Break in a bone because of trauma or excess stress, leading to hemorrhage, edema, and local muscle and tissue damage

Types of Fracture

- **Incomplete fracture** occurs when the fracture is not completely through the bone.
- **Complete fracture** occurs when the fracture is completely through the bone.

- **Open fracture** occurs when the fracture penetrates the skin.
- **Closed fracture** occurs when the fracture does not penetrate the skin.

Complications

- **Fat embolism** occurs when yellow bone marrow releases fat into the bloodstream, resulting in emboli.
- **Delayed union** is a fracture that is not joined within 6 months.
- **Compartment syndrome** occurs when nerves, blood vessels, and muscles in a closed space are compressed by a facture, leading to tissue necrosis.
- **Deep vein thrombosis (DVT)** occurs when clots form as a result of immobility from a fracture.
- **Misalignment** occurs when bone pieces are not anatomically aligned.
- **Muscle wasting** is the deterioration of muscle as a result of immobilization related to the fracture.

Signs and Symptoms

- Edema resulting from an inflammatory reaction
- Abnormal range of motion
- Local bleeding

Medical Tests

- Computes tomography (CT) scan shows fracture.
- X-ray shows fracture.
- Bone scan shows increased cellular activity in fracture.

Treatment

- Immobilize and splint the fracture.
- Reduce and cast the fracture.
- Administer pain medication.

Intervention

- Monitor vital signs.
- Monitor circulation in the area of the fracture.
- Monitor signs of bleeding (increased pulse, increased respiration, and decreased blood pressure).
- Perform range-of-motion exercises to maintain muscle tone.
- Instruct the patient:
  - Not to insert objects into the cast, which can cause breakdown of the skin.

1.4   Gout

Gout is a chronic metabolic disorder in which purine-based proteins are not adequately metabolized, leading to the accumulation of uric acid crystals in the joints (big toe) and crystallization of uric acid in the kidneys, which leads to kidney stones. This is also secondary to treatment with thiazide diuretics and chemotherapy.

Signs and Symptoms

- Swollen joint
- Red, tender joint
- Joint pain, especially at night
- Nephrolithiasis

Medical Tests

- Arthrocentesis: Shows uric acid crystals
- Erythrocyte sedimentation rate: Increase
- Serum uric acid level: Increase
- Urinary uric acid levels: Increase

Treatment

- Do not administer aspirin, because aspirin retains uric acid.
- Administer:
  - NSAIDs to decrease inflammation to aid in pain relief
    - Indomethacin, ibuprofen, naproxen
  - Xanthine oxidase inhibitor to reduce uric acid level
    - Allopurinol
  - Colchicine for acute episode
  - Uricosuric to reduce uric acid level
    - Probenecid, sulfinpyrazone

Intervention

- Monitor serum uric acid levels.
- Immobilize the joint.
- Don't touch the joint.
- Instruct the patient:
  - To drink 3 L of fluid per day to avoid crystallization of uric acid
  - To follow a low-fat, low-cholesterol diet
  - To avoid foods high in purine protein, such as turkey, organ meats, sardines, smelts, mackerel, anchovies, herring, and bacon
  - To avoid alcohol, which inhibits renal excretion of uric acid

1.5   Osteoarthritis

Destruction of the articular cartilage through wearing leads bones to rub, injuring bone tissue. Regrowth of bone tissue results in bone spurs that project into joints and soft tissue, causing pain on movement.

Signs and Symptoms

- Crepitus
- Joint pain on movement relieved with rest
- Stiff joints for a short time in the morning, usually 15 minutes or less
- Heberden's nodes
- Enlargement of joint

Medical Tests

- X-ray: Shows bone spurs
- C-reactive protein test: Positive
- Erythrocyte sedimentation rate: Increase
- Rheumatoid factor: Negative
- Cyclic citrullinated peptide antibody: Negative

Treatment

Administer:

- NSAIDs to decrease inflammation to aid in pain relief
  - Indomethacin; ibuprofen; naproxen
- Analgesics to decrease pain
  - Anacin, Tylenol (acetaminophen)
- Capsaicinoids to decrease pain
  - Capsaicin cream

Intervention

- Pain management
- Instruct the patient:
  - To exercise to maintain mobility
  - To reduce weight to decrease stress on the joints

1.6 Osteomyelitis

Trauma or an acute infection results in a secondary bone infection commonly caused by *Staphylococcus aureus* bacteria. This condition is more common in adolescents and children and has been seen in patients who have recently undergone antibiotic treatment.

Signs and Symptoms

- Pain
- Malaise

- Fever
- Chills

Medical Tests

- White blood cell count (WBC) increased
- Bone scan shows increased cellular activity at site of infection
- X-ray shows location of decreased bone density (osteolytic lesions)
- Bone biopsy to collect issue sample
- Culture and sensitivity to identify microorganism and medication

Treatment

- Débridement
- Drain infection
- Immobilize bone
- Amputation if gangrene is present
- Administer:
  - Analgesics to decrease pain
  - Anacin, Tylenol (acetaminophen); Advil, Motrin (ibuprofen); Aleve, Naprosyn (naproxen);
  - OxyContin, Roxicodone (oxycodone), Vicodin (hydrocodone)
- Antibiotics orally (6 to 8 weeks) parenteral (4 to 6 weeks)
  - Nafcillin, vancomycin, penicillin G, piperacillin, ticarcillin/clavulanate, ampicillin/sulbactam, piperacillin/tazobactam, clindamycin, cefazolin, linezolid, ceftazidime, ciprofloxacin

Intervention

- Monitor the site for signs of infection.
- Monitor the vital signs.
- Monitor the intravenous (IV) site for patency.
- Instruct the patient:
  - To take antibiotics for the full length of time the medication is prescribed

1.7   Osteoporosis

Bone density decreases at the rate that replacement bone is exceeded by bone reabsorption. This leads to brittle bones and increased risk of fractures, particularly in the hip, vertebrae, pelvis, and distal radius. This condition is caused by age, decreased physical activity, prolonged periods of immobility, medication, and poor nutrition. This condition is secondary to underlying disease.

Signs and Symptoms

- Asymptomatic
- Decreased height

- Kyphosis
- Unexplained fractures
- Back pain

Medical Tests

- Dual-energy X-ray absorptiometry (DEXA): Shows decreased bone density
- X-ray: Shows demineralization

Treatment

Administer:

- Selective estrogen receptor modulator postmenopause to prevent osteoporosis
  - Evista (raloxifene)
- Bisphosphonate inhibits bone reabsorption
  - Fosamax (alendronate); Boniva (ibandronate); APD, Aredia (pamidronate); Zometa, Aclasta (zoledronate); Didronel (etidronate); Bonefos, Loron (clodronate); Actonel (risedronate)
- Forteo (teriparatide) stimulates collagenous bone.
- Calcium 1,000 to 1,500 mg per day to enhance absorption
  - Vitamin D enhances the absorption of calcium.

Interventions

- Bisphosphonates:
  - Take on an empty stomach.
  - Take first thing in the morning with a full glass of water.
  - Do not lie down for 30 to 60 minutes afterward.
- Explain to the patient how to:
  - Perform weight-bearing activity.
  - Perform range-of-motion exercises.

Solved Problems

1.1   What is carpal tunnel syndrome?

Carpal tunnel syndrome is compression of the median nerve in the anterior wrist, causing pain and numbness in the fingers.

1.2   What is the underlying cause of carpal tunnel syndrome?

The underlying cause of carpal tunnel syndrome is repetitive hand movement.

1.3   What are signs of carpal tunnel syndrome?

Signs of carpal tunnel syndrome are weakness and pain, paresthesia, tingling, and numbness in the hand.

1.4   What is a positive Tinel's sign?

A positive Tinel's sign is tapping over the carpal tunnel area that causes tingling, numbness, or pain in the hand.

1.5   What is a nonsurgical treatment for carpal tunnel syndrome?

A nonsurgical treatment for carpal tunnel syndrome is to splint the wrist in a neutral or slightly extended position for 2 weeks to decrease compression.

1.6   What is the purpose of administering cortisol to a patient with carpal tunnel syndrome?

The purpose of administering cortisol to a patient with carpal tunnel syndrome is to decrease inflammation.

1.7   What is an incomplete fracture?

An incomplete fracture occurs when the fracture is not completely through the bone.

1.8   What is a complete fracture?

A complete fracture occurs when the fracture is completely through the bone.

1.9   What is an open fracture?

An open fracture occurs when the fracture penetrates the skin.

1.10   What is compartment syndrome?

Compartment syndrome occurs when nerves, blood vessels, and muscles in a closed space are compressed by the fracture, leading to tissue necrosis.

1.11   What is a delayed union?

A delayed union is a fracture that is not joined within 6 months.

1.12   What is a fat embolism?

A fat embolism occurs when yellow bone marrow releases fat into the bloodstream, resulting in emboli.

1.13   What is muscle wasting?

Muscle wasting is the deterioration of muscle as a result of immobilization related to a fracture.

1.14   What are the signs of bleeding?

Signs of bleeding are increased pulse, increased respiration, and decreased blood pressure.

1.15   Why should a patient perform range-of-motion exercises?

A patient should perform range-of-motion exercises to maintain muscle tone.

1.16   Why should a patient not insert objects into a cast?

Inserting objects into a cast can cause the breakdown of skin.

1.17   What is gout?

Gout is a chronic metabolic disorder in which purine-based proteins are not adequately metabolized, leading to the accumulation of uric acid crystals in joints (big toe) and crystallization of uric acid in the kidneys, leading to kidney stones.

1.18   In a patient with gout, what will arthrocentesis reveal?

Arthrocentesis will reveal uric acid crystals in a patient with gout.

1.19   Why should a patient with gout avoid taking aspirin?

A patient with gout should avoid taking aspirin because it retains uric acid.

1.20   What is the purpose of administering allopurinol to a patient with gout?

The purpose of administering allopurinol to a patient with gout is to reduce uric acid levels.

1.21   What foods are high in purine proteins?

Foods that are high in purine proteins are turkey, organ meats, sardines, smelts, mackerel, anchovies, herring, and bacon.

1.22   What is osteoarthritis?

Osteoarthritis is the destruction of the articular cartilage through wearing, which leads bones to rub, thereby injuring bone tissue.

1.23   What causes pain when a patient with osteoarthritis moves?

Bone spurs that project into joints and soft tissue cause pain when a patient with osteoarthritis moves.

1.24   What is osteomyelitis?

Osteomyelitis is a bone infection.

1.25   How are bisphosphonates administered?

- Take them on an empty stomach.
- Take them first thing in the morning with a full glass of water.
- Do not lie down for 30 to 60 minutes.

CHAPTER 2

Immune System

2.1 Definition

The immune system protects the body against invading microorganisms and toxins. The major histocompatibility complex (MHC), also known as the human leukocyte antigen (HLA), marks cells in the patient's body, identifying those cells as the patient's cells. Cells or any matter not so marked are identified as foreign and are attacked by the immune system. Cells of the immune system identify, isolate, and destroy invading microorganisms.

Immunodeficiency disorders occur when the body does not produce sufficient mature cells of the immune system to identify, isolate, and destroy invading microorganisms. As a result, the patient is prone to infection. Autoimmune disorders occur when the cells of the immune system identify the body's own cells as an invading microorganism and destroy the body's cells.

Leukocytes (White Blood Cells)

All white blood cells (WBCs) begin in bone marrow as stem cells and can form into any type of leukocytes. There are three major types of leukocytes: (1) granulocytes, (2) lymphocytes, and (3) monocytes.

Granulocytes
There are three types of granulocytes:

1. **Neutrophils:** Neutrophils move through the bloodstream and into tissues, where they are attracted to foreign material such as bacteria, viruses, and toxins. Neutrophils engulf the foreign material and release enzymes and chemicals, and destroy the foreign material. Dead neutrophils and the foreign material form pus.

2. **Eosinophils:** Eosinophils are similar to neutrophils, except they focus on parasites usually found on the skin and in the lungs.

3. **Basophils:** Basophils increase in number when a foreign material is detected, releasing histamine along with mast cells to dilate capillaries, thereby enabling more blood (leukocytes) to flow into the area where the foreign material is located. This is referred to as *inflammation*.

Lymphocytes

Lymphocytes focus on bacterial and viral infections. There are two classes of lymphocytes:

1. **T Cells:** T cells, also known as killer T cells, begin in bone marrow and mature in the thymus. A T cell is attracted to bacteria and the patient's cells that contain a virus and kills them. There are two support lymphocytes that help sensitize T cells:

   a. *Helper T cells:* Helper T cells are activated by macrophages (see monocytes). Helper T cells then release chemicals to activate B cells (see B cells below) to produce antibodies to fight future infections by that foreign material.

   b. *Suppressor T cells:* Suppressor T cells are also known as *regulatory T cells*. Treg cells turn off T cells and therefore regulate the immune system.

2. **B Cells:** B cells begin and mature in bone marrow and form plasma cells. B cells also become sensitized to a specific foreign material, which is known as an *antibody*. This antibody remains in the blood to protect the body from future infections from that foreign material.

   a. Classes of antibodies:

      (1) *Immunoglobulin A (IgA):* Protects body surfaces (nose, breathing passages, digestive tract, ears, eyes, and vagina) that are exposed to the outside.

      (2) *Immunoglobulin D (IgD):* Unclear how this works.

      (3) *Immunoglobulin E (IgE):* Reacts against pollen, fungus spores, and animal dander. High in people with allergies.

      (4) *Immunoglobulin G (IgG):* Reacts to bacterial and viral infections and crosses the placenta to protect the fetus.

      (5) *Immunoglobulin M (IgM):* First to respond to an infection

Monocytes

Monocytes begin in bone marrow and float in the bloodstream. When a monocyte enters tissue the monocyte matures into a macrophage. Macrophages remain in tissue and also enter the bloodstream. Macrophages are part of the healing process by cleaning up dead neutrophils and foreign material (pus).

Leukocyte (White Blood Cell) Differential

Leukocyte differential in a blood test helps to identify inflammation and infection based on values of types of leukocytes. Here are common values:

- **Neutrophils:** Increase in bacterial infection and inflammatory disease

- **Eosinophils:** Increase in allergic disorders, skin inflammation, and parasitic infection

- **Basophils:** Increase in chronic inflammation, leukemia, and hypersensitivity to food

- **Lymphocytes:** Increase in viral infection, bone marrow cancer, and leukemia. Decrease in disorders affecting the immune system (i.e., lupus, HIV).

- **Monocytes:** Increase in all infections and inflammation and leukemia. Decrease in bone marrow injury

2.2   Acquired Immunodeficiency Syndrome (AIDS)

T cells are invaded by the human immunodeficiency virus (HIV), causing destruction of T cells and resulting in immunodeficiency. Most often affected are the CD4 lymphocytes, B lymphocytes, and macrophages.

Signs and Symptoms

- Malnutrition caused by decreased protein synthesis
- Fatigue caused by high rate of cell death
- Anorexia caused by the side effects of medications
- Night sweats caused by low WBC

Medical Tests

- Complete blood test: CD4 lymphocyte <200 cells/µg
- HIV antibody titer: Positive. Must be administered 6 weeks after infection
- Western blot test: Positive confirming HIV antibody titer

Treatment

Administer:

- Antibiotic prophylaxis
  - Trimpex, Proloprim, Primsol (trimethoprim); Gantanol (sulfamethoxazole)
- Antiviral nucleoside analogs to decrease HIV replication
  - Videx (didanosine); Retrovir (zidovudine); Zerit (stavudine); Hivid (zalcitabine); Viread (tenofovir)
- Protease inhibitors to decrease HIV replication
  - Saquinavir (Fortovase); Norvir (ritonavir); Crixivan (indinavir); Viracept (nelfinavir)
- Nonnucleoside reverse transcriptase inhibitors to decrease HIV replication
  - Viramune (nevirapine); Rescriptor (delavirdine); Sustiva, Stocrin (efavirenz)
- Antiemetic for nausea
  - Compazine (prochlorperazine)
- Antifungal for fungal infections
  - Diflucan (fluconazole)
- High-calorie and high-protein diet to increase weight

Interventions

- Avoid exposure to blood.
- Instruct the patient:
  - To maintain activity as tolerated
  - To schedule rest periods
  - To use condoms

2.3   Anaphylaxis

Histamines are released in response to an allergen. Histamines cause capillary dilation and contraction of smooth muscle, resulting in hypotension, angioedema, respiratory distress, and urticaria.

Signs and Symptoms

- Rales resulting from fluid build up in the lungs
- Rhonchi caused by bronchospasm
- Dyspnea resulting from swelling of the larynx
- Hypotension resulting from vasodilation
- Anxiety related to dyspnea

Medical Tests

- Tryptase test: Measures the number of mast cells. Mast cells increase in anaphylaxis.
- Allergy skin testing: After episode

Treatment

Administer:

- Emergency medications
- Epinephrine to decrease bronchospasm
  - Corticosteroids to decrease immune response
- Antihistamines decrease histamines
- Circulatory volume expanders
  - Crystalloid solutions
    - 0.9% normal saline, lactated Ringer's solution (contains electrolytes)
  - Fresh-frozen plasma
- Catecholamines to increase blood pressure
  - Dopamine, epinephrine, norepinephrine

Interventions

- Administer 2 to 4 L of oxygen.
- Insert endotracheal tube to maintain airways.
- Insert intravenous line (IV) with 14G catheter (use largest).
- Monitor vitals every 15 minutes.
- Instruct the patient:
  - To call 911 at the first sign of anaphylaxis
  - To avoid allergens

2.4 Ankylosing Spondylitis (AS)

Ankylosing spondylitis (AS) is a progressive form of arthritis in which joints between the spine and pelvis are inflamed, resulting in acute painful exacerbations and remissions. This is genetically influenced and affects <1% of the population.

Signs and Symptoms

- Reduced lumbar spine motion caused by the pain of inflammation
- Severe lower back pain (if inactive) caused by inflammation

Medical Tests

- Blood serum: Positive for HLA-B27 antigen
- Complete blood test: Increased erythrocyte sedimentation rate (ESR)
- Spinal x-ray: Shows arthritic erosion or bamboo spine

Treatment

- Physical therapy to maintain flexibility
- Administer:
  - Anti-inflammatory agent (not corticosteroids) to decrease inflammation and pain
  - Aspirin; Advil, Motrin (ibuprofen); Indocin (indomethacin); Azulfidine (sulfasalazine); Clinoril (sulindac)

Interventions

- Massage the lumbar spine for relief.
- Wear a back brace to maintain posture.
- Employ stretching exercises to maintain flexibility.
- Heat the lumbar spine for relief.
- Instruct the patient:
  - To sit in a high-back chair for posture
  - To maintain an erect posture

2.5   Kaposi's Sarcoma (KS)

Herpes virus (KSHV) invades lymphatic and skin tissue, causing overgrowth of blood vessels that lead to malignant lymphatic tissue and skin cancer. This is common in advanced AIDS.

Signs and Symptoms

- Dyspnea if cancer metastasized to lungs
- Red, brown, or purple lesions on the lips, gums, tongue, and palate

Medical Tests

- Computed tomography (CT) scan to determine metastasis if the cancer has metastasized
- Biopsy to identify the HIV virus

Treatment

- Radiation to reduce tumors
- Laser surgery to remove lesions
- Administer:
  - Chemotherapy to destroy cancer cells
    - Adriamycin, Rubex (doxorubicin); Eposin, Etopophos, VePesid (etoposide); Velbe (vinblastine); Oncovin (vincristine)
  - Antiemetic for side effects of radiation and chemotherapy
    - Tebamide, Tigan (trimethobenzamide)

Interventions

- Daily weights
- Monitor for new skin lesions
- Instruct the patient:
  - To change to a high-protein, high-calorie diet
  - To schedule rest periods
  - To consider hospice care

2.6   Lymphoma

Overgrowth of lymph cells (cancer), resulting in immature lymph cells that are unable to function normally. This is caused by a disruption of cells during differentiation.

Types of Lymphoma

- **Hodgkin's disease:** Malignant lymphoma. Reed-Sternberg cells are present. Stages of Hodgkin's disease:
  - *Stage I:* Reed-Sternberg cells appear in one lymph node region.
  - *Stage II:* Reed-Sternberg cells appear in multiple lymph node regions on the same side of the diaphragm.
  - *Stage III:* Reed-Sternberg cells appear in multiple lymph node regions on both sides of the diaphragm.
  - *Stage IV:* Reed-Sternberg cells appear throughout the body.
- **Non-Hodgkin's lymphoma:** Cancer of the B lymphocytes. Reed-Sternberg cells are absent.

Signs and Symptoms

- Painless, swollen lymph nodes in abdomen, pelvis, or cervical region
- Night sweats
- Anorexia related to increased cell growth

Medical Tests

- *Hodgkin's:* Reed-Sternberg cells in lymph node biopsy
- *Non-Hodgkin's:* follicular type cells in bone marrow biopsy

Treatment

- Hodgkin's
  - Radiation to shrink nodes
  - Chemotherapy to destroy cancer cells
    - Adriamycin, Rubex (doxorubicin), Blenoxane (bleomycin), Oncovin (vincristine), DTIC (dacarbazine)
- Non-Hodgkin's
  - Bone marrow transplant to replace bone marrow
  - Radiation to shrink nodes
  - Chemotherapy to destroy cancer cells
    - Adriamycin, Rubex (doxorubicin), Oncovin (vincristine), DTIC (dacarbazine), Cytoxan (cyclophosphamide), Rituximab
  - Anti-inflammatory agent to decrease inflammation and reduce pain
    - Prednisone

Interventions

- Monitor vital signs.
- Palpate lymph nodes to monitor disease progress.
- Instruct the patient:
  - To eat a diet high in calories, protein, iron, calcium, and vitamins and minerals because of weight loss
  - Not to use over-the-counter medications before consulting with the health care provider
  - To increase fluid intake

2.7   Rheumatoid Arthritis

The synovial lining of joints swells because of an autoimmune reaction, causing pain and limiting movement to wrists, hands, knees, and feet. The cause is unknown, although there is a genetic tendency. Onset is 20 to 40. Two percent of the population is affected. Rheumatoid arthritis can affect organs and go into remission.

Signs and Symptoms

- Enlarged joints resulting from inflammation
- Limited range of motion resulting from inflammation
- Morning stiffness with pain resulting from the inflammation

Medical Tests

- X-rays: Show deformed joints
- Blood test:
  - Positive rheumatoid factor
  - Positive antinuclear antibody (ANA)
  - Increased ESR

Treatment

- Cold and heat therapy for anti-inflammatory effect
- Occupational therapy to maintain independence
- Physical therapy to maintain range of motion
- Splints to maintain joints in position
- Administer:
  - Nonsteroidal anti-inflammatory drugs (NSAIDs) to decrease inflammation and pain
    - Advil, Motrin (ibuprofen); Indocin (indomethacin); Clinoril (sulindac); Ansaid (flurbiprofen); Aleve, Naprosyn (naproxen); Dolobid (diflunisal)
  - Disease modifying anti-rheumatology drugs (DMARDs)
    - Trexall, Rheumatrex (methotrexate); TNF1; Enbrel (etanercept); Remicade (infliximab); HUMIRA (adalimumab)
  - Antimalarials
    - Plaquenil (hydroxychloroquine)
  - Anti-inflammatories (corticosteroids) to decrease inflammation and pain
    - Prednisone
  - Antacids to protect stomach
  - Milk of Magnesia (magnesium hydroxide); Amphojel (aluminum hydroxide)

Interventions

- Exercise to maintain flexibility and range of motion.
- Lose weight to place less stress on the joints.
- Instruct the patient:
  - To avoid stress
  - To avoid cold
  - To get a full night's sleep

2.8 Scleroderma

Connective tissue is destroyed by an autoimmune response leading to the formation of scar tissue (fibrosis) on organs, resulting in systemic sclerosis. Onset is seen in ages 30 to 50 and the cause is unknown. It may go into remission.

Signs and Symptoms

- Thickening of skin resulting from fibrosis
- Stiffness resulting from fibrosis
- Pain resulting from fibrosis

Medical Tests

- Skin biopsy: Shows thickening dermis
- Blood test:
  - Positive ANA

Treatment

- Physical therapy to maintain joint mobility

Interventions

- Monitor for hypertension. Renal failure secondary to hypertension is the leading cause of death.
- Instruct the patient:
  - To avoid the cold
  - To schedule rest periods

2.9 Mononucleosis

A viral infection transmitted by contact with saliva.

Signs and Symptoms

- Swollen lymph nodes
- Sore throat
- Malaise
- Headache
- Muscle pain

Medical Tests

- Monospot test is positive
- Heterophil antibody test is positive
- Throat culture to rule out streptococcal infection

Treatment

- Rest
- Treat symptomatically

- Administer:
  - NSAID to decrease pain
    - Aspirin; Advil, Motrin (ibuprofen); Aleve, Naprosyn (naproxen)
  - Antipyretic to decrease fever
    - Anacin, Tylenol (acetaminophen)

Interventions

- Increase fluids.
- Increase nutritional intake.
- Monitor vital signs.
- Instruct the patient:
  - To rest

2.10 Epstein-Barr Virus/Chronic Fatigue Syndrome

An interference of the immune system by one of five viruses can result in decreased effectiveness of the immune system. It is not fully understood and is chronic, with remissions and exacerbations.

Viruses

- Epstein-Barr virus
- Cytomegalovirus
- Coxsackievirus B
- Adenovirus type I
- Human herpes virus 6

Signs and Symptoms

- Headache
- Arthralgias
- Persistent fatigue unrelieved by rest
- Impaired concentration
- Myalgias
- Impaired memory
- Change in sleeping patterns

Medical Tests

- Rule out other etiologies for symptoms.

Treatment

- Treat symptomatically

- Physical therapy
- Administer:
  - Analgesics: NSAIDs to decrease pain
    - Aspirin; Advil, Motrin (ibuprofen); Aleve, Naprosyn (naproxen)
    - Anacin, Tylenol (acetaminophen)

Interventions

- Increase fluids.
- Increase nutritional intake.
- Monitor vital signs.
- Instruct the patient:
  - To rest
  - To exercise

2.11   Lyme Disease

The *Ixodes dammini* tick bite transmits the *Borrelia burgdorferi* bacteria, causing a bull's-eye rash and other symptoms up to 3 weeks after the bite.

Signs and Symptoms

- Bull's-eye rash at bite site
- Muscle pain (myalgias)
- Skin redness (erythema)
- Fever

Medical Tests

- Lyme titers increase
- IgM antibody is increased

Treatment

- Administer:
  - Antibiotics
    - Doryx (doxycycline)
    - Parenteral (aqueous penicillin)
    - Rocephin (ceftriaxone)
  - Analgesics
    - NSAIDs to decrease pain
    - Aspirin; Advil, Motrin (ibuprofen); Aleve, Naprosyn (naproxen)
    - Anacin, Tylenol (acetaminophen)

Interventions

- Monitor for fever.
- Instruct the patient:
  - To cover the skin while outside
  - To inspect the skin for ticks when returning from outside
  - To inspect pets for ticks when returning from outside
  - To remove ticks from skin by lifting the tick's head straight up using tweezers

2.12 Septic Shock

Bacteria enter the blood (bacteremia), causing an inflammatory reaction and leading to vascular permeability in which both infected and noninfected blood leaks from blood vessels, resulting in a systematic infection.

Signs and Symptoms

- Lactic acidosis from poor oxygenation
- Tachypnea in reaction to acidosis by trying to remove acid (CO_2)
- Nausea resulting from fluid leakage
- Temperature over 101 °F resulting from infection
- Hypotension from vasodilation
- Tachycardia from hypotension

Medical Tests

- Culture and sensitivity test to identify bacteria and antibiotic
- Complete blood count:
  - WBC >15,000 because of infection
  - Platelet count decrease
  - Prothrombin time decrease
  - Partial thromboplastin time decrease

Treatment

Antibiotics per results of culture and sensitivity test

- Circulatory volume expanders
  - Crystalloid solutions
    - 0.9% normal saline; lactated Ringer's solution (contains electrolytes)
- Fresh-frozen plasma
  - Analgesics: NSAIDs to decrease pain
    - Aspirin; Advil, Motrin (ibuprofen); Aleve, Naprosyn (naproxen)
    - Anacin, Tylenol (acetaminophen)

Interventions

- Monitor vital signs.
- Measure fluid intake and output to prevent fluid overload.
- Instruct the patient:
  - To rest. No bathroom privileges.

2.13 Systemic Lupus Erythematosus

Systemic lupus erythematosus (SLE) is an autoimmune inflammatory response to DNA and RNA that causes swelling and pain of organs. The cause is unknown. Likelihood is raised for particular populations according to gender (young women) and genetic tendency. There are remissions and exacerbations.

Signs and Symptoms

- Joint pain related to inflammation
- Anemia related to inflammation
- Fatigue related to anemia
- Malaise
- Butterfly rash on face related to immunoglobulin in the skin

Medical Tests

- Blood test:
  - Positive rheumatoid factor
  - Positive ANA

Treatment

- Administer:
  - NSAIDs to decrease inflammation and pain
    - Advil, Motrin (ibuprofen); Indocin (indomethacin); Clinoril (sulindac); Ansaid (flurbiprofen); Aleve, Naprosyn (naproxen); Dolobid (diflunisal)
  - Antimalarials
    - Plaquenil (hydroxychloroquine)
  - Anti-inflammatories (corticosteroids) to decrease inflammation and pain
    - Prednisone
  - Immunosuppressants if no response to corticosteroids
    - Imuran, Azasan (azathioprine); Cytoxan (cyclophosphamide)

Interventions

- Reduce stress.
- Monitor for infections.

- Instruct the patient:
  - To avoid sunlight. Use sunblock when outdoors.
  - To use cosmetics to cover the butterfly rash

Solved Problems

2.1   What is AIDS?

T cells are invaded by the HIV, causing destruction of T cells and resulting in immunodeficiency.

2.2   Why might an AIDS patient show signs of malnutrition?

An AIDS patient might show signs of malnutrition because of decreased protein synthesis.

2.3   What is the purpose of the Western blot test?

The Western blot test confirms the HIV antibody titer.

2.4   Why is an HIV antibody titer inconclusive if given 2 weeks after exposure to the virus?

The test must be administered 6 weeks after infection.

2.5   What T cell is used to measure the progress of an AIDS patient?

CD4 lymphocyte is the T cell used to measure the progress of an AIDS patient.

2.6   Why might an AIDS patient be administered antibiotic prophylaxis?

An AIDS patient might be administered antibiotic prophylaxis because the patient's immune system is compromised, exposing him or her to the risk of bacterial infection.

2.7   What is anaphylaxis?

Histamines are released in response to an allergen. Histamines cause capillary dilation and contraction of smooth muscle, resulting in hypotension, angioedema, respiratory distress, and urticaria.

2.8   What causes rhonchi in a patient experiencing anaphylaxis?

Rhonchi in a patient experiencing anaphylaxis is caused by bronchospasm related to smooth muscle contraction caused by histamines.

2.9   What causes dyspnea is a patient experiencing anaphylaxis?

Dyspnea in a patient experiencing anaphylaxis is caused by swelling of the larynx.

2.10 What causes rales in a patient experiencing anaphylaxis?

Rales in a patient experiencing anaphylaxis is caused by fluid buildup in the lungs.

2.11 What is the purpose of the tryptase test?

The tryptase test measures the number of mast cells. Mast cells increase in anaphylaxis.

2.12 What is Kaposi's sarcoma?

Herpes virus (KSHV) invades lymphatic and skin tissue, causing overgrowth of blood vessels that lead to malignant lymphatic tissue and skin cancer. This is common in advanced AIDS.

2.13 What is a cardinal sign of Kaposi's sarcoma?

A cardinal sign of KS is red, brown, purple lesions on the lips, gums, tongue, and palate.

2.14   What is Hodgkin's disease?

Hodgkin's disease is malignant lymphoma. Reed-Sternberg cells are present.

2.15   What is non-Hodgkin's lymphoma?

Non-Hodgkin's lymphoma is cancer of the B lymphocytes. Reed-Sternberg cells are absent.

2.16   What is a cardinal sign of lymphoma?

A cardinal sign of lymphoma is painless, swollen lymph nodes in the abdomen, pelvis, or cervical region.

2.17   How is non-Hodgkin's lymphoma diagnosed?

Non-Hodgkin's lymphoma is diagnosed through follicular-type cells in bone marrow biopsy.

2.18   What is rheumatoid arthritis?

Rheumatoid arthritis is the synovial lining of joints swelling because of an autoimmune reaction causing pain and limit movement to wrists, hands, knees, and feet.

2.19   What is the cause of rheumatoid arthritis?

The cause of rheumatoid arthritis is unknown, although there is a genetic tendency.

2.20   What is the purpose of physical therapy in rheumatoid arthritis?

The purpose of physical therapy in rheumatoid arthritis is to maintain range of motion.

2.21   What is scleroderma?

Connective tissue is destroyed by an autoimmune response, leading to the formation of scar tissue (fibrosis) on organs and resulting in systemic sclerosis.

2.22   How is mononucleosis transmitted?

Mononucleosis is transmitted by contact with saliva.

2.23   What is Lyme disease?

An *Ixodes dammini* tick bite transmits the *Borrelia burgdorferi* bacteria, causing a bull's-eye rash and other symptoms up to 3 weeks after the bite.

2.24   What is septic shock?

Bacteria enters the blood (bacteremia), causing an inflammatory reaction leading to vascular permeability in which both infected and noninfected blood leaks from the blood vessels, resulting in a systematic infection.

2.25   What is systemic lupus erythematosus?

SLE is an autoimmune inflammatory response to DNA and RNA that causes swelling and organ pain. The cause is unknown, although there is a gender (young women) and genetic tendency. There are remissions and exacerbations.

CHAPTER 3

Hematologic System

3.1 Definition

The hematologic system includes:

- Blood
- Blood vessels
- Blood-forming organs: Bone marrow, spleen, liver, lymph system, and thymus gland

The hematologic system plays a role in:

- Hormone transport
- Inflammatory response
- Immune response
- Temperature regulation
- Fluid-electrolyte balance
- Acid-base balance

Bone Marrow

- Occupies the interior of spongy bones and center of long bones
- Function is to form blood cells (hematopoiesis)
- Red bone marrow
  - Found in flat bones (i.e., ribs, vertebral column)
  - Site of hematopoiesis
- Yellow bone marrow
  - Found in long bones
  - Red bone marrow that changed to fat
  - Does not contribute to hematopoiesis

Blood

- All blood cells start as stem cells in bone marrow.

- Stem cells develop into specific types of cells.

- Fifty-five percent of blood is composed of plasma.

- Forty-five percent of blood is composed of cellular components.

- Pulmonary circulation contains 1300 mL of blood.

- Systematic circulation contains 3000 mL of blood.

Blood is separated using a centrifuge.

- The top layer is plasma.

- The middle layer is leukocytes (white blood cells, WBCs) and platelets.

- The bottom later is erythrocytes (red blood cells, RBCs).

Plasma

- The liquid part of blood

- Yellow

- Contains serum (fluid) and fibrinogen

- Contains plasma proteins

- Albumin regulates intravascular plasma volume and osmotic pressure

- Serum globulins (antibodies)

- Fibrinogen, prothrombin, plasminogen for clotting

Cellular Components

- Erythrocytes (RBCs)

  - No nucleus. Basically a sac containing hemoglobin

  - Responsible for oxygen transport

  - Required to produce erythrocytes (iron, vitamin B_{12}, folic acid, pyridoxine)

  - Hemolysis: Destruction of erythrocytes

  - Mature RBCs have a 120-day life span and are removed by liver and spleen

  - Bilirubin: A by-product of hemoglobin when RBC is destroyed. Excreted in bile.

- Leukocytes (WBCs)

  - Protect against bacteria and foreign substances

  - Granulocytes

- Eosinophils

  - Involved in phagocytosis and allergic reactions

    - Basophils

      - Involved in prevention of clotting and allergic reactions

- Neutrophils
  - Involved in short-term phagocytosis
  - Bacterial infection
  - Mononuclear
    - Monocytes
      - Involved in long-term phagocytosis
  - Lymphocytes
    - Immune cells

Spleen

- The spleen filters blood, removing imperfect cells, and stores RBCs and platelets
- Involved in antibody production by plasma cells

Liver

The liver produces clotting factors.

Lymph System

- This is a network of lymph vessels and lymph nodes that removes antigens from the body.

Thymus Gland

- Produces T cells used to combat antigens

3.2 Anemia

Anemia is low RBC leading to low hemoglobin, decreasing the blood's ability to carry oxygen and oxygenate tissues. The underlying cause can be blood loss, hemolysis, or nutritional deficiency, particularly deficiency in folic acid, vitamin B_{12}, and iron or bone marrow disorder.

Signs and Symptoms

- Lightheadedness/headache caused by hypoxia
- Fatigue caused by decreased oxygenation
- Pallor caused by decreased oxygenation
- Tachycardia caused by the need for increased oxygen throughout the body
- Angina caused by decreased oxygenation
- Jaundice caused by increased levels of bilirubin
- Bone pain caused by increased erythropoiesis

Medical Tests

- RBCs decrease
- Hematocrit decreases

- Hemoglobin decreases
- Reticulocyte increases
- Red cell distribution width increases

Treatment

Treat the underlying cause.

Interventions

- Minimize interventions during periods of fatigue.
- Monitor vital signs.
- Monitor blood labs.
- Monitor for angina.
- Instruct the patient:
  - To schedule rest periods
  - To call the health care provider if chest pains occur

3.3   Aplastic Anemia (Pancytopenia)

Bone marrow disorder reduces production of RBCs, WBCs, and platelets, increasing the risk of bleeding and infection. The cause might be unknown or related to radiation, chemotherapy, or toxins.

Signs and Symptoms

- Lightheadedness/headache caused by hypoxia
- Fatigue caused by decreased oxygenation
- Pallor caused by decreased oxygenation
- Infection increase caused by decreased WBCs
- Ecchymosis and petechiae caused by decreased platelets
- Jaundice caused by increased levels of bilirubin
- Bone pain caused by increased erythropoiesis

Medical Tests

- Bone marrow biopsy: cell count decreases
- RBCs decrease
- Hematocrit decreases
- Hemoglobin decreases
- Reticulocyte increases
- Red cell distribution width increases
- Platelets decrease

- WBCs decrease
- Positive fecal occult blood test

Treatment

Administer:

- Hematopoietic growth factor to increase WBCs
- Erythropoietin (EPO); Epogen, Procrit (epoetin alfa)
- Human granulocyte colony-stimulating factor (G-CSF) to increase WBCs
- Neupogen (filgrastim); Leukine (sargramostim)
- Packed RBCs to increase RBCs
- Fresh-frozen plasma to increase platelets
- Immunosuppressive antithymocyte globulin (ATG); corticosteroids
- Splenectomy to remove enlarged spleen

Interventions

- Prevent bruising.
- Monitor intake and output of fluids.
- Monitor vital signs for changes.
- No intramuscular (IM) injection because of the risk of bleeding.
- No aspirin because of the antiplatelet aggregation factor.
- Instruct the patient:
  - To call the health care provider at the first sign of bruising
  - To plan rest periods to reduce fatigue
  - To use an electric razor to decrease the risk of bleeding

3.4   Iron Deficiency Anemia

Iron deficiency anemia occurs when a decreased amount of iron in blood serum leads to decreased RBCs and decreased hemoglobin, resulting in decreased capacity of RBCs to carry oxygen. Causes are dietary deficiency, blood loss, lactation, and pregnancy.

Signs and Symptoms

- Lightheadedness/headache caused by hypoxia
- Fatigue caused by decreased oxygenation
- Pallor caused by decreased oxygenation
- Spoon nails (Koilonychia): thin, concave-shaped nails raised at edges
- Tachycardia caused by need for increased oxygen throughout the body

Medical Tests

- Peripheral blood smear: poikilocytosis
- RBCs decrease
- Hemoglobin decreases
- Platelets increase
- Mean corpuscular volume decreases
- Mean corpuscular hemoglobin decreases
- Serum ferritin decreases
- Serum iron decreases
- Transferrin saturation decreases
- Serum iron-binding capacity increases

Treatment

Administer

- Iron (oral therapy 3 to 6 months)
  - Ferrous sulfate, ferrous gluconate, ferrous fumarate
- Parenteral iron (patients with continued bleeding or gastrointestinal illness)
  - IM or intravenous (IV) iron dextran (Z-track), IV iron sodium gluconate, IV iron sucrose complex

Interventions

- Monitor intake and output.
- Monitor vital signs.
- Monitor for reactions to therapy.
- Increase dietary intake of iron.
- Instruct the patient:
  - To call the health care provider at the first sign of bleeding

3.5 Pernicious Anemia

Pernicious anemia is a disorder of the gastric mucosa that prevents the secretion of the intrinsic factor by the parietal cells, resulting in an inability of vitamin B_{12} to be absorbed in the intestine. Vitamin B_{12} is needed in the synthesis of hemoglobin.

Signs and Symptoms

- Tingling in hands and feet caused by demyelination of spinal cord nerves
- Fatigue caused by decreased oxygenation
- Pallor caused by decreased oxygenation

- Atrophic glossitis

- Decreased balance caused by cerebral effect

- Decreased position sense

- Dementia later in the disease

Medical Tests

- RBCs decrease

- Hemoglobin decreases

- Mean corpuscular volume increases

- Romberg test to check balance is positive

- Schilling test to check vitamin B_{12} absorption is positive

- Hypochlorhydria

Treatment

Administer

- Vitamin B_{12} by IM injection weekly, then monthly

- Packed RBCs in severe cases

Interventions

- Injury prevention. Patient is at high risk for injury caused by paresthesias and poor balance.

- Instruct the patient:

  o To avoid risky activities to prevent injury

  o To inspect feet daily for injury caused by paresthesia

  o To replace vitamin B_{12} on a lifelong basis, which is necessary to avoid the adverse effects of vitamin B_{12} deficiency, such as dementia

  o To avoid activities that could lead to injury resulting from paresthesias or changes in balance

3.6   Disseminated Intravascular Coagulation (DIC)

Disseminated intravascular coagulation (DIC) is an underlying disease that causes an increasing number of small blood clots to form, resulting in decreased amounts of platelets and coagulation proteins. The patient is at risk for bleeding.

Signs and Symptoms

- Hemolytic anemia caused by RBCs destroyed while passing through blood clots

- Purpura (bleeding under skin) caused by decreased clotting factor

- Unexplained bleeding caused by decreased clotting factor

- Petechiae (ruptured capillaries) caused by decreased clotting factor
- Tissue hypoxia caused by blood clots

Medical Tests

- Prothrombin time (PT) and partial thromboplastin time (PTT) increase
- Fibrin degradation products (FDPs) increase
- D-dimer increases
- Platelet count decreases

Treatment

- Fresh-frozen plasma: Replaces coagulation factor
- Administer platelets to increase clotting factor
- Cryoprecipitate: Replaces fibrinogen
- Packed RBCs: Replace RBC loss caused by bleeding

Interventions

- Monitor for bleeding, including urine and gastrointestinal (GI) tract.
- Do not clean exposed clots.
- Instruct the patient:
  - To call the health care provider immediately at the first sign of bleeding
  - Not to pick or clean exposed clots
  - To use an electric razor
  - To use a soft toothbrush
  - To avoid flossing

3.7   Hemophilia

Hemophilia occurs when normal blood clotting does not take place because the patient is missing a coagulation factor. This is an X-linked recessive inherited disorder affecting males; it rarely affects females. There are two types of hemophilia:

1. **Hemophilia A:** Missing clotting factor VIII
2. **Hemophilia B:** Missing clotting factor IX. This is called Christmas disease.

Signs and Symptoms

- Tarry stool caused by GI bleeding
- Hematuria caused by bleeding
- Swelling of joints caused by bleeding

Medical Tests

- Clotting factor VIII decreased in hemophilia A
- Clotting factor IX decreased in hemophilia B
- PTT increased
- PT normal
- Fibrinogen normal

Treatment

- Cryoprecipitate: Replaces fibrinogen
- Clotting factor VIII for hemophilia A
- Clotting factor IX for hemophilia B
- DDAVP, Stimate, Minirin (desmopressin) for mild deficiency

Interventions

- No IM injections
- Instruct the patient:
  - To refrain from taking aspirin
  - To call the health care provider immediately at the first signs of injury
  - Not to pick or clean exposed clots
  - To use an electric razor
  - To use a soft toothbrush
  - To avoid flossing
  - To wear a medical alert identification

3.8   Leukemia

Leukemia is cancer of the blood and bone marrow, resulting in increased leukocytes. Leukemia is classified as a combination of acute/chronic and lymphocytic/myelocytic. The cause is unknown but may be related to exposure to high levels of radiation, benzene, or chemotherapy.

- **Acute leukemia** is the increase of immature WBCs, leading to decrease in healthy WBCs. It has a rapid progression and metastasizes to organs via blood. This is common in children who have leukemia.
- **Chronic leukemia** is the increase of abnormal, mature WBCs and progresses over months to years.
- **Lymphocytic leukemia** is the increase in immature lymphocytes that infiltrate the central nervous system, spleen, and lymph nodes.
- **Myelocytic leukemia** is the increase of myeloid stem cells that infiltrate all blood cell types.

Signs and Symptoms

- Acute patients
  - Lymphadenopathy

- Splenomegaly
- Hepatomegaly
- Fatigue
- Headache
- Bone pain
- Weight loss
- Nausea/vomiting
- Poor appetite
- Fever
- Ecchymosis
- Epistaxis
- Petechiae
- Gingival (gum) bleeding
- Chronic patients
  - Lymphadenopathy
  - Splenomegaly
  - Fatigue
  - Weight loss
  - Poor appetite

Medical Tests

- RBCs decrease
- Hemoglobin decreases
- Platelets decrease
- WBCs increase
- Bone marrow biopsy: Shows an increase immature WBCs

Treatment

- Acute myelogenous leukemia
  - Anthracycline antibiotics
    - Idamycin (idarubicin), Cerubidine (daunorubicin), cytarabine
  - Antineoplastics
    - Oncovin (vincristine), Elspar (asparaginase)
  - Immunosuppressive to avoid transplant rejection
    - Prednisone
  - Platelets: To increase clotting factor
  - G-CSF
    - Neupogen (filgrastim)

- Chronic myelogenous leukemia
    - Signal transduction inhibitor
        - Imatinib
    - Chemotherapy
        - Busulfex (busulfan), interferon-α, hydroxyurea
- Chronic lymphocytic leukemia
    - Alkylating agents
        - Cytoxan (cyclophosphamide), Leukeran (chlorambucil)
    - Antineoplastics
        - Oncovin (vincristine)
    - Immunosuppressive to avoid transplant rejection
        - Prednisone
    - Chemotherapy
        - Adriamycin (doxorubicin), Fludara (fludarabine)
    - Monoclonal antibody-targeted therapy
        - Campath (alemtuzumab), Rituxan (rituximab)
    - Whole blood
    - Packed RBCs: Replaces RBCs lost by bleeding
    - Platelets: To increase clotting factor

Interventions

- Monitor for infection.
- Maintain a high-protein diet.
- Eat small, frequent meals.
- Monitor for bleeding.
- Instruct the patient:
    - To avoid aspirin
    - To call the health care provider immediately at the first signs of injury or infection
    - Not to pick or clean exposed clots
    - To use an electric razor
    - To use a soft toothbrush
    - To avoid flossing
    - To wear a medical alert identification
    - To avoid infection

3.9 Multiple Myeloma

Multiple myeloma occurs when malignant plasma cells in bone marrow lead to destructive lesions in bone marrow, causing decreased immune system function. Patients, usually older adults, are at risk for infection. The cause is unknown.

Signs and Symptoms

- Anemia caused by decreased production of RBCs by bone marrow
- Osteoporosis
- Pain in the back or ribs
- Spinal cord compression
- Skeletal fractures
- Renal failure caused by protein
- Increased risk of infection

Medical Tests

- CBC:
  - RBCs decrease
  - Hematocrit decreases
  - Hemoglobin decreases
  - Reticulocytes increase
- Red cell distribution width increases
- Calcium increases
- Erythrocyte sedimentation rate increases
- X-rays show bone lytic lesions
- Bone marrow biopsy shows abnormal plasma cells
- Urine analysis shows Bence-Jones protein
- Serum protein electrophoresis shows a monoclonal protein spike
- Peripheral smear shows rouleaux formation

Treatment

- Chemotherapy
  - Melphalan, prednisone, thalidomide, dexamethasone, Oncovin (vincristine), Adriamycin (doxorubicin), dexamethasone, bortezomib, lenalidomide
- Packed RBCs
- Bone marrow transplant

Interventions

- Monitor input and output
- Reduce risk from falling
- High carbohydrate, protein, vitamins, and minerals diet
- Small frequent meals
- Perform muscle strengthening exercises

- Instruct the patient:
  - To avoid activities that risk fall or injury
  - To avoid lifting
  - To notify the health care provider if he or she falls

3.10 Polycythemia Vera

Polycythemia vera is an overproduction of all blood cells leading to thickening of blood that decreases circulation, resulting in organ damage caused by thrombosis and tissue hypoxia. The cause is unknown.

Signs and Symptoms

- Splenomegaly
- Tinnitus
- Headache
- Blurred vision
- Facial plethora
- Hypertension
- Itching worsens
- Difficulty concentrating
- Thrombosis

Medical Tests

- Increase in:
  - RBCs
  - Hemoglobin
  - Hematocrit
  - WBC count
  - Basophils
  - Eosinophils
  - Platelet count
  - Uric acid level
  - Potassium
  - Vitamin B_{12} level
- Bone marrow iron stores absent

Treatment

- Radiation therapy
- Weekly phlebotomy to remove 500 mL of blood, decreasing the hematocrit level to <45

- Increased hydration
- Administer:
  - Anticoagulants
    - Aspirin, Coumadin (warfarin)
  - Myelosuppressive chemotherapy
    Hydroxyurea, anagrelide, radioactive phosphorus 32
  - Antigout medication to decrease uric acid
    - Zyloprim, Aloprim (allopurinol)
  - Alkylating agents
    - Alkeran (melphalan), Busulfex (busulfan)
  - Antihistamine for pruritus
    - Benadryl (diphenhydramine)

Interventions

- Increase fluid intake.
- Monitor for signs of bleeding.
- Monitor for signs of infection.
- Monitor vital signs.
- Monitor for bleeding.
- Monitor for signs of infection.
- Keep the patient mobilized to decrease the chance of clot formation.
- Increase the fluid intake.
- Instruct the patient:
  - To maintain activity to decrease the risk of clot formation
  - To abstain from activities that can cause injury
  - To use an electric razor
  - To use a soft toothbrush
  - To avoid flossing

3.11   Sickle Cell Anemia

Sickle cell anemia occurs when the RBC dehydrates to a form a crescent-like shape called sickling caused by an autosomal recessive gene. Hemolytic anemia results. Clumps of sickled cells are unable to pass easily through small blood vessels. A patient may inherit sickle cell anemia or the trait for sickle cell anemia from his or her parents.

Signs and Symptoms

- Fatigue caused by anemia
- Fever caused by acute sickling episode

- Swollen and painful joints
- Enlarged heart
- Acute pain
- Hepatomegaly

Medical Tests

- Hemoglobin electrophoresis shows majority hemoglobin S
- Blood smear shows sickle cells
- Blood smear shows Howell-Jolly bodies and target cells
- Decreased RBC count
- Increased WBC count
- Increased reticulocytes
- Increased indirect bilirubin

Treatment

Administer:

- Analgesics
- Packed RBCs
- IV fluids for hydration
- 2 to 4 L of O_2 if hypoxic
- Hydrate with IV fluids

Interventions

- Apply warm compresses to the joint.
- Monitor IV fluids for fluid overload.
- Monitor intake and output.
- Instruct the patient:
  - To schedule daily rest periods
  - To increase fluid intake
  - To avoid the cold

3.12 Deep Vein Thrombosis

A blood clot forms when a vein located deep in the legs or arms or the vein becomes inflamed (thrombophlebitis). Platelets and WBCs adhere to walls of the blood vessel, decreasing blood flow and increasing blood pressure. A portion of the clot may form emboli, resulting in a pulmonary embolism and causing respiratory distress. This is caused by hormonal changes, obesity, and immobility.

Signs and Symptoms

- Asymptomatic
- Warmth over the site

- Unilateral pain in leg or arm
- Unilateral swelling of leg or arm

Medical Tests

- Positive Homan's sign
- Doppler flow study shows blockage
- Impedance plethysmography shows blockage
- Magnetic resonance imaging MRI shows blockage
- Venous duplex ultrasound shows blockage
- D-dimer increase

Treatment

- Thrombectomy to remove clot
- Umbrella filter to trap future emboli if condition is chronic
- Administer:
  - Anticoagulants
    - Heparin (IV), Coumadin (warfarin), enoxaparin (Lovenox)
  - Tissue plasminogen (t-P) activator
    - t-P

Interventions

- Elevate the leg.
- Apply a warm compress to the site.
- Rest in bed.
- Monitor the vital signs.
- Monitor the signs of pulmonary embolism.
  - Dyspnea, tachycardia, tachypnea, diaphoresis, chest pains
- Monitor PT, PTT, international normalized ratio (INR) during anticoagulant therapy
- Monitor for bleeding
- Instruct the patient:
  - To avoid massaging the site
  - To avoid participating in activities that can cause injury
  - To use an electric razor
  - To use a soft toothbrush
  - To avoid flossing
  - To call the health care provider at the first sign of bleeding

3.13   Idiopathic Thrombocytopenic Purpura (ITP)

Antibodies develop against the patient's platelets in the spleen, resulting from an autoimmune disorder and leading to bleeding.

Signs and Symptoms

- Petechiae
- Menorrhagia
- Epistaxis
- Purpura

Medical Tests

- RBCs decrease
- Hematocrit decreases
- Hemoglobin decreases
- Platelets decrease
- PT normal
- PTT normal

Treatment

- Splenectomy provides remission
- Stem cell transplant
- Prednisone to stop bleeding
- IV immunoglobulin to restore antibodies
- Immunosuppressive therapy
  - Oncovin (vincristine); Imuran, Azasan (azathioprine); cyclosporine; Cytoxan (cyclophosphamide); Rituxan (rituximab)

Interventions

- Monitor vital signs for changes.
- Monitor for signs of bleeding.
- Instruct the patient:
  - To avoid infection
  - To avoid massaging the site
  - To avoid participating in activities that can cause injury
  - To use an electric razor
  - To use a soft toothbrush
  - To avoid flossing
  - To call the health care provider at the first sign of bleeding

Solved Problems

3.1   What is anemia?

Anemia is a low RBC count leading to low hemoglobin, decreasing the blood's ability to carry oxygen and oxygenate tissues.

3.2   What is an underlying cause of anemia?

The underlying cause can be blood loss, hemolysis, nutritional deficiency, particularly deficiency in folic acid, vitamin B_{12}, and iron or bone marrow disorder.

3.3   When are lightheadedness and headache signs of anemia?

Lightheadedness and headache are signs of anemia when they are caused by hypoxia.

3.4   What is the treatment for anemia?

The treatment for anemia is to take care of the underlying cause.

3.5   What is pancytopenia?

Pancytopenia is aplastic anemia. Bone marrow disorder reduces production of RBCs, WBCs, and platelets, increasing the risk of bleeding and infection.

3.6   When is ecchymosis a sign of pancytopenia?

Ecchymosis is a sign of pancytopenia when it is caused by decreased platelets.

3.7   What is the purpose of administering hematopoietic growth factor in pancytopenia?

The purpose of administering hematopoietic growth factor in pancytopenia is to increase WBC count.

3.8   When should IM injections not be administered to a patient who has pancytopenia?

IM injections should not be administered to a patient who has pancytopenia caused by risk of bleeding.

3.9   Why should a patient who has pancytopenia use an electric razor?

A patient who has pancytopenia should use an electric razor to decrease the risk of bleeding.

3.10   What is pernicious anemia?

Pernicious anemia is the inability of vitamin B_{12} to be absorbed in the intestine, which is needed to synthesize hemoglobin.

3.11   Why is vitamin B_{12} not absorbed in a patient who has pernicious anemia?

Disorder of the gastric mucosa prevents the secretion of the intrinsic factor by the parietal cells, resulting in an inability of vitamin B_{12} to be absorbed in the intestine.

3.12   What is a later sign of pernicious anemia?

Dementia is a later sign of pernicious anemia.

3.13   What is DIC?

DIC is the formation of an increasing number of small blood clots, resulting in decreased amounts of platelets and coagulation proteins. The patient is at risk for bleeding.

3.14   What are the signs and symptoms of DIC?

The signs and symptoms of DIC are hemolytic anemia caused by RBCs being destroyed while passing through blood clots, purpura (bleeding under skin) caused by decrease in clotting factor, unexplained bleeding caused by decreased clotting factor, petechiae (ruptured capillaries) caused by decrease in clotting factor, and tissue hypoxia caused by blood clots.

3.15   What should you tell a patient who has DIC and clots form on the skin from a cut?

Do not clean or pick the exposed clots.

3.16   Why should a patient who has DIC use a soft toothbrush?

A patient who has DIC should use a soft toothbrush to avoid the risk of bleeding.

3.17   What is hemophilia A?

Hemophilia A is a condition in which normal blood clotting does not occur because the patient is missing the coagulation factor VIII.

3.18   A patient who is concerned because hemophilia runs in his family asks the likelihood of his daughter developing hemophilia. How would you respond?

This is an X-linked recessive inherited disorder affecting males and rarely affects females.

3.19   What are signs and symptoms of hemophilia?

The signs and symptoms of hemophilia are tarry stool caused by GI bleeding, hematuria caused by bleeding, and swelling joints caused by bleeding.

3.20   What is leukemia?

Leukemia is cancer of blood and bone marrow, resulting in increased leukocytes.

3.21   What is acute leukemia?

Acute leukemia is the increase of immature WBCs, leading to the decrease in healthy WBCs. This has a rapid progression and metastasizes to organs via blood. This is common in children who have leukemia.

3.22   What is lymphocytic leukemia?

Lymphocytic leukemia is the increase in immature lymphocytes that infiltrate the central nervous system, spleen, and lymph nodes.

3.23   What is multiple myeloma?

Multiple myeloma is characterized by malignant plasma cells in bone marrow leading to destructive lesions in bone marrow and causing a decrease in immune system function. Usually older adults are at risk for infection. The cause is unknown.

3.24   What is ITP?

ITP occurs when antibodies develop against the patient's platelets in the spleen, resulting from an autoimmune disorder and leading to bleeding.

3.25   What is deep vein thrombosis?

Deep vein thrombosis occurs when a blood clot forms within a vein located deep in the legs or arms or the vein becomes inflamed (thrombophlebitis). Platelets and WBCs adhere to walls of the blood vessel, decreasing blood flow and increasing blood pressure. A portion of the clot may form an emboli, resulting in a pulmonary embolism and causing respiratory distress. This is caused by hormonal changes, obesity, and immobility.

CHAPTER 4

Cardiovascular System

4.1 Definition

The four chambers of the heart:

1. Left atrium: Left upper chamber
2. Right atrium: Right upper chamber
3. Left ventricle: Left lower chamber
4. Right ventricle: Right lower chamber

The septal wall separates the right side from the left side of the heart.

Valves

- **Atrioventricular (AV) valves:** Control blood flow between the upper and lower chambers
- **Tricuspid valve:** On the right side between the atria and the ventricles
- **Mitral valve:** On the left side between the atria and the ventricles
- **Pulmonic valve:** Controls the flow between the right ventricle and the pulmonary artery
- **Aortic valve:** Controls the flow between the left ventricle and the aorta

Electrical Conduction

- Sinoatrial (SA) node:
  - Located in the right atrium
  - Initiates the heart beat
- AV node:
  - Located in the superior portion of the ventricular septum
  - Atria repolarizes
- Right and left bundle of His:
  - Ends in the Purkinje fibers
  - Spread through the ventricles
  - Cause ventricular contraction

Blood Flow

1. Unoxygenated blood empties into the right atrium from the systemic circulation via the inferior vena cava and superior vena cava.

2. The right atrium contracts and the tricuspid valve opens, allowing the blood to flow into the right ventricle.

3. The right ventricle contracts and the pulmonic valve opens, allowing the unoxygenated blood to enter the pulmonary artery to go to the lungs to pick up oxygen.

4. Oxygenated blood returns from the lungs to the heart via the pulmonary vein and enters the left atrium.

5. The left atrium contracts and the mitral valve opens, allowing the blood to flow into the left ventricle. The left ventricle contracts and the aortic valve opens, allowing the blood to flow into the aorta and systemic circulation.

6. Blood returns to the heart from the lower body via the inferior vena cava and from the upper body via the super vena cava.

Heart Sounds

- Mitral and tricuspid valves closing create the first heart sound (S1).
- Aortic pulmonic valve closing creates the second heart sound (S2).

4.2 Aortic Aneurysm

Atherosclerosis, degeneration of the middle aortic muscle layer, trauma, infection, or congenital defects can weaken the aortic wall. Pressure from blood flow causes the wall to bulge. Blood becomes turbulent, resulting in an increased dilation of the weakened wall. The aneurysm may rupture, causing a drop in circulation, severe hypotension, syncope, and possibly death.

Signs and Symptoms

- Asymptomatic
- Restlessness and anxiety
- Increased thready pulse and decreased pulse pressure
- Decreased femoral pulses
- Abdominal pulsation
- Back pain radiating to posterior legs
- Abdominal pain

Medical Tests

- Chest X-ray, abdominal ultrasound, computed tomography (CT) scan, or magnetic resonance imaging (MRI) to display the aortic aneurysm
- Auscultation of bruit (swishing sound of turbulent blood) over the iliac or femoral arteries or abdominal aorta

Treatment

- Administer:
  - Morphine sulfate or oxycodone to decrease oxygen demand

    o Antihypertensives to reduce blood pressure

    o Analgesics to reduce pain associated with tearing of the aortic wall and the pressure the aortic aneurysm is placing on the nerves

- Surgically resect the aortic aneurysm

Interventions

- Limit activity and encourage the patient to rest in a quiet place to reduce anxiety.
- Palpate the abdomen for pulsating mass or distention. Distention may signify imminent rupture.
- Listen for abdominal bruits.
- Monitor for:
  - Numbness and tingling
  - Decreased temperature of extremities
  - Increased thready pulse
  - Change in skin color in extremities
  - Pale clammy skin, indicating decreased circulation
  - Restlessness, indicating increased anxiety and decreased oxygenation
  - Intake and output and urine quality. Low urine output and high specific gravity of urine indicate hypovolemia.
- Hypovolemic shock:
  - Decreased blood pressure caused by rupture of the aortic aneurysm
  - Decreased peripheral pulse resulting from decrease in blood pressure
  - Increased heart rate as heart tries to meet increased demand for oxygen
  - Increased respiration to increase demand for oxygen
- Decreased pulse pressure resulting from less filling time between cardiac contractions and decreased circulating volume of blood
- Severe back pain caused by rupture or dissection

4.3   Angina (Angina Pectoris)

Arteriosclerosis of the coronary artery narrows blood flow to cardiac muscles. Chest pain, pressure, heaviness, squeezing, or tightness occurs when cardiac muscle demand for oxygen exceeds the supply of oxygen. The three categories of angina are:

1. **Stable angina:** Chest pain occurs after exercise or stress and is relieved by rest or nitrates.
2. **Unstable angina:** Chest pain occurs at rest with increasing intensity and duration and is not relieved by rest; it is slow to respond to nitrates.
3. **Prinzmetal's or vasospastic angina:** Chest pain occurs at night at rest with minimal exertion.

Signs and Symptoms

- Chest pain, pressure, heaviness, squeezing, tightness for up to 5 minutes; radiates to the jaw, back, or arms; occurs at rest, after exercise or stress, which increases oxygen demands on the heart
- Shortness of breath (dyspnea) caused by increased respiration related to increased demand for oxygen
- Tachycardia caused by increased need to pump oxygenated blood
- Increased anxiety resulting from decreased oxygen to cardiac muscles
- Sweating (diaphoresis) caused by anxiety and increased cardiac workload

Medical Tests

- Electrocardiogram (ECG) during attack:
  - T-wave inverted: First sign of initial ischemia
  - ST-segment changes: Indicate myocardium injury
  - Abnormal Q-waves: Indicate myocardium infarction
- Cardiac panel: Troponin, isoenzyme of creatine kinase with muscle and brain subunits (CK-MB), electrolytes
- Routine blood workup: complete blood count (CBC), blood chemistry, prothrombin time (PT), partial thromboplastin time (PTT), international normalized ratio (INR), brain natriuretic peptide (BNP), cholesterol panel
- Holter monitoring for 24 to 48 hours provides continuous cardiac monitoring.
- Stress test: Assess cardiac function under pharmacologic or exercise stress.
- Coronary arteriography: Assess arteriosclerosis of the coronary artery.
- Cardiac positron emission tomography (PET): Assess arteriosclerosis of the coronary artery.
- Chest X-ray: Assess for heart failure.
- Echocardiogram or stress-echo: Assess cardiac abnormality caused by ischemia.

Treatment

- Rest: Reduces cardiac demand for oxygen
- Administer:
  - 2 to 4 L of oxygen to increase oxygen supply
  - Analgesic (morphine) to decrease cardiac workload and pain
  - Nitrates (nitroglycerin) to dilate blood vessels, increasing blood flow to cardiac muscles
  - Beta-adrenergic blocker to decrease cardiac workload
    - Inderal (propranolol), Corgard (nadolol), Tenormin (atenolol), Lopressor (metoprolol)
  - Aspirin to reduce formation of platelets
- Procedures:
  - Percutaneous transluminal coronary angioplasty: An inflated balloon within the coronary artery compresses the blockage against the artery wall.
  - Coronary artery stent: A mesh tube is inserted into the coronary artery, reducing the blockage.
  - Coronary artery bypass graph (CABG): A vein from a leg or artery from an arm or chest is graphed to coronary arteries, bypassing the blockage.
- Diet:
  - Low cholesterol
  - Low sodium
  - Low fat

Interventions

- Place the patient in a semi-Fowler's position and avoid stress.
- Monitor his or her vital signs:
  - Hold the nitrate order if the systolic blood pressure is <90 mm Hg because of the risk of reduced blood to the brain.

- o Hold beta-adrenergic blocker if the heart rate is <60 beats per minute because of the risk of low cardiac output.
- Monitor the patient with a 12-lead ECG during each attack.
- Monitor the intake and output to assess renal function.
- Instruct the patient:
  - o To take one sublingual dose every 5 minutes for a maximum of three doses at the first signs of angina
  - o To rest immediately
  - o To call 911 if the signs of angina continue for more than 10 minutes
  - o To avoid the stress that brings about angina
  - o To adhere to the diet
  - o To stop smoking

4.4   Myocardial Infarction (MI)

Blockage of coronary arteries reduces oxygen supply to cardiac muscle, resulting in necrosis of an area of cardiac muscle known as a myocardial infarction. Blockage is caused by atherosclerosis, which results in a buildup of plaque on the wall of the artery.

Signs and Symptoms

- Restlessness, feeling of impending doom, anxiety
- Chest pain radiating to arms, jaw, back, and/or neck that is unrelieved by rest or nitroglycerin, unlike angina
- Cool, clammy pale skin caused by decreased circulation
- Diaphoresis (sweating) caused by anxiety
- Tachycardia caused by pain and low cardiac output
- Nausea or vomiting possible caused by decreased cardiac output
- Variable blood pressure resulting from decreased cardiac output
- Shortness of breath in elderly and women
- Asymptomatic (silent heart attack) in diabetics

Medical Tests

- Labs:
  - o Increased white blood cells (WBC) resulting from inflammatory response to infarction
  - o Elevated CK-MB released by injured tissue; follows a predetermined curve reflecting tissue damage and repair
  - o Elevated troponin I and troponin T-proteins within 1 hour of infarction released by injured tissue
- Urine output: <25 mL/hr caused by lack of renal blood flow
- ECG
  - o T wave: Inversion indicates ischemia
  - o ST segment: Elevated or depressed indicates cardiac tissue injury
  - o Q waves: Significant indicates infarction
- Decreased pulse pressure caused by decreased cardiac output

Treatment

Administer:

- 2 to 4 L of oxygen to increase oxygen supply
- Aspirin to reduce formation of platelets
- Antiarrhythmics to control cardiac arrhythmias
  - Cordarone (amiodarone), Lidocaine, Pronestyl (procainamide)
- Antihypertensive to decrease blood pressure
  - Apresoline (hydralazine)
- Thrombolytic therapy within 3 to 12 hours of an attack to reduce blockage
  - Activase (alteplase), Streptase (streptokinase), Eminase (anistreplase), Retavase (reteplase)
- Heparin to prevent clots after thrombolytic therapy
- Calcium channel blockers for non–Q-wave infarction to prevent reinfarction
  - Isoptin (verapamil), Cardizem (diltiazem)
- Beta-adrenergic blockers to decrease duration of pain
  - Inderal (propranolol), Corgard (nadolol), Lopressor (metoprolol)
- Analgesics to decrease pain and cardiac workload
  - Morphine
- Nitrates to dilate blood vessels
  - Nitroglycerin
- Electrical cardioversion in unstable ventricular tachycardia to re-establish sinus rhythm
- Percutaneous revascularization to restore cardiac blood flow

Interventions

- Maintain the patient on bed rest without bathroom privileges.
- Place the patient in a semi-Fowler's position and avoid stress.
- Monitor his or her vital signs.
- Use 12-lead ECG monitoring for an episode.
- Instruct the patient:
  - To eat a low-fat, low-cholesterol, low-sodium diet
  - To reduce stress, reduce weight, and engage in moderate exercise
  - To stop smoking
  - To identify MI pain and angina pain
  - To recognize when to take nitroglycerin and when to call 911

4.5   Coronary Artery Disease (CAD)

Plaque buildup on the walls of the coronary artery from deposits reduces blood flow to the cardiac muscle. Cardiac muscle is deprived of oxygen and nutrients, injuring the muscle. Plaque buildup is the result of high levels of cholesterol and fat intake, smoking, hypertension, and diabetes.

Signs and Symptoms

- Angina pain radiating to arms, jaw, back, and/or neck lasting 3 to 5 minutes after stress or at rest caused by decreased oxygen to cardiac muscle
- Asymptomatic

Medical Tests

- Labs:
  - Total cholesterol: Increased
  - High-density lipoproteins (HDL): Decreased
  - Low-density lipoproteins (LDL): Increased
- ECG during attack
  - T wave: Inversion indicates ischemia
  - ST segment: Elevated or depressed indicates cardiac tissue injury
  - Q waves: Significant indicates infarction

Treatment

Administer:

- Aspirin to reduce formation of platelets
- Beta-adrenergic blockers to decrease duration of pain
  - Inderal (propranolol), Corgard (nadolol), Lopressor (metoprolol)
- Calcium channel blockers for non–Q-wave infarction to prevent reinfarction
  - Isoptin (verapamil), Cardizem (diltiazem)
- Nitrates to dilate blood vessels
  - Nitroglycerin
- Platelet inhibitor to decrease platelet formation
  - Persantine (dipyridamole), Plavix (clopidogrel), Ticlid (ticlopidine)
- Statin 3-hydroxy-3-methylglutaryl coenzyme A (HMG CoA) reductase inhibitors decrease cholesterol formation
  - Mevacor (lovastatin), Zocor (simvastatin), Lipitor (atorvastatin), Lescol (fluvastatin), Pravachol (pravastatin), Crestor (rosuvastatin)
- Fibric acid derivatives to increase breakdown of very low-density lipoproteins (VLDL)
  - Lopid (gemfibrozil)
- Bile acid–binding resins to bind intestinal bile acid
  - Colestid (colestipol)
- Nicotinic acid to decrease production of VLDL
  - Niacin

Interventions

- Monitor:
  - Vital signs for hypertension and irregular heart rate
  - Liver function if patient is taking statin HMG CoA reductase inhibitors

- Instruct the patient:
  - ○ To eat a low-fat, low-cholesterol, low-sodium, high-fiber diet
  - ○ To reduce stress, reduce weight, and engage in moderate exercise
  - ○ To stop smoking

4.6 Peripheral Arterial Disease

Atherosclerosis, a blood clot or inflammation, narrows peripheral arteries and reduces blood flow to tissues. Acute peripheral arterial disease is caused by a temporary narrowing of peripheral arteries. Chronic peripheral arterial disease is caused by a permanent narrowing of peripheral arteries and can lead to skin ulceration and gangrene.

Signs and Symptoms

- Weak or absent pulse in area caused by decreased circulation
- Pallor or mottling (patchy coloring) skin and decreased skin temperature in area caused by decreased circulation
- Intermittent claudication (pain, numbness, and weakness with walking) caused by increased oxygen demand on muscle
- Dependent rubor (redness) when legs are lower
- Sudden pain in area caused by decreased oxygenation of muscle
- Hair loss in area caused by decreased circulation

Medical Tests

- Ankle brachial index (ABI) measures arterial insufficiency
- Doppler ultrasonography to assess size of blockage
- Arteriography: An X-ray of the blockage using dye

Treatment

- Atherectomy: Plaque is ground from the artery wall using a catheter containing a grinding tool.
- Amputation: The affected limb is surgically removed.
- Embolectomy: The emboli are surgical removed from the affected artery.
- Femoropopliteal bypass graft: The blockage is bypassed by grafting a vein or artery from another part of the body.
- Laser angioplasty: The blockage is removed by a laser-tipped catheter.
- Percutaneous transluminal angioplasty: A balloon catheter is inflated, causing the artery to stretch. The healing process removes the plaque buildup.
- Thromboendarterectomy: The atherosclerotic tissue is surgically removed.
- Stent: A tube is inserted to keep the artery open.

Administer:

- Platelet inhibitor to decrease platelet formation
  - ○ Trental (pentoxifylline), Pletal (cilostazol), aspirin, Plavix (clopidogrel), Persantine (dipyridamole), Ticlid (ticlopidine)

- Anticoagulant to prevent formation of blood clots
  - Heparin, Coumadin (warfarin)

Interventions

- Check the capillary refill.
- Examine the distal pulses and compare the bilateral pulses for decreased circulation.
- Assess the skin in the affected area (temperature, color) to detect decreased tissue perfusion.
- Instruct the patient:
  - To eat a low-fat, low-cholesterol, low-sodium, high-fiber diet
  - To reduce stress, reduce weight, and engage in moderate exercise
  - To stop smoking
  - To wear loose-fitting clothes to avoid restrictions of blood vessels
  - To report pain, numbness, or paralysis immediately to a health care provider
  - Not to elevate leg or apply heat because it is difficult for blood to circulate in that area
  - Not to engage in prolonged sitting because it increases the risk for blood clot formation

4.7   Cardiac Tamponade

In cardiac tamponade, the pericardium fills with fluid, blood, or pus as a result of trauma, postoperative complications, or complications from an MI, cancer, or uremia. Pressure in the pericardium reduces filling of the ventricles, resulting in decreased cardiac output.

Signs and Symptoms

- Muffled cardiac sounds caused by fluid
- Sweating (diaphoresis), tachycardia, and difficulty breathing (dyspnea) caused by the increased demand for oxygen
- Restlessness caused by decreased oxygen to the brain
- Pulsus paradoxus (decrease of 10 mm Hg or more in systolic blood pressure on inspiration) caused by pressure change within the chest on inspiration
- Fatigue caused by increased workload
- Jugular vein distention caused by decreased venous return from the jugular veins

Medical Tests

- Chest X-ray: Assess for enlarged heart
- ECG: Ultrasound image of the heart to assess cardiac structure and function
- ECG: Excludes cardiac disorders
- Cardiac catheterization

Treatment

- Pericardiocentesis: Aspirate fluid from the pericardium
- Administer:

- o 2 to 4 L of oxygen to increase oxygen supply
- o Beta-adrenergic blockers to decrease duration of pain
  - ▪ Inderal (propranolol), Corgard (nadolol), Lopressor (metoprolol)

Interventions

- Monitor the patient's vital signs.

4.8 Cardiogenic Shock

Cardiac tamponade, myocardial ischemia, myocarditis, or cardiomyopathies result in the heart being unable to pump blood, resulting in decreased blood pressure. Blood backs up from the left ventricle into the lungs, causing pulmonary edema. The cardiac rate increases to compensate for the decrease in blood flow. Cardiac muscle oxygenation decreases because the lungs are unable to oxygenate the blood.

Signs and Symptoms

- Distended jugular veins caused by fluid overload
- Hypotension caused by decreased blood flow
- Clammy skin caused by tissue deoxygenation
- Confusion caused by poor perfusion of the brain
- Crackles in lungs indicating fluid buildup and pulmonary edema
- Skin pallor (decreased skin temperature) caused by decreased circulation
- Cyanosis caused by poor perfusion
- Arrhythmias caused by irritability of cardiac muscle from decreased oxygenation
- Oliguria (urine output <30 mL/hr) caused by decreased kidney perfusion
- Tachycardia caused by increased cardiac demand for blood

Medical Tests

- ECG
  - o Q-wave: Enlarged because of cardiac failure
  - o ST waves: Elevated because of ischemia
- Echocardiogram: Ultrasound image of the heart to assess cardiac structure and function

Treatment

- Swan-Ganz catheterization to measure pressure in the pulmonary artery
- Labs:
  - o Arterial blood gas to assess the acid-base balance of blood
- Administer:
  - o Vasodilator to reduce peripheral arterial resistance and decrease cardiac workload—dilates
    - ▪ Nitropress (nitroprusside), nitroglycerin
  - o Adrenergic agent to increase blood pressure and cardiac rate
    - ▪ Epinephrine

o Inotropes to strengthen cardiac contractions

- Dopamine, dobutamine, amiodarone (inamrinone), Primacor (milrinone)

o Vasopressor to increase blood flow to the heart and brain and decrease blood flow to other organs

- Norepinephrine

Interventions

- Place the patient on bed rest.
- Administer 2 to 4 L of oxygen to increase the oxygen supply.
- Monitor the vital signs. The patient is at risk for respiratory distress.
- Measure fluid intake and output to assess for adequate renal perfusion.
- Weigh the patient daily, and notify the health care provider if the patient's weight increases 3 lb (4.4 kg).
- Instruct the patient:

  o To notify the health care provider if the patient is short of breath or shows sign of fluid retention (dependent edema)

  o To eat a low-sodium, low-fat diet

  o To rest frequently

4.9　Cardiomyopathy

The myocardium is weakened and stretches, resulting in enlargement of the heart, decreased cardiac contraction, and decreased cardiac output. The cause is idiopathic.

There are three types of cardiomyopathy:

1. **Dilated:** The myocardium becomes thick, leading to congestive heart failure and decreased ventricular pumping action.
2. **Hypertrophic:** The ventricular myocardium thickens, leading to restriction of blood flow.
3. **Restrictive:** The myocardium becomes stiff, leading to decreased filling of the ventricles. This condition is secondary to open heart surgery.

Signs and Symptoms

- Asymptomatic
- S3 heart sound caused by vibration of the ventricular when filling
- S4 heart sound caused by vibration when the atria contracts and fill the ventricles
- Murmur: Turbulence of abnormal blood flow
- Chest pain caused by narrowing of coronary arteries related to increased thickness of the myocardium and increased cardiac oxygen demand
- Syncope caused by cardiac arrhythmias
- Dyspnea caused by increased pressure on the lungs

Medical Tests

- ECG: Abnormal ST wave
- Echocardiography: Shows enlarged heart

- Chest X-ray: Shows pulmonary congestion and enlarged heart
- Stress test: Identifies decreased cardiac function during exercise

Treatment

- Myectomy: Removal of cardiac tissue
- Implantable cardioverter-defibrillator: Defibrillate heart as necessary (high-risk patients)
- Administer:
  - Diuretics: Decrease fluid volume
    - Lasix (furosemide), Bumex (bumetanide), Zaroxolyn (metolazone) [for dilated], Aldactone (spironolactone) [aldosterone antagonist]
  - Calcium channel blockers: Decrease cardiac workload
    - Isoptin (verapamil)
  - Angiotensin-converting enzyme (ACE) inhibitors: Decrease pressure in the left ventricle
    - Prinivil (lisinopril), Capoten (captopril), Vasotec (enalapril)
  - Beta-adrenergic blockers: Decrease cardiac contractions
    - Inderal (propranolol), Corgard (nadolol), Lopressor (metoprolol)
  - Anticoagulant: Decreases blood coagulation
    - Heparin, Coumadin (warfarin)
  - Inotropic agent: Increases cardiac contractions
    - Dopamine, dobutamine, amiodarone (inamrinone), Primacor (milrinone), Digitalis (digoxin) [for dilated]
  - Stool softener to prevent straining
    - Colace (docusate)

Interventions

- Place the patient on rest and place him or her in a semi-Fowler's position.
- Monitor his or her vitals.
- Weigh the patient daily, and notify the health care provider if the patient's weight increases 3 lb (4.4 kg).
- Measure the fluid intake and output.
- Instruct the patient to follow a low-sodium diet.
- Instruct the patient:
  - To stop straining
  - To stop smoking
  - To stop drinking alcohol

4.10   Endocarditis

An invasive medical procedure or intravenous (IV) drug use introduces microorganisms into the blood. An infection by a microorganism develops in the inner lining of the heart (endocardium) and heart valves, resulting in cardiac inflammation and leading to ulceration and necrosis of heart valves. Endocarditis is also secondary to degenerative heart disease and rheumatic heart disease.

Signs and Symptoms

- Janeway lesions: On the soles and palms
- Petechiae: On fingernails and palate
- Osler nodes: On pads of fingers and feet
- Fatigue: Related to the infection
- Murmurs: Caused by turbulent blood flow
- Fever: Related to the infection

Medical Tests

- Echocardiography: To examine functioning of heart valves
- Transesophageal echocardiography: To examine functioning of heart valves
- Chest X-ray: To examine pulmonary and cardiac abnormalities
- Blood culture and sensitivity test: Three times, 1 hour apart to identify the microorganism and determine treatment

Treatment

- Administer antibiotics according to results of culture and sensitivity tests.
- Replace valves when they are damaged.

Interventions

- Maintain the patient on bed rest to reduce cardiac demand.
- Monitor for renal failure:
  o Decreased urine output
  o Increased blood urea nitrogen (BUN) levels
  o Increased creatinine clearance
- Monitor for embolism:
  o Hematuria
  o Decreased mentation
  o Cough or painful breathing
- Monitor for heart failure:
  o Weight gain and edema
  o Distended neck vein
  o Crackles in lungs
  o Dyspnea
  o Tachycardia
- Instruct the patient:
  o To take all prescribed antibiotics even if he or she is feeling well
  o To tell a health care provider, including a dentist, to administered prophylactic antibiotics before, during, and after an invasive medical procedure

4.11   Congestive Heart Failure (CHF)

Ventricles are unable to contract at full capacity, causing decreased circulation and a backup of blood. This is caused by an MI, hypertension, valve disorder, or endocarditis. Left-sided CHF results in the backup of blood into the lungs. Right-sided CHF results in the backup of blood into the systemic circulation, which causes edema.

Signs and Symptoms

- Early signs:
  - Fatigue
  - S3 heart sound
  - Nocturia
  - Dyspnea on exertion
  - Bilateral rales in lungs
  - Hepatojugular reflux
- Advanced signs:
  - Orthopnea
  - Cardiomegaly
  - Hepatomegaly
  - Cough
  - Anasarca (edema)
  - Cardiac rales
  - Frothy or pink sputum caused by capillary permeability

Medical Tests

- ECG: T-wave sign of ischemia, tachycardia
- Labs:
  - Increased B-type natriuretic peptide
  - Decreased hemoglobin
  - HCT $<3\times$ hemoglobin
  - Increased BUN, increased creatinine clearance, decreased urine output
- Chest X-ray:
  - Enlarged left ventricle (left-sided heart failure)
  - Pulmonary congestion
  - Pleural effusion (right-sided heart failure)
  - Cardiomegaly (right-sided heart failure)

Treatment

Administer:

- Diuretics: Decrease fluid volume
  - Lasix (furosemide), Bumex (bumetanide), Zaroxolyn (metolazone), Aldactone (spironolactone) [aldosterone antagonist]

- ACE inhibitors: Decrease pressure in the left ventricle
  - Prinivil (lisinopril), Capoten (captopril), Vasotec (enalapril)
- Beta-adrenergic blockers: Decrease cardiac contractions
  - Inderal (propranolol), Corgard (nadolol), Lopressor (metoprolol)
- Inotropic agent: Increase cardiac contractions
  - Dopamine, dobutamine, amiodarone (inamrinone), Primacor (milrinone), Digitalis (digoxin)
- Vasodilator to reduce peripheral arterial resistance and decrease cardiac workload—dilates
  - Nitropress (nitroprusside), nitroglycerin
- Anticoagulant: Decrease blood coagulation
  - Heparin, Coumadin (warfarin)

Interventions

- Instruct the patient to rest and place him or her in a high-Fowler's position.
- Monitor his or her vitals.
- Weigh him or her daily. Notify the health care provider if weight increases 3 lb (4.4 kg).
- Measure the fluid intake and output.
- Instruct the patient to maintain a low-sodium diet.
- Administer 2 to 4 L of oxygen to increase the oxygen supply.
- Instruct the patient:
  - To raise his or her legs to reduce dependent edema
  - To eat a low-sodium diet

4.12   Hypertension

Blood vessel pressure increases secondary to an underlying condition or idiopathically.

Classifications of Hypertension:
- Normal <120 mm Hg systolic / <80 mm Hg diastolic
- Prehypertension: 120 to 139 mm Hg systolic / 80 to 89 mm Hg diastolic
- Stage 1 hypertension: 140 to 159 mm Hg systolic / 90 to 99 mm Hg diastolic
- Stage 2 hypertension: ≥160 mm Hg / systolic ≥100 mm Hg diastolic
- Diabetic hypertension: 130 mm Hg systolic / 80 mm Hg diastolic or higher

Signs and Symptoms

- Asymptomatic
- Dizziness
- Headache

Medical Tests

- Blood pressure >140/90 mm Hg on at least three different occasions when lying, sitting, and standing, bilaterally

Treatment

- First: Change lifestyle:
  - o Decrease caloric intake.
  - o Decrease caffeine intake.
  - o Decrease alcohol intake.
  - o Follow a low-sodium diet.
  - o Increase exercise.
  - o Stop smoking.
- Second: Administer medication:
  - o Diuretics to decrease circulation
    - Lasix (furosemide), Bumex (bumetanide), Zaroxolyn (metolazone), Aldactone (spironolactone) [aldosterone antagonist]
  - o Beta-adrenergic blocker to decrease cardiac output
    - Inderal (propranolol), Corgard (nadolol), Lopressor (metoprolol)
  - o Calcium channel blockers to increase peripheral vasodilation
    - Isoptin (verapamil), Cardizem/Dilacor/Tiazac (diltiazem), Cardene (nicardipine)
  - o ACE inhibitors to delay renal disease
    - Prinivil (lisinopril), Capoten (captopril), Vasotec (enalapril)
- Third: Increase medication dosages
- Fourth: Combine medications

Interventions

- Measure the fluid intake and output.
- Maintain a stress-free environment.
- Follow a low-sodium diet.
- Instruct the patient:
  - o To change his or her lifestyle to avoid being prescribed medication
  - o To decrease his or her weight
  - o To take note of the side effects of medications

4.13   Hypovolemic Shock

Hypovolemic shock is a decrease in circulation from hemorrhage, dehydration, or blood moving from blood vessels into tissues, resulting in inadequate organ perfusion.

Signs and Symptoms

- Tachycardia caused by cardiac compensation for reduced blood volume
- Agitation and restlessness caused by decreased brain perfusion
- Hypotension caused by decreased blood volume

- Decreased skin temperature caused by decreased circulation, resulting in peripheral vasoconstriction
- Urine output <25 mL/hr caused by decreased kidney perfusion

Medical Tests

- Decreased blood pressure
- Increased heart rate
- Labs:
  - Decreased hemoglobin (anemia)
  - Increased BUN
  - Increased creatinine clearance
  - Decreased hematocrit
  - Arterial blood gas: Decreased pH, increased partial pressure of carbon dioxide (PCO_2), decreased partial pressure of oxygen (PO_2)
- Decreased urine output (renal failure)

Treatment

Administer:

- Catecholamines to increase blood pressure
  - Dopamine, epinephrine, and norepinephrine
- Inotropic agent to increase blood pressure
  - Dobutamine
- IV use largest catheter (14 G)
- Crystalloid solutions to expand intravascular and extravascular fluid volume
  - 0.9% normal saline, lactated Ringer's solution (contains electrolytes)
- Fresh-frozen plasma for clotting
- Blood replacement (type O negative universal donor)

Interventions

- Monitor the patient's vital signs every 15 minutes.
- Administer 2 to 4 L of oxygen (increase oxygen if <80 mm Hg systolic).
- Measure urine output hourly using indwelling urinary catheter. Increase the fluid intake if the urine output is <30 mL/hr.
- Monitor the lungs for crackles and dyspnea caused by fluid overflow.
- Instruct the patient:
  - How to avoid hypovolemic shock

4.14 Myocarditis

Infection from chronic alcohol abuse, disease, and drug use causes the cardiac muscle to become inflamed. Inflammation can degenerate the cardiac muscle, leading to CHF.

Signs and Symptoms

- Dyspnea related to CHF
- Chest pain caused by infection and inflammation
- Fever caused by infection and inflammation
- S3 gallop related to CHF
- Tachycardia caused by increased cardiac workload

Medical Tests

- Labs: Increased CK-MB and increased troponins related to cardiac cell injury
- Chest X-ray shows cardiomegaly
- Echocardiogram shows cardiomegaly
- ECG: Abnormal ST segment related to inflammation
- Endomyocardial biopsy to identify microorganism

Treatment

- Treat underlying cause
- Administer:
  - Antiarrhythmics to stabilize arrhythmia
    - Quinidine, Pronestyl (procainamide)

Interventions

- Maintain the patient on bed rest.
- Do not allow bathroom privileges.
- Monitor his or her vital signs.
- Instruct the patient:
  - To return to normal activities gradually
  - To avoid competitive activities

4.15   Pericarditis

Infection by a microorganism, autoimmune disease, acute MI or a reaction from medication causes inflammation of the pericardium. Acute pericarditis is typically caused by a viral infection. Chronic pericarditis is typically caused by disease or a medication reaction.

Signs and Symptoms

- Acute:
  - Anxiety caused by pain and respiratory changes
  - Sharp pain over the pericardium radiating to the neck, shoulders, back, and arm relieved by leaning forward or sitting up related to common nerve

- o Pain in the teeth or muscles related to common nerve
- o Arrhythmias related to irritated heart
- o Dyspnea related to inflammation
- o Tachypnea related to increased oxygen demand
- o Pericardial friction rub caused by inflammation
- Chronic:
  - o Hepatomegaly related to decrease in cardiac output and fluid overflow
  - o Ascites related to decrease in cardiac output and liver fluid overflow
  - o Increased fluid retention related to decrease in cardiac output
  - o Pericardial friction rub related to inflammation

Medical Tests

- Chest X-ray shows fluid in pericardium
- ECG shows ST segment elevation
- Echocardiograph shows fluid in pericardium
- Labs:
  - o Increased aspartate transaminase (AST) and alanine transaminase (ALT) levels caused by injury of liver cells
  - o Increased CK level caused by injury of heart cells
  - o Increased WBC count caused by inflammation
  - o Increased sedimentation rate caused by inflammation
  - o Increased lactic dehydrogenase (LDH) level caused by tissue damage

Treatment

- Pericardiocentesis to remove fluid from pericardium
- Pericardial biopsy to identify infecting microorganism
- Administer:
  - o Corticosteroids to decrease inflammation
    - ▪ Medrol (methylprednisolone)
  - o Nonsteroidal anti-inflammatory drugs (NSAIDs) to decrease inflammation
    - ▪ Aspirin, Indocin (indomethacin)

Interventions

- Instruct the patient to rest.
- Do not allow bathroom privileges.
- Encourage coughing and deep breathing exercises to decrease discomfort.
- Place the patient in a high-Fowler's position to ease breathing.
- Instruct the patient:
  - o To reduce ongoing fatigue by scheduling rest periods
  - o To resume normal activities slowly
  - o To ease anxiety by knowing that there will be a recovery

4.16 Pulmonary Edema

Decreased pumping action of the left side of the heart causes fluid to build up in the lungs. This is caused by congestive heart disease or acute MI.

Signs and Symptoms

- Restlessness caused by decreased oxygenation of brain
- Capillary permeability resulting in frothy/pink sputum
- Tachypnea caused by increased demand for oxygen
- Cool, clammy skin caused by decreased circulation
- Crackles in lungs caused by increased fluid in lungs
- Distended jugular vein caused by fluid overload
- Cyanosis caused by decreased oxygenated blood
- Dyspnea when sitting upright caused by increased fluid in lungs

Medical Tests

- Chest X-ray shows cardiomegaly
- Echocardiogram to assess cardiac ejection fraction
- Oxygen saturation to assess whether oxygen saturation is <90%

Treatment

Treat underlying cause.

Administer:
- Analgesics to decrease cardiac workload and pain
  - Morphine
- Vasodilator to dilate blood vessels and decrease cardiac workload
  - Nitropress (nitroprusside), nitroglycerin, Dilatate (isosorbide dinitrate)
- Inotropes to improve cardiac contractions
  - Dopamine, Dobutamine, Amiodarone (inamrinone), Primacor (milrinone), Digitalis (digoxin)
- Diuretics to decrease fluid
  - Lasix (furosemide), Bumex (bumetanide), Zaroxolyn (metolazone), Aldactone (spironolactone)

Interventions

- Monitor the vital signs and capillary refill.
- Administer 2 to 4 L of oxygen.
- Place patient in a full-Fowler's position.
- Maintain the patient on bed rest.
- Prescribe a low-sodium diet to prevent fluid retention.
- Decrease fluid intake caused by the existing fluid overload.
- Measure the intake and output of fluids to assess renal perfusion.

- Weigh the patient daily, and notify the health care provider if the weight increases 3 lb (4.4 kg).
- Instruct the patient:
  - To elevate his or her head when sleeping by placing blocks under the head side of the bed frame or use three pillows
  - To notify the health care provider if he or she is short of breath and fatigued

4.17 Raynaud's Disease

Raynaud's disease is characterized by decreased blood flow to the extremities caused by vasospasm of peripheral arteries resulting from emotional stress or cold or secondary to inflammatory or connective tissue disease.

Signs and Symptoms

- Numbness and tingling of extremities caused by decreased blood flow
- Pale, blue and red discoloration of extremities caused by decreased blood flow

Medical Tests

- Arteriograph detects vasospasm.

Treatment

Treat the underlying cause.

Administer:

- Calcium channel blockers decrease cardiac workload and increase contractions and peripheral vasodilation
  - Isoptin (verapamil), Cardizem/Dilacor/Tiazac (diltiazem), Cardene (nicardipine), Procardia (nifedipine)
- Vasodilator to dilate blood vessels and decrease cardiac workload
  - Nitropress (nitroprusside); nitroglycerin, Dilatate (isosorbide dinitrate)

Interventions

- Warm the affected area.
- Instruct the patient:
  - To avoid cold to prevent vasospasm
  - To avoid stress to prevent vasospasm
  - To avoid smoking because smoking causes vasoconstriction
  - To wear mittens

4.18 Rheumatic Heart Disease

Rheumatic heart disease is a valve disease secondary to a group A streptococcus upper respiratory infection (rheumatic fever). Typically the mitral valve is affected.

Signs and Symptoms

- S3 murmur caused by turbulence blood flow
- Friction rub caused by inflammation
- Temperature >100.3 °F
- Join pain caused by inflammation

Medical Tests

- Labs:
  - o Increased WBC
  - o Increased CK
  - o Increased C-reactive protein
  - o Increased sedimentation rate
- Echocardiogram to identify valve damage

Treatment

Repair or replace the valve.

Administer:
- Antibiotics for infection
  - o Clindamycin, erythromycin, penicillin
- NSAIDs to decrease inflammation
  - o Indocin (indomethacin), aspirin
- Anticoagulant decreases coagulation
  - o Coumadin (warfarin), heparin

Interventions

- Monitor vital signs
- Instruct the patient:
  - o To slowly return to normal activities
  - o To contact the health care provider if experiencing shortness of breath or unexplained weight gain
  - o To avoid infectious people

4.19 Thrombophlebitis

A thrombus (blood clot) in a vein causes inflammation of a vein, usually in the lower extremities. This may be caused by trauma, poor circulation, coagulation disorder, or medication.

Signs and Symptoms

- Asymptomatic
- Cramps caused by decreased blood flow

- Positive Homans' sign
- Tenderness and warmth in affected area caused by inflammation
- Edema caused by decreased blood flow
- Clot moved to lungs
  - Dyspnea caused by clot in lungs
  - Tachypnea caused by clot in lungs
  - Crackles in lungs caused by fluid buildup

Medical Tests

- Photoplethysmography to assess blood flow in affected area
- Ultrasound to detect blood flow in affected area

Treatment

Administer:

- NSAIDs to decrease inflammation
  - Aspirin, Indocin (indomethacin)
- Anticoagulant to decrease coagulation
  - Heparin, Coumadin (warfarin), Fragmin (dalteparin), Lovenox (enoxaparin)

Interventions

- Elevate the affected area.
- Limit activity. Maintain the patient on bed rest with bathroom privileges.
- Apply warm, moist compresses on the affected area to increase the blood flow.
- Monitor the therapeutic level of the anticoagulant.
- Monitor for tachypnea and dyspnea, which may indicate an embolus in the lungs.
- Instruct the patient:
  - To avoid crossing the legs, which causes decreased circulation
  - To avoid oral contraceptives, which cause an increase in clotting
  - To wear support hose
  - To move frequently once the condition is resolved to prevent future clot formation
  - To contact the health care provider if he or she experiences shortness of breath or signs of bleeding

4.20 Atrial Fibrillation

The atria stops beating and quivers, resulting in ineffective contractions. This is caused by abnormal cardiac impulses. It is not life threatening; however, the patient is at risk for strokes and blood clots.

Signs and Symptoms

- Asymptomatic
- Dyspnea caused by decreased oxygenation related to decreased circulation

- Faint feeling and lightheadedness caused by decreased circulation
- Irregular pulse caused by arrhythmia
- Palpitations caused by arrhythmia

Medical Tests

- Echocardiogram: Shows structural abnormalities
- Thyroid function tests to rule out hyperthyroidism
- ECG:
  - QRS complexes: Irregular
  - PR interval: Barely visible
  - P-wave: Absent

Treatment

- Patient unstable: Synchronized cardioversion to reestablish normal sinus rhythm
- Patient stable:
  - Internal pacemaker
- Administer:
  - Antiarrhythmics to stabilize arrhythmia
    - Cordarone (amiodarone), digitalis (digoxin), Cardizem, Dilacor, Tiazac (diltiazem), Isoptin (verapamil)
- After 72 hours administer:
  - Anticoagulant to decrease coagulation and reduce risk of thromboembolism
    - Heparin, Coumadin (warfarin), Fragmin (dalteparin), Lovenox (enoxaparin)

Interventions

- Limit the patient's activity to decrease the cardiac workload.
- Maintain the patient on bed rest to decrease his or her cardiac workload.
- Allow bathroom privileges.
- Monitor for hypoperfusion (cool extremities, increased heart rate, decreased pulse pressure, altered mentation).
- Instruct the patient:
  - To contact the health care provider if feeling dizzy
  - To abstain from nicotine, caffeine, and alcohol, which can trigger an arrhythmia

4.21 Asystole

Asystole is cardiac standstill resulting in no circulation. Asystole can be caused by arrhythmia, cardiac tamponade, pulmonary embolism, sudden cardiac death, acute MI, or hypovolemia.

Signs and Symptoms

- No blood pressure
- No pulse

- Apnea
- Cyanosis

Medical Tests

- ECG: No wave

Treatment

- Cardiopulmonary resuscitation within 2 minutes
- Advanced cardiac life support within 8 minutes
- Transcutaneous pacing
- Endotracheal intubation
- Administer:
  - Buffering agent to correct acidosis
    - Sodium bicarbonate
  - Antiarrhythmics to control arrhythmia
    - Atropine, epinephrine

Interventions

- Cardiopulmonary resuscitation

4.22   Ventricular Fibrillation

Erratic impulses cause ventricles to quiver, resulting in disruption of circulation. This is caused by electrolyte disturbances, drug toxicities, ventricular tachycardia, electric shock, or MI.

Signs and Symptoms

- Apnea
- No blood pressure
- No pulse

Medical Tests

- ECG:
  - P wave: Not noticeable
  - Ventricular rhythm: Chaotic
  - QRS complex: Irregular and wide

Treatment

- Cardiopulmonary resuscitation
- Endotracheal intubation

- Advanced cardiac life support
- Defibrillation
- Administer:
  - Buffering agent to correct acidosis
    - Sodium bicarbonate
  - Antiarrhythmics to control arrhythmia
    - Bretylium, epinephrine, lidocaine, procainamide

Interventions

- Employ cardiopulmonary resuscitation.
- Defibrillate.

4.23   Ventricular Tachycardia

Erratic impulses cause ventricles to contract >160 beats per minute, resulting in inadequate filling of the ventricles and decreased cardiac output. This is caused by mitral valve prolapse, coronary artery disease, or acute MI. It may suddenly start and stop.

Signs and Symptoms

- Hypotension caused by decreased circulation
- Decreased pulse caused by insufficient heart rate
- Decreased breathing
- Dizziness caused by decreased oxygenation of blood
- Unconsciousness
- Apnea

Medical Tests

- ECG:
  - P wave: Not noticeable
  - Rhythm: Chaotic; >160 bpm
  - QRS complex: Abnormal
  - Ventricular tachycardia may suddenly start and stop, depending on the irritability of the heart
  - Ventricles contract >160 per minute

Treatment

Treatment consists of establishing a regular rate and rhythm.

- Cardiopulmonary resuscitation
- Endotracheal intubation
- Advanced cardiac life support
- Synchronized cardioversion

- Administer:
  - Buffering agent to correct acidosis
    - Sodium bicarbonate
  - Antiarrhythmics to control arrhythmia
    - Bretylium, epinephrine, lidocaine, procainamide, Cordarone (amiodarone)

Interventions

- Employ cardiopulmonary resuscitation.
- Employ synchronized cardioversion.

4.24   Aortic Insufficiency (AI)

In aortic insufficiency (AI), the aortic valve leaks, leading to blood flowing back into the left ventricle. The left ventricle dilates, becoming hypertropic and decreasing the output of the heart. This is caused by structural problems in the aortic valve, connective tissue disorder, endocarditis, arteriosclerosis, hypertension, or rheumatic heart disease.

Signs and Symptoms

- Palpitations caused by decreased blood flow
- Fatigue caused by decreased oxygenation
- Dyspnea caused by decreased cardiac output
- Orthopnea caused by decreased cardiac output

Medical Tests

- Chest X-ray shows enlarged left ventricle
- Echocardiograph shows enlarged left ventricle

Treatment

- Repair or replace the aortic valve
- Anticoagulant after surgery to decrease coagulation and reduce risk of thromboembolism
  - Heparin, Coumadin (warfarin), Fragmin (dalteparin), Lovenox (enoxaparin)

Interventions

- Administer 2 to 4 L of oxygen.
- Maintain the patient on bed rest with no bathroom privileges.
- Maintain the patient in a high-Fowler's position to ease breathing.
- Advise the patient to maintain a low-sodium, low-fat diet.
- Weigh the patient daily. Notify the health care provider if the patient's weight increases by 3 lb (4.4 kg).
- Instruct the patient:
  - To reduce ongoing fatigue by scheduling rest periods

4.25 Mitral Insufficiency

Blood flows back into the left atrium and lungs from the left ventricle. This is caused by a leak in the mitral valve and is called mitral regurgitation. It results from rheumatic fever, structural damage to the mitral valve, endocarditis, or coronary artery disease.

Signs and Symptoms

- Fatigue caused by decreased oxygenation
- Dyspnea caused by decreased cardiac output
- Orthopnea caused by decreased cardiac output
- S3 gallop

Medical Tests

- Chest X-ray shows enlarged left ventricle
- Echocardiograph shows enlarged left ventricle
- Cardiac catheterization to measure pressure in atrium

Treatment

- Vasodilator to dilate blood vessels and decrease cardiac workload
  - o Nitropress (nitroprusside), nitroglycerin, Dilatate (isosorbide dinitrate)
- Repair or replace the aortic valve
- Anticoagulant after surgery to decrease coagulation and reduce risk of thromboembolism
  - o Heparin, Coumadin (warfarin), Fragmin (Dalteparin), Lovenox (enoxaparin)

Interventions

- Administer 2 to 4 L of oxygen.
- Maintain the patient on bed rest, without bathroom privileges.
- Maintain the patient in a high-Fowler's position to ease breathing.
- Advise the patient to follow a low-sodium, low-fat diet.
- Weigh the patient daily, and notify the health care provider if his or her weight increases by 3 lb (4.4 kg).
- Instruct the patient:
  - o To reduce ongoing fatigue by scheduling rest periods

4.26 Mitral Stenosis

The mitral valve narrows, caused by scar tissue related to rheumatic fever. Blood flow between the left ventricle and left atrium decreases, causing an increase in cardiac workload.

Signs and Symptoms

- Fatigue caused by increased cardiac workload
- Palpitations caused by increased cardiac workload

- Dyspnea on exertion
- Murmur

Medical Tests

- Chest X-ray shows enlarged left atrium and left ventricle
- ECG shows notched P wave
- Cardiac catheterization measures pressure in the mitral valve

Treatment

- Repair or replace the aortic valve
- Anticoagulant after surgery to decrease coagulation and reduce risk of thromboembolism
  - Heparin, Coumadin (warfarin), Fragmin (dalteparin), Lovenox (enoxaparin)

Interventions

- Administer 2 to 4 L of oxygen.
- Maintain the patient on bed rest, without bathroom privileges.
- Maintain the patient in a high-Fowler's position to ease breathing.
- Advise the patient to follow a low-sodium, low-fat diet.
- Weigh the patient daily, and notify the health care provider if his or her weight increases by 3 lb (4.4 kg).
- Instruct the patient:
  - To reduce ongoing fatigue by scheduling rest periods

4.27 Mitral Valve Prolapse

Mitral valve prolapse is a congenital disorder that causes valve leaflets of the mitral valve to slightly bulge into the left atrium, resulting in blood flow back from the left ventricle into the left atrium.

Signs and Symptoms

- Asymptomatic
- Fatigue
- Syncope
- Systolic click
- Dyspnea
- Palpitations
- Chest pain

Medical Tests

- ECG shows irregular P-wave

Treatment

It is not considered serious unless the patient's activities of daily life are affected.

- Antiarrhythmics to control arrhythmia
  - o Bretylium, epinephrine, lidocaine, procainamide
- Repair or replace the aortic valve.
- Anticoagulant after surgery to decrease coagulation and reduce risk of thromboembolism
  - o Heparin, Coumadin (warfarin), Fragmin (dalteparin), Lovenox (enoxaparin)

Interventions

If the patient's activities of daily life are affected:

- Administer 2 to 4 L of oxygen.
- Maintain the patient on rest, without bathroom privileges.
- Maintain the patient in a high-Fowler's position to ease breathing.
- Advise the patient to follow a low-sodium, low-fat diet.
- Weigh the patient daily, and notify the health care provider if his or her weight increases by 3 lb (4.4 kg).
- Instruct the patient:
  - o To reduce ongoing fatigue by scheduling rest periods

4.28   Tricuspid Insufficiency

The tricuspid value prolapses, resulting in a leaking valve and allowing blood from the right ventricle to backflow into the right atrium. This leads to increased atrium pressure and increased resistance to incoming venous blood. This condition is caused by endocarditis, MI, or an overload of the right or left ventricles.

Signs and Symptoms

- S3 murmur (inspiration)
- Distended jugular venous
- Dyspnea
- Fatigue
- Hepatic congestion

Medical Tests

- ECG shows wide QRS complex and wide P-wave
- Echocardiography shows enlarged right side heart
- X-ray shows enlarged right atrium/ventricle

Treatment

- Repair or replace the aortic valve.
- Anticoagulant after surgery to decrease coagulation and reduce risk of thromboembolism
  - o Heparin, Coumadin (warfarin), Fragmin (dalteparin), Lovenox (enoxaparin)

Interventions

- Administer 2 to 4 L of oxygen.

- Maintain the patient on bed rest, without bathroom privileges.

- Maintain the patient in a high-Fowler's position to ease breathing.

- Advise the patient to follow a low-sodium, low-fat diet.

- Weigh the patient daily, and notify the health care provider if his or her weight increases by 3 lb (4.4 kg).

- Instruct the patient:

  o To reduce ongoing fatigue by scheduling rest periods

Solved Problems

4.1   What sounds identify an aortic aneurysm?

A bruit (swishing sound of turbulent blood) over the iliac or femoral arteries or abdominal aorta is the sound that identifies an aortic aneurysm.

4.2   Why are antihypertensives administered to a patient with an aortic aneurysm?

Antihypertensives are administered to a patient with an aortic aneurysm to reduce blood pressure.

4.3   What might a distended abdomen indicate in a patient with an aortic aneurysm?

Distention may signify imminent rupture.

4.4   What might restlessness indicate in a patient?

Restlessness might indicate increased anxiety and decreased oxygenation.

4.5   What are signs of hypovolemic shock?

Signs of hypovolemic shock are decreased blood pressure caused by rupture of the aortic aneurysm, decreased peripheral pulse resulting from a decrease in blood pressure, increased heart rate as the heart tries to meet increased demand for oxygen, and increased respiration to increase the demand for oxygen.

4.6   What might decreased pulse pressure indicate?

Decreased pulse pressure might indicate less filling time between cardiac contractions and a decreased circulating volume of blood.

4.7   What is stable angina?

Stable angina is chest pain that occurs after exercise or stress and is relieved by rest or nitrates.

4.8   What is unstable angina?

Unstable angina is chest pain that occurs at rest with increasing intensity and duration, is not relieved by rest, and is slow to respond to nitrates.

4.9   What is vasospastic angina?

Vasospastic angina is chest pain that occurs at night at rest with minimal exertion.

4.10   In angina, why does the patient have tachycardia?

Tachycardia is caused by an increased need to pump oxygenated blood.

4.11   What is a Holter monitor?

A Holter monitor checks 24 to 48 hours of continuous cardiac monitoring.

4.12   Why is an analgesic administered to a patient having angina?

Analgesic (morphine) is administered to a patient having angina to decrease cardiac workload and decrease pain.

4.13   Why are beta-adrenergic blockers administered to a patient having angina?

Beta-adrenergic blockers are administered to a patient having angina to decrease the cardiac workload.

4.14   What is a coronary artery stent?

A coronary artery stent is a mesh tube inserted into the coronary artery to reduce the blockage.

4.15   What is a coronary artery bypass graph (CABG)?

A coronary artery bypass graph (CABG) is carried out when a vein from a leg or artery from an arm or chest is graphed to coronary arteries bypassing the blockage.

4.16   What should the patient do if he or she has an angina attack?

If a patient has an angina attack, he or she should take one sublingual dose every 5 minutes for a maximum of three doses at the first sign of angina, rest immediately, and then call 911 if the signs of angina continue for more than 10 minutes.

4.17   What is cardiac tamponade?

The pericardium fills with fluid, blood, or pus as a result of trauma, postoperative complications, or complications from an MI, cancer, or uremia.

4.18   What is pulsus paradoxus?

Pulsus paradoxus is a decrease of 10 mm Hg or more in systolic blood pressure on inspiration.

4.19   What is pericardiocentesis?

Pericardiocentesis is aspiration of fluid from the pericardium.

4.20   What is the function of vasopressors?

Vasopressors increase blood flow to the heart and brain and decrease blood flow to other organs.

4.21   Why should the health care provider be notified if a cardiac patient's weight increases by 3 lb in a day?

This weight increase is an indicator of fluid retention as a result of poor circulation.

4.22   What is cardiomyopathy?

The myocardium is weakened and stretches, resulting in an enlargement of the heart, decreased cardiac contraction, and decreased cardiac output.

4.23   What is dilated cardiomyopathy?

The myocardium becomes thick, leading to CHF and decreased ventricular pumping action.

4.24   Why might a cardiac patient be prescribed a stool softener?

A cardiac patient might be prescribed a stool softener to prevent straining.

4.25   What is endocarditis?

Endocarditis is an infection by a microorganism that develops in the inner lining of the heart (endocardium) and heart valves, resulting in cardiac inflammation and leading to ulceration and necrosis of heart valves.

CHAPTER 5

Respiratory System

5.1 Definition

- Parts of the respiratory system:
  - Nasal cavities: Nose and linked air passages
  - Mouth
  - Larynx
  - Trachea
  - Bronchi
  - Bronchioles: Small, thin tubes
  - Alveoli: Air sacs connected to the bronchioles
  - Capillaries: A network of tiny blood vessels that cover the alveoli. Capillaries connect to a network of arteries and veins.
  - Pulmonary artery: Delivers blood containing carbon dioxide to the capillaries of the alveoli.
  - Diaphragm: The main muscle for breathing located below the lungs; it separates the chest cavity from the abdominal cavity.
  - Intercostal muscles: Located between the ribs, intercostal muscles assist in breathing.
  - Abdominal muscles: Used to exhale when breathing fast.
  - Accessory muscles (neck and collarbone): Used for breathing when the patient is having difficulty breathing.
- Respiratory system function:
  - Nose and mouth wet and warm the air. Lungs are irritated by cold. Dry air irritates lungs.
  - Cilia in the nose and airway trap germs and other foreign particles in the air. Particles are swallowed, coughed, or sneezed out of the body.
  - Air then travels through the trachea and into two bronchial tubes, then into the lungs.
  - The lungs exchange oxygen and carbon dioxide from blood vessels.

- The pulmonary artery delivers blood containing carbon dioxide to the capillaries of the alveoli. Gas exchange takes place, replacing carbon dioxide from hemoglobin in red blood cells with oxygen.
- The pulmonary vein delivers blood containing oxygen from the lungs to the heart.
- The heart pumps the oxygenated blood throughout the system's circulation.

- Respiration
  - Airway: Carries oxygenated air to the lungs and removes carbon dioxide
  - Muscle around the lungs expand and contract to force the lungs to exhale and inhale. These muscles are:
    - Inhalation
      - Diaphragm contracts, moving down increased space in the chest cavity, and enabling lungs to expand. Intercostal muscles pull the rib cage out and up, enlarging the chest cavity.
      - Air sucked through the nose and mouth as the lungs expand and travels down the trachea and bronchi, bronchioles and alveoli, where gas exchange occurs.
    - Exhalation
      - The diaphragm and intercostal muscles contract, reducing space in the chest cavity and forcing air out of the lungs.

- Respiratory control
  - The medulla oblongata portion of the brain controls breathing. Sensors in the carotid artery and aorta detect carbon dioxide and oxygen levels in the blood. These sensors signal when respiration should increase or decrease. Sensors in the airways detect irritants and trigger the brain to cause coughing or sneezing by tightening smooth muscles around the airway, increasing the air pressure on exhalation. Sensors in the alveoli detect fluid buildup and signal the brain to trigger rapid, shallow breathing.

5.2   Acute Respiratory Distress Syndrome (ARDS)

Shock, trauma, or sepsis causes fluid to build up in lung tissue and alveoli, resulting in stuffiness and impaired ventilation. This causes an inflammatory response and damage to surfactant in the alveoli, resulting in collapse of the alveolar and impaired gas exchange.

Signs and Symptoms

- Dyspnea
- Pulmonary edema
- Tachypnea
- Rales (crackles)
- Hypoxemia
- Accessory muscle use for respirations
- Decreased breath sounds
- Cyanosis
- Rhonchi
- Anxiety
- Restlessness resulting from decreased oxygen levels

Medical Tests

- Arterial blood gases show respiratory acidosis
- Pulse oximetry shows lowered oxygen levels
- Chest X-ray shows infiltrates within the lung

Treatment

- Positive end-expiratory pressure mechanical ventilation
- Continuous positive airway pressure (CPAP) mechanical ventilation
- Endotracheal intubation
- Administer:
  - Analgesic to decrease pain
    - Morphine
  - Diuretics to decrease fluid
    - Lasix (furosemide), Edecrin (ethacrynic acid), Bumex (bumetanide)
  - Anesthetic during endotracheal intubation
    - Diprivan (propofol)
  - Neuromuscular blocking agent during mechanical ventilation
    - Pavulon (pancuronium), Norcuron (vecuronium)
  - Proton pump inhibitors decrease risk of aspiration and gastric stress ulcer
    - Zantac (ranitidine), Pepcid (famotidine), Axid (nizatidine), Prilosec (omeprazole)
  - Anticoagulants: decrease coagulation
    - Heparin, Coumadin (warfarin), Fragmin (dalteparin), Lovenox (enoxaparin)
  - Steroids to decrease inflammation
    - Hydrocortisone; Medrol (methylprednisolone)
  - Exogenous surfactant
    - Survanta (beractant)

Interventions

- Bed rest
- Record intake and output of fluid
- Monitor for fluid overload
- Weigh daily
- No overexertion
- Instruct the patient:
  - To employ coughing and deep-breathing exercises
  - To call the health care provider at the first sign of respiratory distress

5.3 Asbestosis

Inhalation of asbestos fibers results in asbestos fibers infiltrating bronchioles and alveoli, causing inflammation and fibrosis and leading to decreased gas exchange and impaired breathing. Symptoms may take 15 years to develop.

Signs and Symptoms

- Tachypnea
- Dyspnea
- Dry cough
- Chest pain
- Rales
- Frequent respiratory infections

Medical Tests

- Pulmonary function test shows decreased vital capacity
- Pulse oximetry shows decreased O_2
- Chest X-ray shows linear irregular, linear opacities
- Computed tomography (CT) scan shows Opacities
- Arterial blood gases show respiratory acidosis

Treatment

- No specific treatment

Interventions

- Chest percussion loosens secretions
- Oxygen therapy 1 to 2 L/min
- Instruct the patient:
  - To avoid infections
  - To use oxygen therapy

5.4 Asthma

An allergen or nonallergen factor triggers inflammation of the airway and/or bronchospasm, resulting in dyspnea. There are two types of asthma:

1. Atopic (extrinsic) asthma, caused by allergens
2. Nonatopic (intrinsic) asthma, caused by a nonallergic factor such as cold air, humidity, or respiratory tract infection

Signs and Symptoms

- Asymptomatic between asthma attacks
- Dyspnea
- Bronchoconstriction
- Tachypnea
- Wheezing on expiration

- Cough
- Use of accessory muscles to breath
- Tachycardia

Medical Tests

- Arterial blood gases show respiratory acidosis
- Chest X-ray shows hyperinflated lungs
- Pulse oximetry shows decreased O_2
- Complete blood count (CBC) shows eosinophils increase
- Sputum shows positive eosinophils
- Pulmonary function test shows decreased force on expiration during attack

Treatment

- 3 L of fluid daily to liquefy any secretions
- Remove allergens and triggers
- Administer:
  - Beta$_2$ adrenergic bronchodilators
    - Salmeterol, formoterol, albuterol, pirbuterol, metaproterenol, terbutaline, levalbuterol
  - Leukotriene modulators anti-inflammatory
    - Zafirlukast, zileuton, montelukast
  - Anticholinergic to reduce bronchospasm
    - Ipratropium inhaler, tiotropium inhaler
  - Antacids
    - Aluminum hydroxide/magnesium hydroxide, calcium carbonate
  - Histamine (H$_2$) blockers
    - Ranitidine, famotidine, nizatidine, cimetidine
  - Proton pump inhibitor
    - Omeprazole, lansoprazole, esomeprazole, rabeprazole, pantoprazole
  - Mast cell stabilizer
    - Cromolyn, nedocromil
  - Steroids to decrease inflammation
    - Hydrocortisone; Medrol (methylprednisolone); prednisolone
  - Methylxanthines for bronchodilation
    - Aminophylline, theophylline

Interventions

- High-Fowler's position
- Oxygen therapy 1 to 2 L/min
- Monitor vital signs

- Instruct the patient:
  - To avoid allergen
  - To identify signs of asthma attack
  - How to use inhaler

5.5 Atelectasis

Atelectasis is a collapsed lung because of airway obstruction, pleural space infusion, tumor, anesthesia, immobility or no deep-breathing exercise postoperatively resulting in decreased gas exchange.

Signs and Symptoms

- Decreased breath
- Diaphoresis
- Dyspnea
- Hypoxemia
- Tachypnea
- Tachycardia
- Cyanosis
- Anxiety
- Use of accessory muscle

Medical Tests

- Chest X-ray shows shadows in collapsed area.
- CT scan shows collapsed area.

Treatment

- Administer:
  - Beta$_2$ adrenergic bronchodilators
    - Salmeterol, formoterol, albuterol, pirbuterol, metaproterenol, terbutaline, levalbuterol
  - Mucolytics to loosen secretions
    - Acetylcysteine inhaled, guaifenesin oral

Interventions

- Oxygen therapy 1 to 2 L/min
- Provide humidified air
- Monitor breathing
- Instruct the patient:
  - To use the incentive spirometer
  - To cough and use deep-breathing exercises every 2 hours

5.6   Bronchiectasis

The bronchi become obstructed with excessive mucus because of abnormal dilation of bronchi and bronchioles related to infection and inflammation. The patient may develop atelectasis and bronchitis.

Signs and Symptoms

- Hemoptysis
- Dyspnea
- Cyanosis
- Cough when lying down
- Foul-smelling cough
- Crackles on inspiration
- Rhonchi on inspiration
- Bronchial infections
- Weight loss
- Anemia

Medical Tests

- Pulmonary function test shows decreased vital capacity.
- Chest X-ray shows shadows.
- CT scan shows bronchiectasis.
- Culture and sensitivity of sputum identifies microorganism and medication.

Treatment

- Bronchoscopy to remove excessive secretions
- Postural drainage uses gravity to move mucus from lungs to throat
- Administer:
  - $Beta_2$ adrenergic bronchodilators
    - Salmeterol, formoterol, albuterol, pirbuterol, metaproterenol, terbutaline, levalbuterol
  - Antibiotics to treat infection

Interventions

- Oxygen therapy 1 to 2 L/min
- Chest percussion loosens secretions.
- Monitor vital signs.
- Instruct the patient's family:
  - To perform chest percussion
  - To do postural drainage

5.7 Bronchitis

Infection or airborne irritants cause increased mucus production, leading to blocked airways and decreased gas exchange.

- Acute bronchitis is reversible within 10 days.
- Chronic bronchitis is not reversible and is classified as chronic obstructive pulmonary disease (COPD)

Signs and Symptoms

- Productive cough (acute bronchitis)
- Chronic productive cough for 3 months (chronic bronchitis)
- Cough because of mucus production and irritation of airways
- Dyspnea
- Wheezing
- Use of accessory muscles to breathe
- Fever
- Weight gain because of edema from right-sided heart failure (chronic bronchitis)

Medical Tests

- Arterial blood gases show respiratory acidosis.
- Hemoglobin increases.
- Chest X-ray shows infiltrate related to infection.
- Pulmonary function testing shows
  - Forced vital capacity decreases
  - Forced expiratory volume in 1 second (FEV_1) decreases
  - Residual volume (RV) increase

Treatment

Administer:
- Beta$_2$ adrenergic bronchodilators
  - Salmeterol, formoterol, albuterol, pirbuterol, metaproterenol, terbutaline, levalbuterol
- Steroids to decrease inflammation
  - Hydrocortisone, Medrol (methylprednisolone), prednisolone
- Methylxanthines for bronchodilation
  - Aminophylline, theophylline
- Diuretics to decrease fluid
  - Lasix (furosemide), Edecrin (ethacrynic acid), Bumex (bumetanide)
- Proton pump inhibitor decrease risk of aspiration and gastric stress ulcer
  - Zantac (ranitidine), Pepcid (famotidine), Axid (nizatidine), Prilosec (omeprazole)
- H$_2$ blockers
  - Ranitidine, famotidine, nizatidine, cimetidine

- Antacid
  - Aluminum hydroxide/magnesium hydroxide, calcium carbonate
- Expectorant to liquefy secretions
  - Guaifenesin
- Anticholinergic to reduce bronchospasm
  - Ipratropium inhaler, tiotropium inhaler

Interventions

- Use incentive spirometer
- High-Fowler's position
- 3 L of fluid daily to help liquefy secretions
- Oxygen therapy 1 to 2 L/min via nasal cannula
- Monitor vital signs
- Weigh patient daily. Notify health care provider of weight gain of 2 lb in 1 day
- Monitor sputum changes
- Monitor fluid intake and output
- Increase fluids to keep mucus thinner and easier to expel
- Instruct the patient:
  - To administer oxygen
  - To turn, cough, and employ deep-breathing exercises
  - To increase calories and protein in the diet
  - To increase vitamin C

5.8 Cor Pulmonale

Cor pulmonale is right-sided heart failure resulting from COPD, leading to pulmonary hypertension and enlargement of the right ventricle.

Signs and Symptoms

- Productive cough
- Edema
- Weight gain
- Orthopnea
- Dyspnea
- Tachycardia
- Cyanosis
- Fatigue
- Tachypnea
- Wheezing

Medical Tests

- Pulse oximetry shows lowered oxygen levels.
- Hemoglobin level is elevated.
- Arterial blood gases show respiratory acidosis.
- Chest X-ray shows enlarged right ventricle and enlarged pulmonary arteries.
- Echocardiography shows enlarged right ventricle.
- Pulmonary artery catheterization shows increased pulmonary artery and right ventricular pressure.

Treatment

- Administer:
  - Calcium channel blockers to decrease blood pressure and thereby decrease heart rate
    - Isoptin (verapamil); Cardizem, Tiazac (diltiazem); Procardia (nifedipine); Cardene (nicardipine); Norvasc (amlodipine)
  - Potassium channel activator to dilate pulmonary artery
    - Diazoxide, hydralazine, nitroprusside
  - Angiotensin-converting enzyme (ACE) inhibitor
    - Captopril, enalapril
  - Diuretics to decrease fluid
    - Lasix (furosemide), Edecrin (ethacrynic acid), Bumex (bumetanide)
  - Anticoagulant: Decreases coagulation
    - Heparin, Coumadin (warfarin), Fragmin (dalteparin), Lovenox (enoxaparin)
  - Cardiac glycoside
    - Digitalis (digoxin)

Interventions

- Bed rest
- Monitor vital signs
- Weigh patient daily. Notify the health care provider of weight gain of 2 lb in 1 day.
- No overexertion
- Oxygen therapy 1 to 2 L/min via nasal canula
- Monitor digoxin level to avoid toxic effect
- Monitor serum potassium levels if given ACE inhibitors and diuretics
- Instruct the patient:
  - To maintain a low-sodium diet
  - To limit fluid to 2 L each day

5.9 Emphysema

Chronic inflammation of the lungs results in decreased flexibility of the alveoli walls, leading to overdistention of the alveolar walls and trapped air. This causes decreased gas exchange and is linked to smoking. It can be caused by inherited alpha 1-antitrypsin deficiency, but this is a less frequent cause.

Signs and Symptoms

- Difficulty breathing (dyspnea)
- Use of accessory muscles to breathe
- Barrel chest
- Loss of weight

Medical Tests

- Pulmonary function test shows increase residual volume.
- Arterial blood gases show respiratory acidosis
- Chest X-ray shows flattened diaphragm and overinflated lungs

Treatment

- Administer:
  - Beta$_2$ adrenergic bronchodilators
    - Salmeterol, formoterol, albuterol, pirbuterol, metaproterenol, terbutaline, levalbuterol
  - Anticholinergic to reduce bronchospasm
    - Ipratropium inhaler, tiotropium inhaler
  - Methylxanthines for bronchodilation
    - Aminophylline, theophylline
  - Steroids to decrease inflammation
    - Hydrocortisone, Medrol (methylprednisolone), prednisolone
  - Antacid
    - Aluminum hydroxide/magnesium hydroxide, calcium carbonate
  - H$_2$ blockers
    - Ranitidine, famotidine, nizatidine, cimetidine
  - Proton pump inhibitor
    - Omeprazole, lansoprazole, esomeprazole, rabeprazole, pantoprazole
  - Expectorant to liquefy secretions
    - Guaifenesin
  - Diuretics to decrease fluid
    - Lasix (furosemide), Edecrin (ethacrynic acid), Bumex (bumetanide)
- Selected based on results of culture and sensitivity study or given empirically
- Administer alpha$_1$ antitrypsin therapy for patients with deficiency
- Teach patient use of the incentive spirometer—to encourage deep breathing and enhance coughing and expelling of mucus
- Teach patient use of flutter valve to increase the expiration force
- Nocturnal negative-pressure ventilation for hypercapnic patients (those with elevated CO_2 levels)

Interventions

- Oxygen therapy 1 to 2 L/min via nasal canula
- 3 L of fluid daily to help liquefy secretions

- Monitor sputum changes
- Use incentive spirometer
- High-Fowler's position
- Monitor intake and output
- Monitor vital signs
- Weigh patient daily. Notify health care provider of weight gain of 2 lb in 1 day.
- Instruct the patient:
  - To administer oxygen
  - To turn, cough, and employ deep-breathing exercises
  - To avoid infection

5.10   Lung Cancer

Lung cancer is an uncontrolled, abnormal cell growth resulting in a tumor in the lung. Primary lung cancer occurs when the tumor consists of lung tissue. Secondary lung cancer occurs when the tumor from other parts of the body metastasizes to the lung. This is caused by exposure to inhaled irritants such as cigarette smoke.

Categories of Lung Cancer:

- Small cell:
  - Oat cell: Early metastasis, fast growing
- Non–small cell:
  - Adenocarcinoma: Early metastasis, moderate growing
  - Squamous cell late metastasis, slow growing
  - Large cell early metastasis, fast growing

Signs and Symptoms

- Hemoptysis
- Coughing
- Dyspnea
- Weight loss
- Fatigue
- Pleural effusion
- Chest pains
- Sputum production

Medical Tests

- Sputum study shows cancer cells.
- Bronchoscopy shows cancer cells.
- Chest X-ray shows lung mass.
- Bone scan shows metastasis.

- Biopsy shows cell type
- Computed tomography (CT) scan shows lung mass

Treatment

- Surgical removal of affected lung area
  - Wedge resection
  - Segmental resection
  - Lobectomy
  - Pneumonectomy
- Radiation therapy to decrease tumor size

Administer:

- Chemotherapy
  - Cyclophosphamide, doxorubicin, vincristine, etoposide, cisplatin
- Antiemetics for side effects of chemotherapy
  - Ondansetron, prochlorperazine
- Analgesics for pain control
  - Morphine, fentanyl

Interventions

- Semi-Fowler's position
- Oxygen therapy 2 to 4 L/min
- High-protein, high-calorie diet
- Monitor vital signs
- Assist patient with turning, coughing, and employing deep breathing exercises.
- Instruct the patient:
  - To schedule rest periods
  - To turn, cough, and employ deep-breathing exercises

5.11 Pleural Effusion

The pleural sac fills with serous fluid, blood (hemothorax) or pus (empyema), restricting lung expansion, displaying lung tissue and interfering with gas exchange. Causes include postoperative complication, congestive heart failure, renal failure, pulmonary infarction, infection, trauma, lupus erythematosus, or cancer.

Signs and Symptoms

- Dyspnea
- Decreased breath sounds
- Increased respiration
- Increased pulse

- Decreased blood pressure (hemothorax)
- Chest pain if inflamed
- Fever (empyema)
- Dullness on percussion over the affected area

Medical Tests

- Pulse oximeter shows decreased oxygen saturation.
- Chest X-ray shows pleural effusion.
- Chest CT scan shows pleural effusion.
- Chest ultrasound shows pleural effusion.

Treatment

- Thoracentesis to remove fluid
- Chest tube to drain fluid
- Administer antibiotics (empyema)

Interventions

- Oxygen therapy 2 to 4 L/min
- Monitor chest tube drainage and patency
- Monitor vital signs
- Instruct the patient:
  - To turn, cough, and employ deep-breathing exercises.

5.12 Pneumonia

Inhalation of bacteria, viruses, parasites, or irritating agents or aspiration of liquids or foods leads to infection and inflammation, resulting in increased mucus production, thickening alveolar fluid, and decreased gas exchange.

Signs and Symptoms

- Dyspnea
- Crackles
- Rhonchi
- Discolored, blood-tinged sputum
- Cough
- Fever
- Chills
- Pain on respiration
- Tachypnea
- Tachycardia
- Myalgia

Medical Tests

- Pulse oximeter shows decreased oxygen saturation.
- Chest X-ray shows infiltration.
- White blood cell (WBC) count is elevated.
- Arterial blood gases show respiratory acidosis.
- Culture and sensitivity of the sputum

Treatment

- Administer:
  - Antipyretics when fever is > 101 °F for patient comfort
    - Tylenol (acetaminophen), Advil, Motrin (ibuprofen)
  - Bronchodilators
    - Albuterol, metaproterenol, levalbuterol
  - Antibiotics for bacterial infection
    - Azithromycin, clarithromycin, levofloxacin, moxifloxacin, amoxicillin/clavulanate, cefotaxime, ceftriaxone, cefuroxime axetil, cefpodoxime, ampicillin/sublactam, telithromycin

Interventions

- Oxygen therapy 2 to 4 L/min
- Incentive spirometer every 2 hours
- Monitor fluid intake and output
- Monitor vital signs
- Monitor sputum characteristics
- Instruct the patient:
  - To drink 3 L of fluid daily to help liquefy secretions
  - To use the incentive spirometer every 2 hours

5.13 Pneumothorax

The lung is partially or completely collapsed as a result of air entering the pleural sac. Types of pneumothorax are:

- Open pneumothorax: Penetrating chest wound
- Closed pneumothorax: Blunt trauma
- Spontaneous pneumothorax: Caused by underlying disease
- Tension pneumothorax: Displacement of the mediastinum causes unaffected lung to collapse

Signs and Symptoms

- Sharp chest pain aggravated by coughing
- Tracheal deviation toward the unaffected side with tension pneumothorax
- Subcutaneous emphysema

- Absent breath sounds over the affected area
- Tachypnea
- Tachycardia

Medical Tests

- Pulse oximeter shows decreased oxygen saturation.
- Chest X-ray shows infiltration.
- Arterial blood gases show respiratory acidosis.

Treatment

Chest tube connected to suction to re-expand lung

- Administer analgesic
  - Morphine

Interventions

- High-Fowler's position
- Bed rest
- Oxygen therapy 2 to 4 L/min
- Monitor chest tube drainage and patency
- Monitor vital signs
- Instruct the patient:
  - To turn, cough, and employ deep-breathing exercises

5.14 Respiratory Acidosis

Blood becomes more acid as a result of acute or chronic respiratory, hypoventilation, asphyxia, or central nervous system disorders. Carbon dioxide (acid) increases, resulting in increased respiration, retention bicarbonate and sodium, and excreting hydrogen ions by the kidneys to compensate.

Signs and Symptoms

- Dyspnea
- Hypoxemia
- Headache
- Irritability
- Confusion
- Restlessness
- Cardiac arrhythmia

Medical Tests

- Arterial blood gas:
  - Carbon dioxide (CO_2) > 50 mm Hg
  - pH of blood < 7.35

Treatment

- Treat underlying cause.
- Mechanical ventilation
- Administer:
  - Bronchodilators
    - Albuterol, metaproterenol, levalbuterol

Interventions

- Oxygen therapy 2 to 4 L/min
- Monitor vitals
- Monitor blood chemistry
- Instruct the patient:
  - To turn, cough, and employ deep-breathing exercises

5.15 Tuberculosis

Tuberculosis is a lung infection by the *Mycobacterium tuberculosis* bacteria transmitted by coughing, sneezing, or talking. It can infect other organs.

- Primary tuberculosis occurs when the patient is initially infected with the *M. tuberculosis* bacteria.
- Secondary tuberculosis is reactivation of the *M. tuberculosis* bacteria from a previous infection.
- Exposure to *M. tuberculosis* bacteria resulting in negative test and no symptoms.
- Patients may or may not have tuberculosis.
- Latent tuberculosis results in positive test results and no symptoms.

Signs and Symptoms

- Low-grade fever
- Productive cough
- Blood-tinged sputum
- Fatigue
- Night sweats
- Anorexia
- Weight loss
- Shortness of breath

Medical Tests

- Positive Mantoux (purified protein derivative, or PPD) skin test.
- Sputum test is positive for *M. tuberculosis* bacteria.
- Chest X-ray shows areas of granuloma or cavitation.

Treatment

Administer:

- Antitubercular agents
  - Isoniazid, rifampin, pyrazinamide, ethambutol, streptomycin

Interventions

- Respiratory isolation
- Increase carbohydrates, protein, vitamin C in diet
- Monitor vitals
- Monitor intake and output
- Instruct the patient:
  - To drink 3 L of fluid daily to help liquefy secretions
  - To schedule rest periods
  - To prevent the spread of tuberculosis

5.16   Acute Respiratory Failure

Insufficient ventilation reduces adequate gas exchange in the lungs, resulting in increased carbon dioxide and decreased oxygen in blood. Acute respiratory failure occurs because of depression of the central nervous system, resulting from medication or trauma or decompensation of a respiratory illness.

Signs and Symptoms

- Dyspnea
- Orthopnea
- Tachypnea
- Coughing
- Fatigue
- Diminished breath sounds
- Hemoptysis
- Diaphoresis
- Crackles
- Rhonchi
- Cyanosis

Medical Tests

- Arterial blood gas:
  - ○ Oxygen alveolar -arterial difference in partial pressure (Pao_2) <60 mmHg
  - ○ Carbon dioxide (CO_2) >50 mm Hg
  - ○ Oxygen saturation (Sao_2) <90%
  - ○ Blood pH <7.30
- Pulse oximeter shows decreased oxygen saturation
- Increased WBC count

Treatment

- Treat underlying cause
- Mechanical ventilation
- Administer:
  - ○ Bronchodilators
    - ▪ Albuterol, metaproterenol, levalbuterol
  - ○ Anticholinergics to reduce bronchospasm
    - ▪ Ipratropium inhaler, tiotropium inhaler
  - ○ Anesthetic to ease intubation
    - ▪ Propofol
  - ○ Neuromuscular blocking agent to ease mechanical ventilation ventilator
    - ▪ Pancuronium, vecuronium, atracurium
  - ○ Steroids to decrease inflammation
    - ▪ Hydrocortisone, methylprednisolone, prednisone
  - ○ Anticoagulant to decrease coagulation
    - ▪ Heparin, Coumadin (warfarin), Fragmin (dalteparin), Lovenox (enoxaparin)
  - ○ Antacid
    - ▪ Aluminum hydroxide/magnesium hydroxide, calcium carbonate
  - ○ H_2 blockers
    - ▪ Ranitidine, famotidine, nizatidine, cimetidine
  - ○ Proton pump inhibitor
    - ▪ Omeprazole, lansoprazole, esomeprazole, rabeprazole, pantoprazole
  - ○ Analgesic for discomfort and decrease myocardial oxygen demand
    - ▪ Morphine

Interventions

- High-Fowler's position
- Oxygen therapy 2 to 4 L/min
- Monitor vitals
- Change position every 2 hours

- Monitor intake and output
- Instruct the patient:
  - To turn, cough, and employ deep-breathing exercises

5.17 Pulmonary Embolism

Gas exchange is impaired because of alveoli collapse resulting from an obstruction of blood flow in the lungs caused by thrombus, air emboli, or fat emboli. Small area of atelectasis self-resolve. A large area of atelectasis is fatal.

Signs and Symptoms

- Sudden dyspnea
- Chest pain
- Tachypnea
- Tachycardia
- Crackles at site of emboli
- Coughing
- Hemoptysis

Medical Tests

- Lung scan shows perfusion mismatch.
- Chest X-ray shows dilated pulmonary artery.
- Pulmonary angiography shows clot.
- Helical CT scan shows clot in pulmonary arteries.
- Arterial blood gases show respiratory acidosis.
- D-dimer is positive when a thromboembolic event has occurred.
- Pulse oximetry shows decreased oxygen saturation.

Treatment

- Surgical insertion of a vena cava filter
- Surgical removal of the emboli
- Administer:
  - Anticoagulant to decrease coagulation
    - Heparin, Coumadin (warfarin), Fragmin (dalteparin), Lovenox (enoxaparin)
  - Analgesic for discomfort and to decrease myocardial oxygen demand
    - Morphine
  - Thrombolytics to remove clot within 3 to 12 hours of blockages
    - Urokinase, alteplase

Interventions

- Bed rest
- High-Fowler's position
- Oxygen therapy 2 to 4 L/min
- Monitor vitals
- Instruct the patient:
  - To turn, cough, and employ deep-breathing exercises
  - Not to cross the legs
  - Not to sit or stand for too long
  - To call the health care provider at the first sign of bleeding
  - To call the health care provider at the first sign of respiratory increase

5.18   Influenza

Influenza is a viral infection of the upper layer of cells in the respiratory tract transmitted by inhaling droplets or direct contact with virus-containing droplets. This can lead to secondary bacterial infection.

Signs and Symptoms

- Myalgia
- Fever >101 °F
- Malaise
- Diaphoresis
- Nonproductive cough
- Abrupt onset of symptoms
- Headache
- Watery discharge
- Sore throat

Medical Tests

- Nasopharyngeal viral culture identifies virus.
- Rapid diagnostic test is positive for virus.

Treatment

Administer:

- Antipyretics when fever is >101°F for patient comfort
  - Tylenol (acetaminophen), Advil, Motrin (ibuprofen)
- Antiviral medications
  - Zanamivir, oseltamivir, amantadine, rimantadine

Interventions

- Monitor vital signs
- Instruct the patient:
  - To increase fluid intake
  - To increase electrolyte intake

Solved Problems

5.1   What is the purpose of pulse oximetry?

The purpose of pulse oximetry is to measure the oxygen saturation of blood.

5.2   What is ARDS?

Shock, trauma, or sepsis causes fluid to build up in lung tissue and alveoli, causing stuffiness and impaired ventilation and resulting in an inflammatory response and damage to surfactant in the alveoli, which in turn cause collapse of the alveolar and impaired gas exchange.

5.3   What is the purpose of administering diuretics?

The purpose of administering diuretics is to decrease fluids.

5.4   What is the purpose of administering a proton pump inhibitor for ARDS?

The purpose of administering a proton pump inhibitor for ARDS is to decrease risk of aspiration and gastric stress ulcer.

5.5   What is asbestosis?

Asbestosis is the inhalation of asbestos fibers resulting in asbestos fibers infiltrating bronchioles and alveoli and causing inflammation and fibrosis, which lead to decreased gas exchange and impaired breathing.

5.6   What is asthma?

Asthma occurs when an allergen or nonallergen factory triggers inflammation of the airway and/or bronchospasm resulting in dyspnea.

5.7   What is extrinsic asthma?

Extrinsic asthma is atopic asthma caused by allergens.

5.8   What is intrinsic asthma?

Intrinsic asthma is nonatopic asthma caused by a nonallergic factor such as cold air, humidity, or respiratory tract infection.

5.9   What should be found in the sputum of an asthma patient?

The sputum of an asthma patient should show positive eosinophils.

5.10   Why are anticholinergics administered to asthma patients?

Anticholinergics reduce bronchospasm.

5.11   In what position should you place an asthma patient who is having an asthma attack?

Place an asthma patient who is having an asthma attack in the high-Fowler's position.

5.12   What is atelectasis?

Atelectasis is a lung collapsed because of airway obstruction, pleural space infusion, tumor, anesthesia, immobility, or no deep-breathing exercise postoperatively, resulting in decreased gas exchange.

5.13   What is bronchiectasis?

Bronchiectasis occurs when the bronchi become obstructed with excessive mucus because of abnormal dilation of bronchi and bronchioles related to infection and inflammation. The patient may develop atelectasis and bronchitis.

5.14   What is the purpose of using bronchoscopy in a patient who has bronchiectasis?

The purpose of using bronchoscopy in a patient who has bronchiectasis is to remove excessive secretions.

5.15   What is bronchitis?

Bronchitis is an infection or airborne irritants that cause increased mucus production, leading to blocked airways and decreased gas exchange.

5.16   What is acute bronchitis?

Acute bronchitis is bronchitis that is reversible within 10 days.

5.17   What is chronic bronchitis?

Chronic bronchitis is not reversible and is classified as COPD.

5.18   What is cor pulmonale?

Cor pulmonale is right-sided heart failure resulting from COPD, leading to pulmonary hypertension and enlargement of the right ventricle.

5.19   What is emphysema?

Emphysema is chronic inflammation of the lungs resulting in decreased flexibility of the alveoli walls leading to overdistention of the alveolar walls and trapped air, causing decreased gas exchange. Emphysema is linked to smoking and can be caused by inherited alpha$_1$- antitrypsin deficiency, although this cause is less frequent.

5.20   What is small cell lung cancer?

Small cell lung cancer metastasizes early and is fast growing.

5.21   What is pleural effusion?

The pleural sac fills with serous fluid, blood (hemothorax), or pus (empyema), restricting lung expansion, displacing lung tissue, and interfering with gas exchange. Causes include postoperative complication, congestive heart failure, renal failure, pulmonary infarction, infection, trauma, lupus erythematosus, or cancer.

5.22   What is pneumonia?

Pneumonia is inhalation of bacteria, viruses, parasites, or irritating agents or aspirating liquids or foods that leads to infection and inflammation, resulting in increased mucus production, thickening alveolar fluid, and decreased gas exchange.

5.23   What is pneumothorax?

Pneumothorax occurs when the lung is partially or completely collapsed as a result of air entering the pleural sac.

5.24   What is an open pneumothorax?

An open pneumothorax is a penetrating chest wound.

5.25   What is a pulmonary embolism?

Gas exchange is impaired because of alveoli collapse as a result of an obstruction of blood flow in the lungs caused by thrombus, air emboli, or fat emboli. A small area of atelectasis self-resolves. A large area of atelectasis is fatal.

CHAPTER 6

Nervous System

6.1 Definition

Nervous system divisions:

- Central nervous system:
  - Brain
  - Spinal cord
- Peripheral nervous system
  - Spinal nerves
  - Peripheral nerves
- Neuron (nerve cell)
  - Nucleus: Within the cell body
  - Dendrites: Receive impulse
  - Axons: Send impulse
    - Axon terminal: Transmits impulses
  - Synapse (gap between neurons)
  - Neurotransmitters: Chemicals released by the neuron to enhance impulse transmission
  - Neurotransmitter receptor sites: Locations on the neuron that receive neurotransmitters
  - Afferent neurons: Neurons with no dendrite transmit impulses from the peripheral nervous system to the central nervous system
  - Efferent (motor) neurons: Neurons that transmit impulses from the central nervous system to glands or muscles
  - Myelin coating: White outer surface of neuron restrict impulse transmission along neuron cell membrane
  - Impulse transmission: Electronically charged ions that transmit signals along the neuron cell membrane
- Brain
  - Cerebral cortex
    - Outermost layer
    - Gray
    - Composed of neuron cell bodies

- Divisions
  - Right hemisphere
    - Controls the left side of the body
    - Temporal relationships
    - Spatial relationships
    - Analyzing nonverbal information
    - Communicating emotion
  - Left hemisphere
    - Controls the right side of the body
    - Produce and understand language
  - Corpus callosum: Controls communication between right and left hemispheres
- Cerebellum
  - Balance
  - Cardiac, vasomotor, respiratory centers
  - Posture
- Brain stem
  - Motor and sensory pathway
  - Cardiac, vasomotor, respiratory centers
- Lobes
  - Frontal lobe
    - Inhibition
    - Judgment
    - Skilled movements
    - Creative thought
    - Abstract thought processes
    - Intellect
    - Problem solving
    - Movement
    - Behavior
    - Attention
    - Sense of smell
    - Libido
    - Muscle movements
  - Parietal lobe
    - Language and reading functions
    - Response to internal stimuli
    - Sense of touch
  - Occipital lobe
    - Vision
    - Reading

- o Temporal lobe
  - Visual memories
  - Auditory memories
  - Fear
  - Sense of identity
  - Memory
- Glands
  - o Hypothalamus
    - Maintains homeostasis
    - Hormonal body processes
    - Sexual maturation
    - Moods and motivation
    - Temperature regulation
  - o Pituitary
    - Sexual maturation
    - Sexual functioning
    - Hormonal body processes
    - Physical maturation
    - Growth (height and form)
- Spinal cord
  - o Conduit of impulses for sensation and movement
  - o Protected by the vertebral column
  - o Efferent (motor) neurons located along the anterior horns of the spinal column
  - o Afferent neurons located along the posterior horns of the spinal column
  - o Ventricles and cerebral aqueduct
    - Contains the cerebrospinal fluid
    - Bathes the brain and spinal cord
- Brain stem
  - o Controls breathing, heart beat, and blood pressure
  - o Pons
    - Motor control
    - Sensory analysis
  - o Medulla oblongata
    - Controls breathing
    - Heart rate
  - o Midbrain
    - Vision
    - Hearing
    - Eye movement
    - Body movement

6.2　Cerebral Hemorrhage

A cerebral hemorrhage is characterized by bleeding within the brain, the layers covering the brain, or between the skull and the dura mater. It can occur at the time of the injury or hours or days later. The types of cerebral hemorrhages are:

- Epidural hematoma: Bleeding from an artery with blood accumulating between the dura and skull
- Subdural hematoma: Bleeding from a vein in the area between the dura mater and the arachnoid mater resulting in slow, chronic bleeding
- Subarachnoid hemorrhage: Bleeding between the arachnoid mater, and the pia mater, the location of cerebrospinal fluid
- Intracerebral hemorrhage: Bleeding within brain tissue caused by shearing or tearing of small vessels within the brain and between the cerebrum and brain stem
- Concussion: Blunt-force trauma that thrusts the brain against the inside of the skull, resulting in bruising
- Cerebral contusion: Blunt-force trauma thrusting the brain against the inside of the skull, resulting in cerebral edema, cerebral hemorrhage, and loss of consciousness longer than that from a concussion
- Coup injury: Blunt-force trauma that thrusts the brain against the inside of the skull at the point of the blunt force trauma
- Contrecoup injury: Blunt-force trauma that causes the head to recoil, thrusting the brain against the inside of the skull at a point opposite the blunt force trauma
- Cerebral edema: Fluid within the skull moves to the third space, resulting in increased cranial pressure

Signs and Symptoms

- Nausea
- Vomiting
- Disorientation
- Headache
- Unequal pupil size
- Diminished or absent pupil reaction
- Cognitive changes
- Speech changes
- Motor movement changes
- Decreased level of consciousness or
- Loss of consciousness
- Amnesia

Medical Tests

- Computed tomography (CT) scan shows cerebral edema and hemorrhage.
- Magnetic resonance imaging shows edema and hemorrhage.

Treatment

- Craniotomy
  - o Stops bleeding surgically

      o Débride wound and tissue necrosis

      o Decompress cerebral pressure by drilling bur holes to remove hematoma surgically

- Intubation to open airway
- Mechanical ventilation to assess breathing
- Administer:
  - Osmotic diuretics to decrease cerebral edema
    - Mannitol
  - Loop diuretics to decrease edema and circulating blood volume
    - Lasix (furosemide)
  - Analgesics
    - Acetaminophen (Tylenol)
  - Antibiotics (open head wound) to prevent infection
  - Opioids (low-dose) for restlessness, agitation, and pain (if on ventilator)
    - Morphine sulfate, fentanyl citrate

Interventions

- Follow seizure precautions.
- Monitor vital signs.
- Monitor signs of increased intracranial pressure: Widening pulse pressure, increased blood pressure, slow pulse.
- Eat a high-protein, high-calorie, high-vitamin diet
- Monitor intake and output.
- Monitor for diabetes insipidus caused by injury to the pituitary gland.
- Monitor neurologic status (Glasgow Coma Scale).
- Instruct the patient:
  - To call the health care provider if he or she becomes lethargic, experiences change in personality, or is drowsy
  - About seizure precautions

6.3 Amyotrophic Lateral Sclerosis (ALS)

Commonly called Lou Gehrig's disease, amyotrophic lateral sclerosis (ALS) is a progressive, degenerative disorder of the upper and lower motor neurons leading to paralysis of the motor system, except for the eyes. There is no change in mental status or sensory function. Onset is usually between the ages of 40 and the late sixties and affects men. It has been linked to an abnormality in chromosome 21.

Signs and Symptoms

- Atrophy of muscles
- Slurred speech
- Dysphagia
- Fasciculation (muscle twitching)
- Fatigue

Medical Tests

- Creatinine kinase is increased.
- Muscle biopsy shows neuron degeneration.
- Pulmonary function test shows decreased vital capacity.
- Electromyogram (EMG) shows fibrillation and fasciculation.

Treatment

- Administer:
  - Spasmolytic agent for ALS to slow progression
    - Riluzole
  - BIPAP (bi-level positive airway pressure) to assist respiration

Interventions

- Assess gag reflex.
- Monitor vital signs.
- Monitor fluid input and output.
- Develop a communication method.
- Maintain adequate nutrition.
- Suction oral pharynx to remove secretions or food particles.
- Instruct the patient:
  - To tuck the chin while drinking or eating to decrease aspiration

6.4 Bell's Palsy

This is facial paralysis of the seventh cranial nerve affecting one side of the face related to inflammation and is common in diabetics, leading to the patient being unable to close the eyelid, smile, or raise the eyebrow. Patients may have change in taste and pain around the ear. This disorder is self-resolving in most patients.

Signs and Symptoms

- Unilateral facial paralysis
- Change in taste
- Ear and jaw pain

Medical Tests

- EMG to assess recovery time

Treatment

- Administer:
  - Corticosteroids to decrease inflammation

- ○ Prednisone
- ○ Artificial tears to moisten eyes

Interventions

- Monitor for eye irritation.
- Provide meals in private.
- Instruct the patient:
  - ○ How to apply artificial tears properly

6.5 Brain Abscess

Pus collects within the brain as a result of infection from the ear, sinuses, systemic circulation, or from within the brain, leading to cerebral edema. The cause is streptococci, staphylococci, anaerobes, or mixed organism infections.

Signs and Symptoms

- Seizures
- Headache
- Drowsiness
- Confusion
- Ataxia (loss of coordination)
- Widened pulse pressure
- Nystagmus (involuntary eye movement)
- Aphasia (inability to use or understand language)

Medical Tests

- The white blood cell (WBC) count is elevated.
- MRI shows abscess.
- CT shows abscess.
- Biopsy is done to identify organism.

Treatment

- Drain the abscess.
- Administer:
  - ○ Antibiotics
    - Nafcillin sodium (penicillinase-resistant penicillin)
    - Penicillin G benzathine
    - Chloramphenicol
    - Metronidazole
    - Vancomycin

- Corticosteroids
  - Dexamethasone
- Anticonvulsants
  - Phenytoin
  - Phenobarbital
- Osmotic diuretics to decrease cerebral edema
  - Mannitol

Interventions

- Monitor vital signs.
- Monitor mental status.
- Monitor fluid intake and output.
- Monitor movement.
- Monitor senses.
- Instruct the patient:
  - To continue antibiotic treatments

6.6   Brain Tumor

A growth of abnormal cells within the brain leading to increased intracranial pressure. Abnormal cells may be metastasized cancer cells from a site outside the brain (secondary).

- Meningiomas: Benign tumors generated from the meninges
- Gliomas: Malignant rapid growing tumors generated from neuroglial cells
- Astrocytomas: Type of glioma
- Oligodendrogliomas: Slower-growing glioma
- Glioblastomas: Differentiated glioma

Signs and Symptoms

- Parietal lobe
  - Visual-field defect
  - Sensory loss
  - Seizures
- Frontal lobe
  - Anosmia (loss of sense of smell)
  - Personality changes
  - Expressive aphasia
  - Slowing of mental activity
- Occipital lobe
  - Prosopagnosia
  - Impaired vision

- Cerebellum or brain stem
  - Ataxia
  - Lack of coordination
  - Hypotonia of limbs
- Temporal lobe
  - Receptive aphasia
  - Auditory hallucinations
  - Depersonalization
  - Seizures
  - Smell hallucinations
  - Emotional changes
  - Visual field defects

Medical Tests

- CT shows meningioma.
- MRI with contrast shows tumor.

Treatment

- Craniotomy to remove the tumor
- Radiation to decrease tumor size
- Administer:
  - Glucocorticoid to decrease inflammation
  - Dexamethasone
  - Anticonvulsant to decrease seizure activity
  - Phenytoin, phenobarbital, carbamazepine, divalproex sodium, valproic acid, levetiracetam, lamotrigine, clonazepam, topiramate, ethosuximide
  - Osmotic diuretic to reduce cerebral edema
    - Mannitol
  - Proton pump inhibitors to decrease gastric irritation
  - Lansoprazole, omeprazole, esomeprazole, rabeprazole, pantoprazole
  - Histamine (H_2) receptor antagonists: to decrease gastric irritation
    - Ranitidine, famotidine, nizatidine, cimetidine
  - Mucosal barrier fortifier to decrease gastric irritation
    - Sucralfate
  - Chemotherapeutic agents based on cell type
  - Carmustine, lomustine, procarbazine, vincristine, temozolomide, erlotinib, gefitinib

Interventions

- Monitor neurologic function.
- Follow seizure precautions.

- Instruct the patient:
  - On seizure precautions

6.7 Cerebral Aneurysm

Weakening of a blood vessel wall in the brain, resulting in ballooning of the vessel wall, which might lead to a rupture and intracranial bleeding. This can be caused by congenital malformation, infection, a lesion on the blood vessel wall, a trauma, or atherosclerosis.

Signs and Symptoms

- Asymptomatic unless rupture occurs
- Decreased level of consciousness
- Headache caused by hemorrhage and increased intracranial pressure

Medical Tests

- CT shows the aneurysm
- Single photon emission computed tomography (SPECT) shows the aneurysm
- Angiogram shows the aneurysm
- Digital subtraction angiography shows the aneurysm
- Diffusion/perfusion magnetic resonance angiography (MRA) shows the aneurysm

Treatment

- Surgical resection of the aneurysm
- Administer:
  - Glucocorticoid to decrease inflammation
    - Dexamethasone
  - Anticonvulsant to decrease seizure activity
    - Phenytoin, phenobarbital, carbamazepine, divalproex sodium, valproic acid, levetiracetam, lamotrigine, clonazepam, topiramate, ethosuximide
  - Stool softener to decrease need to strain
    - Colace (docusate sodium)

Interventions

- Elevate head of bed 30°.
- Maintain the patient on bed rest.
- Monitor the level of consciousness.
- Monitor the vital signs for indication of increased intracranial pressure (widened pulse pressure and bradycardia).
- Instruct the patient:
  - To report any headache immediately to the health care provider

6.8 Encephalitis

Encephalitis is inflammation of the brain in response to an infection by a virus (common), bacteria, fungus, or protozoa.

Signs and Symptoms

- Fever
- Stiff neck
- Headache
- Nausea and vomiting
- Drowsiness
- Lethargy
- Seizure

Medical Tests

- Blood cultures and sensitivity

Treatment

Administer:

- Glucocorticoid to decrease inflammation
  - Dexamethasone
- Anticonvulsant to decrease seizure activity
  - Phenytoin, phenobarbital, carbamazepine, divalproex sodium, valproic acid, levetiracetam, lamotrigine, clonazepam, topiramate, ethosuximide
- Diuretic to reduce cerebral edema
  - Mannitol, Lasix (furosemide)
- Antipyretics to reduce fever
  - Tylenol (acetaminophen)

Interventions

- Monitor vital signs for indication of increased intracranial pressure (widened pulse pressure and bradycardia).
- Monitor neurologic changes.
- Monitor fluid input and output.
- Provide a quiet environment.
- Perform range-of-motion exercises—active or passive.
- Turn and position patient.
- Instruct the patient:
  - To turn every 2 hours

6.9 Guillain-Barré Syndrome

An autoimmune reaction damages the myelin surrounding the axon on the peripheral nerves resulting in an acute, progressive weakness and paralysis of muscles. This occurs a few weeks after a viral infection, acute illness, or surgery. Damage may be permanent if nerve cells are damaged. Damage may be temporary if axons are damaged.

In ascending Guillain-Barré, the damage begins at the distal lower extremities and moves upward.

In descending Guillain-Barré, the damage begins in the muscles of the face and throat and moves downward, resulting in paralysis of the diaphragm and intercostal muscles, leading to respiratory compromise.

Signs and Symptoms

- Acute illness or infection within the past several weeks
- Absence of deep-tendon reflexes
- Burning or prickling feeling
- Symmetric weakness
- Flaccid paralysis
- Fluctuating blood pressure
- Cardiac dysrhythmias
- Facial weakness
- Difficulty swallowing (dysphagia)

Medical Tests

- Nerve-conduction studies show slowed velocity.
- Pulmonary function tests show diminished tidal volume and vital capacity.
- Lumbar puncture shows increased protein in cerebrospinal fluid.

Treatment

- Plasmapheresis to remove antibodies from blood
- Monitor respirations and support ventilation if necessary.
- Administer:
  - Intravenous (IV) immunoglobulin

Interventions

- Monitor vital signs.
- Monitor for progression of change.
- Monitor gag reflex.
- Insert nasogastric tube if dysphagia present.
- Develop nonverbal communication method (call bell).
- Instruct the patient:
  - To turn every 2 hours

6.10 Huntington's Disease (Chorea)

Huntington's disease is a genetic malady that appears between the ages of 30 and 50 and results in a progressive decline in mental ability and gradual onset of involuntary jerking movements. This is an autosomal-dominant trait located on chromosome 4. Decreased mental ability progresses to dementia and is fatal within 20 years of onset.

The patient may present with either abnormalities of movements or changes in intellectual function. In time, both will be present. The mental status changes will progress to dementia. The disease will prove to be fatal within 10 to 20 years from the time of onset. There is no cure.

Signs and Symptoms

- Psychiatric disturbance
- Restlessness or fidgeting
- Abnormal, jerking movements
- Progressive dementia

Medical Tests

- Genetic testing can detect gene presence before onset.
- Positron emission tomography (PET) shows decrease in glucose uptake in specific areas in brain.
- CT scan shows cerebral atrophy (late in disease).
- MRI shows cerebral atrophy (late in disease).

Treatment

- Administer:
  - Antipsychotic
    - Reserpine, Haldol (haloperidol)

Interventions

- Assist the patient with activities of daily living.
- Monitor for depression.
- Instruct the patient:
  - On the benefits of genetic counseling

6.11 Meningitis

Infection of the meningeal coverings of the brain and spinal cord commonly caused by bacteria (*Streptococcus pneumoniae,* pneumococcal; *Neisseria meningitides,* meningococcal; or *Haemophilus influenzae*) but can also be caused by a virus, fungus, protozoa, or toxic exposure. Bacterial meningitis is transmitted when people live in close quarters. Viral meningitis may follow a viral infection and is self-limiting. Fungal meningitis may occur in patients who are immunocompromised.

Signs and Symptoms

- Fever
- Nuchal rigidity (pain when flexing chin toward chest)
- Stiff neck
- Petechial rash on skin and mucus membranes
- Photophobia (sensitivity to light)
- Headache
- Malaise and fatigue
- Seizures
- Nausea and vomiting
- Myalgia (muscle aches)

Medical Tests

- Lumbar puncture to sample cerebrospinal fluid
- Polymerase chain reaction (PCR) test of cerebrospinal fluid for organisms
- Culture and sensitivity of cerebrospinal fluid and blood
- CT brain to rule out lesion

Treatment

- Administer:
  - Glucocorticoid to decrease inflammation
    - Dexamethasone
  - Anticonvulsant to decrease seizure activity
    - Phenytoin, phenobarbital, carbamazepine, divalproex sodium, valproic acid, levetiracetam, lamotrigine, clonazepam, topiramate, ethosuximide
  - Diuretic to reduce cerebral edema
    - Mannitol, Lasix (furosemide)
  - Antipyretics to reduce fever
    - Tylenol (acetaminophen)
  - Antibiotics for bacterial meningitis
    - Penicillin G, ceftriaxone, cefotaxime, vancomycin plus ceftriaxone or cefotaxime, ceftazidime
  - Antifungal medication for fungal infection
    - Amphotericin B, fluconazole, flucytosine

Interventions

- Isolate the patient.
- Darken room.
- Follow seizure precautions.
- Maintain the patient on bed rest.
- Monitor fluid intake and output.

- Monitor neurologic function every 2 hours.
- Instruct the patient:
  - To explain restrictions

6.12 Multiple Sclerosis (MS)

This is demyelination of the white matter of the nervous system resulting in disruption of neural transmission leading to abnormal sensations, mental function, and movements and permanent nerve damage. Many patients experience periods of exacerbation and remission, in which symptoms self-resolve. The cause is unknown but is suspected to be an autoimmune process. Stress aggravates the symptoms.

Primary progressive disease is the progressive deterioration without periods of exacerbation and remission.

Secondary progressive disease is a progressive deterioration regardless of periods of exacerbation and remission.

Signs and Symptoms

- Fatigue
- Muscle weakness
- Ataxia (decreased motor coordination)
- Paresthesia (burning tingling on the skin)
- Memory loss
- Decreased mental focus
- Slurred speech
- Diplopia (double vision)
- Urinary changes

Medical Tests

- MRI shows central nervous system plaques and demyelination
- CT shows central nervous system plaques
- Lumbar puncture to sample cerebrospinal fluid for increased immunoglobulin G in cerebrospinal fluid

Treatment

- Plasmapheresis to remove antibodies from blood
- Administer:
  - Biologic response modifiers on a continuous basis
  - Interferon beta–1a, interferon beta–1b, glatiramer acetate
- Immunosuppressants
  - Cyclophosphamide, azathioprine, methotrexate, cladribine, mitoxantrone
- Glucocorticoid to decrease inflammation
  - Dexamethasone, IV methylprednisolone, prednisone
- Muscle relaxants
  - Dantrolene, baclofen, carisoprodol, metaxalone, tizanidine, diazepam

- Psychostimulants
  - Modafinil, methylphenidate
- Antidepressants
  - Fluoxetine, sertraline, paroxetine, citalopram, escitalopram, venlafaxine, bupropion, duloxetine, amitriptyline
- Administer anticholinergic to improve bladder function
  - Oxybutynin, hyoscyamine sulfate, darifenacin, solifenacin, tolterodine

Interventions

- Schedule rest periods.
- Monitor motor movements.
- Monitor cognitive functions.
- Instruct the patient:
  - How to control the bladder
  - On self-catheterization
  - To develop long-term care

6.13   Myasthenia Gravis

Normal muscle contraction of the face, throat, tongue, and neck is disrupted, caused by antibodies binding to acetylcholine receptor sites, resulting in droopy eyes and mild weakness progressing to respiratory distress. Acetylcholine is required for normal muscle contraction. This is an autoimmune disorder with a family tendency, although not an inherited disorder. There are exacerbations and remissions. It is more likely in young women. Patients may experience hyperplasia of the thymus gland.

Myasthenic crisis is an exacerbation of symptoms caused by insufficient medication. Cholinergic crisis is an exacerbation of weakness caused by overabundance of cholinergic medication.

Signs and Symptoms

- Ptosis (drooping of the eyelids)
- Dry eyes
- Incomplete closing of eyes
- Fatigue
- Dysphagia (difficulty swallowing)
- Diplopia (double vision)
- Muscle weakness
- Bowel incontinence
- Bladder incontinence
- Myasthenic crisis
  - Hypertension
  - Tachycardia
  - Loss of gag reflex

- ○ Tachypnea
- ○ Bowel incontinence
- ○ Bladder incontinence
- ○ Cyanosis
- Cholinergic crisis
  - ○ Hypotension
  - ○ Twitching of facial muscles
  - ○ Miosis (small pupils)
  - ○ Paleness
  - ○ Abdominal cramping
  - ○ Blurred vision
  - ○ Nausea, vomiting, diarrhea

Medical Tests

- Administer edrophonium (Tensilon) or neostigmine bromide (Prostigmin), resulting in temporary relief of symptoms.
- Blood test to detect acetylcholine receptor antibodies
- CT to rule out tumor of the thymus (thymoma)
- Electromyography (EMG) shows decrease muscle response

Treatment

- Plasmapheresis to remove antibodies from blood
- Administer:
  - ○ There are no aminoglycoside antibiotics that can exacerbate symptoms
  - ○ Immunosuppressants
    - ▪ Prednisone, dexamethasone, azathioprine, cyclophosphamide
  - ○ Cholinesterase inhibitors for symptoms
    - ▪ Neostigmine, pyridostigmine, ambenonium
  - ○ Natural tears to keep eyes moist
  - ○ BiPAP or continuous positive airway pressure to assist respiration

Interventions

- Monitor vital signs.
- Follow a high-calorie diet.
- Monitor weight.
- Eye patch if unable to close eyes.
- Monitor fluid intake and output.
- Monitor neurologic changes.
- Monitor gag reflex.
- Develop nonverbal communication method (call bell).

- Instruct the patient:
  ○ To schedule rest periods
  ○ To eat meals an hour following medication to decrease the risk of aspiration
  ○ On the use of an oral-pharyngeal suctioning catheter to clear secretions
  ○ To avoid heat extremes (hot tubs, saunas)
  ○ That alcohol may exacerbate symptoms

6.14 Parkinson's Disease

A gradual degeneration of neurons of the substantia nigra (midbrain) resulting in decreased dopamine neurotransmitter, leading to decreased fine voluntary motor skills. Sympathetic noradrenergic lesions develop, resulting in decreased norepinephrine and leading to excess production of acetylcholine neurotransmitters, leading to increased muscle tone, rigidity, and tremors. There is a genetic tendency in Parkinson's disease, and it can be caused by environmental factors and virus. Onset is after age 60. Mental changes and dementia may develop.

Signs and Symptoms

- Pill-rolling hand movements
- Lead pipe (resists movement)
- Cogwheeling (rhythmic interruption of movement)
- Shuffling gait
- Tremor at rest
- Dyskinesia (unable to control voluntary movements)
- Stooping posture
- Masklike facial expressions
- Handwriting becomes progressively smaller
- Orthostatic hypotension
- Bradykinesia (slow movement)
- Drooling

Medical Tests

- Lumbar puncture to sample cerebrospinal fluid for decreased levels of dopamine

Treatment

- Administer:
  ○ Antiparkinsonian agents
    ▪ Levodopa, carbidopa-levodopa
  ○ Dopamine receptor agonists
    ▪ Pergolide, bromocriptine, pramipexole, ropinirole
  ○ Monoamine oxidase B inhibitor
    ▪ Selegiline

   ○ Catechol-O-methyltransferase (COMT) inhibitors

      ▪ Entacapone, tolcapone

   ○ Acetylcholine-blocking drugs to decrease tremor and rigidity

      ▪ Biperiden, benztropine mesylate, procyclidine, orphenadrine, trihexyphenidyl

Interventions

- Monitor vital signs.
- Monitor the neurologic status for changes.
- Weigh the patient weekly.
- Monitor intake and output.
- Employ physical therapy.
- Instruct the patient:
  ○ To follow a high-protein, high-calorie soft-food diet
  ○ To take time with activities of daily living
  ○ On fall precautions

6.15   Spinal Cord Injury

Spinal cord injury results from pulling, twisting, compressing, or severing the spinal cord resulting in damage to the partial (incomplete) or entire thickness (complete) of the spinal cord. Damage is assessed after inflammation related to trauma subsides. Spinal cord tissue does not regenerate. The level of damage to the spinal cord determines the degree of disability.

Signs and Symptoms

- Tingling (paresthesia)
- Reduced sensation (hypoesthesia)
- Increased sensation (hyperesthesia)
- Weakness (flaccid paralysis)
- Absence of reflexes
- Lack of bowel control
- Loss of bladder control
- Hypotension
- Hypothermia
- Bradycardia
- Loss of motor control

Medical Tests

- CT scan shows injury.
- MRI shows injury.

Treatment

- Administer:
  - Corticosteroid to decrease inflammation
    - Methylprednisolone, prednisone, dexamethasone
  - Plasma expander to increase circulation and oxygen to injured tissues
    - Dextran
  - H_2 receptor antagonists to protect formation of stress ulcer
    - Cimetidine, ranitidine, famotidine, nizatidine
  - Gastric mucosal protective agent to protect formation of stress ulcer
    - Sucralfate
  - Surgical decompression or repair of fracture

Interventions

- Position the patient flat on a rotating bed to prevent pressure ulcers.
- Instruct the patient against flexion.
- Immobilize the spinal cord with traction to decrease irritation.
- Monitor traction to prevent skin irritation.
- Monitor for spinal shock (reflexes loss below injury, bradycardia, hypotension, paralytic ileus, flaccid paralysis).
- Monitor the vital signs.
- Monitor intake and output.
- Monitor mental status.
- Monitor neurologic status.
- Monitor the skin for pressure ulcers.
- Care for cervical traction pin sites.
- Instruct the patient:
  - In the proper transference from wheelchair to bed
  - In the need for regular bowel movement and urination
  - In the need to use the incentive spirometer
  - About turning and positioning

6.16   Cerebrovascular Accident (CVA)

A CVA is an interruption of the blood supply to the brain resulting in infarction (necrosis) in the affective tissue. Patients with high cholesterol, diabetes mellitus, smoking, obesity, oral contraceptive use, or atrial fibrillation have a high risk for cerebrovascular accident. There are three types of CVA. Ischemic stroke (common) is an interruption of arterial blood flow by an obstruction (clot). Hemorrhagic stroke is an interruption of blood flow by rupture or leakage of a blood vessel. Transient ischemic attack (TIA) is a temporary interruption of blood flow that resolves in a few hours.

Signs and Symptoms

- Difficulty speaking (aphasia)
- Personality changes
- Confusion
- Sensory changes
- Numbness
- Weakness
- Severe headache
- Seizure

Medical Tests

- SPECT shows decreased perfusion.
- MRA shows abnormal vessels.
- CT scan shows bleeding.
- MRI shows ischemic vessels.

Treatment

- Carotid artery endarterectomy to remove plaque from carotid artery (ischemic)
- Surgical implantation of a stent in the carotid artery (ischemic)
- Surgical correction of bleeding (hemorrhagic)
- Administer:
  - Thrombolytic agent within 3 hours of onset of symptoms (ischemic)
    - Tissue plasminogen activator (TPA)
  - Anticoagulants after TPA (ischemic)
    - Heparin, warfarin, Lovenox, aspirin
  - Antiplatelet medications to decrease platelet adhesiveness (ischemic)
    - Clopidogrel, ticlopidine hydrochloride, dipyridamole
  - Corticosteroid to decrease inflammation
    - Dexamethasone (Decadron)

Interventions

- Bed rest
- Monitor vital signs.
- Monitor neurologic status.
- Monitor for increased intracranial pressure (decreased level of consciousness, restlessness, confusion, headaches, nausea, and vomiting).
- Develop nonverbal communication method (call bell).
- Physical therapy is done to maintain muscle tone.
- Speech therapy is done to assist swallowing and speech.

- Occupational therapy is done to regain independent living.
- Instruct the patient:
  - On the proper way to transfer from wheelchair to bed
  - On the effects of CVA on activities of daily living

6.17 Seizure Disorder

Sudden uncontrolled discharge of neurons in the brain, resulting in abnormal behavior caused by metabolic disorder, intracranial pressure, tumor, CVA, medication, or seizure disorder. Before the seizure (preictal stage), the patient may experience alterations in sight, sound, or smell. After the seizure (postictal stage), the patient is fatigued, confused, and may not recall the seizure.

Signs and Symptoms

GENERALIZED SEIZURES	
Tonic/clonic	First tonic (limbs rigidity) loss of consciousness
	Then clonic (rhythmic jerking)
Tonic	Limbs rigid, loss of consciousness
Clonic	Rhythmic jerking
Absence	Staring and brief loss of consciousness
Myoclonic	Brief rhythmic jerking
Atonic	Loss of muscle tone
PARTIAL SEIZURES	
Simple partial	No loss of consciousness, unusual sensation, unusual movement, begins with aura
Complex partial	Lip smacking, patting, picking, loss of consciousness

Medical Tests

- CT scan of brain to rule out tumor or bleed
- MRI of brain to rule out tumor or bleed
- Electroencephalogram (EEG) shows abnormal electrical activity in brain

Treatment

- Treat underlying cause.
- Surgically remove seizure focal area.
- Implant vagal nerve stimulator to decrease the frequency of seizures.
- Administer:
  - Antiepileptic
    - Carbamazepine, phenytoin, phenobarbital, clonazepam, valproic acid, lamotrigine, gabapentin, levetiracetam, oxcarbazepine, primidone, tiagabine, topiramate

Interventions

- Seizure precautions
- During seizure:
  - Place the patient on his or her side to decrease the risk of aspiration.
  - Remove objects from around the patient to prevent injury.
  - Note the duration and the patient's actions during the seizure.
  - Monitor for status epilepticus (prolonged seizures or repeated seizures).
  - Do not insert anything in the patient's mouth during seizure.
- Instruct the patient:
  - To explain seizure precautions to his or her family and friends
  - To instruct family and friends what to do during a seizure
  - On the importance of taking medications as prescribed

Solved Problems

6.1   What is an epidural hematoma?

An epidural hematoma is bleeding from an artery with blood accumulating between the dura and skull.

6.2   What is a subarachnoid hemorrhage?

A subarachnoid hemorrhage is bleeding between the arachnoid mater and the pia mater, the location of cerebrospinal fluid.

6.3   What is a concussion?

A concussion is blunt-force trauma that thrusts the brain against the inside of the skull, resulting in bruising.

6.4   What is a coup injury?

A coup injury is blunt-force trauma that thrusts the brain against the inside of the skull at the point of the blunt-force trauma.

6.5   What is a contrecoup injury?

A contrecoup injury is blunt-force trauma that causes the head to recoil, thrusting the brain against the inside of the skull at a point opposite the blunt-force trauma.

6.6   What is ALS?

ALS, commonly called Lou Gehrig's disease, is a progressive degenerative disorder of the upper and lower motor neurons, leading to paralysis of the motor system except for the eyes. There is no change in mental status or sensory function.

6.7   What is Bell's palsy?

Bell's palsy is facial paralysis of the seventh cranial nerve affecting one side of the face related to inflammation and is common in diabetics, leading to the patient being unable to close the eyelid, smile, or raise the eyebrows.

6.8   What is a brain abscess?

A brain abscess occurs when pus collects within the brain as a result of infection from the ear, sinuses, systemic circulation, or from within the brain, leading to cerebral edema.

6.9 What is a meningioma?

A meningioma is a benign tumor generated from the meninges.

6.10 What is a glioma?

A glioma is a malignant rapid-growing tumor generated from neuroglial cells.

6.11 What is a cerebral aneurysm?

A cerebral aneurysm is the weakening of a blood vessel wall in the brain, resulting in ballooning of the vessel wall that might lead to a rupture and intracranial bleeding.

6.12 What can cause a cerebral aneurysm?

A cerebral aneurysm can be caused by congenital malformation, infection, lesion on the blood vessel wall, trauma, or atherosclerosis.

6.13 Why would a health care provider prescribe Colace for a patient who has a cerebral aneurysm?

A health care provider would prescribe Colace for a patient who has a cerebral aneurysm to decrease straining during defecation.

6.14 What is the purpose of using bronchoscopy in a patient who has bronchiectasis?

The purpose of using bronchoscopy in a patient who has bronchiectasis is to remove excessive secretions.

6.15 What is encephalitis?

Encephalitis is inflammation of the brain in response to an infection by a virus (common), bacteria, fungus, or protozoa.

6.16 What is ascending Guillain-Barré syndrome?

Ascending Guillain-Barré syndrome is an autoimmune reaction that damages the myelin surrounding the axon on the peripheral nerves resulting in an acute, progressive weakness and paralysis of muscles beginning at the distal lower extremities and moving upward.

6.17 What is Huntington's disease?

Huntington's disease is a genetic disease that appears between the ages of 30 and 50, resulting in a progressive decline in mental ability and gradual onset of involuntary jerking movements.

6.18 What is meningitis?

Meningitis is an infection of the meningeal coverings of the brain and spinal cord commonly caused by bacteria (*S. pneumoniae,* pneumococcal; *N. meningitides,* meningococcal; or *H. influenzae*) but can also be caused by a virus, fungus, protozoa, or toxic exposure.

6.19 What are signs and symptoms of meningitis?

The signs and symptoms of meningitis are fever, nuchal rigidity (pain when flexing the chin toward the chest), stiff neck, petechial rash on the skin and mucus membranes, photophobia (sensitivity to light), headache, malaise and fatigue, seizures, nausea and vomiting, and myalgia (muscle aches).

6.20 What is multiple sclerosis?

Multiple sclerosis is demyelination of the white matter of the nervous system resulting in disruption of neural transmission, leading to abnormal sensations, mental function, and movements and permanent nerve damage.

6.21   What is myasthenia gravis?

Myasthenia gravis is normal muscle contraction of the face, throat, tongue, and neck disrupted by antibodies binding to acetylcholine receptor sites and resulting in droopy eyes and mild weakness progressing to respiratory distress.

6.22   What is a myasthenic crisis?

A myasthenic crisis is an exacerbation of symptoms of myasthenia gravis caused by insufficient medication.

6.23   What is a cholinergic crisis?

A cholinergic crisis is an exacerbation of weakness related to myasthenia gravis caused by an overabundance of cholinergic medication.

6.24   What is Parkinson's disease?

Parkinson's disease is a gradual degeneration of neurons in the substantia nigra (midbrain), resulting in decreased dopamine neurotransmitters and leading to decreased fine voluntary motor skills. Sympathetic noradrenergic lesions develop, resulting in decreased norepinephrine and leading to excess production of acetylcholine neurotransmitter, which also leads to increased muscle tone, rigidity, and tremors.

6.25   What is a seizure disorder?

A seizure disorder is a sudden uncontrolled discharge of neurons in the brain, resulting in abnormal behavior caused by a metabolic disorder, intracranial pressure, tumor, CVA, medication, or seizure disorder. Before the seizure (preictal stage), the patient may experience alterations in sight, sound, or smell. After the seizure (postictal stage), the patient is fatigued, confused, and may not recall the seizure.

CHAPTER 7

Endocrine System

7.1 Definition

- Glands
  - o Secrete chemical messengers called hormones that control and regulate target cells and organs.
  - o Hormones are released into the blood because of the quantity of the hormone in the blood or in response to another hormone.
  - o Hormones stop being released into the blood based on direct feedback.
  - o Direct feedback is the mechanism whereby changes in hormone levels and bodily functions signal the gland to secrete or withhold secretion of the hormone.
- Hypothalamus
  - o Location: The brain
  - o Secretes:
    - Thyrotropin-releasing hormone
      - – Stimulates thyroid-stimulating hormone (TSH) release from anterior pituitary (primarily)
      - – Stimulates prolactin release from anterior pituitary
    - Dopamine
      - – Inhibits prolactin release from anterior pituitary
    - Growth hormone (GH) – releasing hormone
      - – Stimulates GH release from anterior pituitary
    - Somatostatin
      - – Inhibits GH release from anterior pituitary
      - – Inhibits TSH release from anterior pituitary
    - Gonadotropin-releasing hormone
      - – Stimulates follicle-stimulating hormone (FSH) release from anterior pituitary
      - – Stimulates luteinizing hormone (LH) release from anterior pituitary
    - Corticotropin-releasing hormone
      - – Stimulates adrenocorticotropic hormone (ACTH) release from anterior pituitary

- Oxytocin
  - Uterine contraction
  - Lactation (letdown reflex)
- Vasopressin
  - Promotes water reabsorption
  - Increases blood volume

- Pineal body
  - Location: The brain
  - Secretes:
    - Melatonin
      - Antioxidant
      - Monitors the circadian rhythm
      - Induces drowsiness
    - Dimethyltryptamine
      - Plays a role in dreams

- Pituitary gland
  - Location: At the base of the at the hypothalamus in the brain
  - Anterior pituitary gland
    - GH (somatotropin)
      - Stimulates growth and cell reproduction
      - Stimulates insulin-like growth factor 1 release from liver
    - TSH (thyrotropin)
      - Stimulates thyroxine (T4) and tri-iodothyronine (T3) synthesis and release from thyroid gland
      - Stimulates iodine absorption by thyroid gland
    - Adrenocorticotropic hormone (corticotropin)
      - Stimulates corticosteroid (glucocorticoid and mineralocorticoid) and androgen synthesis and release from adrenocortical cells
    - FSH
      - Females:
        - Stimulates maturation of ovarian follicles in ovary
      - Males:
        - Stimulates maturation of seminiferous tubules
        - Stimulates spermatogenesis
        - Stimulates production of androgen-binding protein from Sertoli cells of the testes
    - LH
      - Females:
        - Stimulates ovulation
        - Stimulates formation of corpus luteum
      - Males:
        - Stimulates testosterone synthesis from Leydig cells (interstitial cells)

- Prolactin
  - Stimulates milk synthesis and release from mammary glands
  - Mediates sexual gratification
- Posterior pituitary gland
  - Oxytocin
    - Uterine contraction
    - Lactation (letdown reflex)
  - Vasopressin
    - Promotes water reabsorption
    - Increases blood volume
- Intermediate pituitary gland
  - Melanocyte-stimulating hormone
  - Stimulates melanin synthesis and release from skin/hair melanocytes
- Thyroid gland
  - Location: The anterior neck overlying the trachea
  - Secretes:
    - T3
      - Stimulates body oxygen consumption
      - Increases the basal metabolic rate
      - Promotes protein synthesis
    - T4 (tetraiodothyronine)
      - Stimulates body oxygen consumption
      - Increases the basal metabolic rate
      - Promotes protein synthesis
    - Calcitonin
      - Stimulates bone construction
      - Inhibits release of calcium from bone
      - Reduces calcium in blood
- Adrenal glands
  - Located: At the top of each kidney in the retro peritoneum
  - Cortex: Secretes
    - Glucocorticoids (cortisol)
      - Stimulates gluconeogenesis
      - Stimulates fat breakdown in adipose tissue
      - Inhibits protein synthesis
      - Inhibits glucose uptake in muscle and adipose tissue
      - Inhibits immunological responses
      - Inhibits inflammatory responses
    - Mineralocorticoids (aldosterone)
      - Stimulate active sodium reabsorption in kidneys
      - Stimulate water reabsorption in kidneys

- Increase blood volume
- Increase blood pressure
- Stimulate potassium
  - Androgens (DHEA and testosterone)
    - Females: Masculinizing effects
- Medulla: Secretes
  - Adrenaline (epinephrine)
    - Increases oxygen to the brain and muscles
    - Increases glucose to the brain and muscles
    - Vasodilation
    - Increases breakdown of lipids
    - Increases glycogen in liver
    - Increases cardiac rate
    - Increases respiration
    - Increases cardiac stroke volume
    - Dilates pupils
    - Decreases digestion and nonemergency bodily functions
    - Decrease the immune system
  - Noradrenaline (norepinephrine)
    - Increases skeletal muscle readiness.
    - Same as adrenaline (epinephrine)
  - Dopamine
    - Increases heart rate
    - Increases blood pressure
  - Enkephalin
    - Regulates pain
- Parathyroid glands
  - Location: Neck
  - Secrete:
    - Parathyroid hormone
      - Releases calcium from bones
      - Regains calcium by kidneys
      - Excretes phosphate
- Testes
  - Location: Testicles
  - Secretes:
    - Androgens (testosterone)
      - Increase muscle mass
      - Increase strength
      - Increase bone density
      - Increase bone growth

- – Maturation of sex organs
- – Growth of beard
- – Growth of auxiliary hair
- – Deepening of voice
  - ▪ Inhibin
    - – Inhibits production of FSH
- Ovarian follicle
  - o Location: Ovaries
  - o Secretes:
    - ▪ Progesterone
      - – Anti-inflammatory
      - – Supports pregnancy
    - ▪ Estrogens (estradiol)
      - – Form female secondary sex characteristics
    - ▪ Inhibin
      - – Inhibits production of FSH

7.2   Hypothyroidism (Myxedema)

Hypothyroidism (myxedema) results from little pressure or absence of thyroid hormone as a result of decreased production of TSH by the pituitary gland, inflammation of the thyroid gland, surgery, treatment for hyperthyroidism or Hashimoto's thyroiditis, in which the thyroid is attacked by antibodies.

Signs and Symptoms

- Weight gain
- Fatigue
- Slow cognitive function
- Hypothermia
- Brittle nails
- Dry skin
- Dry hair

Medical Tests

- Thyroid blood test
  - o Decreased T3, T4
  - o Decreased TSH by the pituitary gland
  - o Increased TSH
  - o Positive thyroglobulin (Hashimoto's thyroiditis)
  - o Positive peroxidase autoantibodies (Hashimoto's thyroiditis)

Treatment

- Administer:
  - o Synthroid (levothyroxine)

Interventions

- Monitor for thyrotoxicosis: Nausea, vomiting, diarrhea, sweating, tachycardia.
- Monitor T3 and T4 levels.
- Monitor vital signs.
- Have patient eat a low-calorie diet.
- Create a warm environment.
- Increase fluids and fiber to decrease risk of constipation.
- Instruct the patient:
  - About lifetime hormone replacement in the morning
  - To monitor for signs of hypothyroidism and hyperthyroidism

7.3   Hyperthyroidism (Graves' Disease)

Hyperthyroidism is overproduction of the thyroid hormone by the thyroid gland as a result of adenomas (benign tumor), overproduction of TSH by the pituitary gland, or autoimmune disease in which antibodies attack the thyroid gland.

Signs and Symptoms

- Exophthalmos (bulging eyes), not reversible
- Goiter (enlarged thyroid gland) related to a tumor
- Weight loss
- Increased appetite
- Diaphoresis
- Nervousness

Medical Tests

- Thyroid scan shows enlarged thyroid
- Thyroid blood test
  - Increased T3, T4
  - Increased TSH (pituitary gland)
- Positive antibodies (Graves' disease)

Treatment

- Surgical reduction or removal of the thyroid if condition complicates breathing or swallowing
- Administer:
  - Beta-blockers to decrease sympathetic activity to control anxiety and tachycardia
    - Inderal (propranolol)
  - Radioactive iodine therapy (Graves' disease) for patients 50 years old or older
    - Lugol's solution, potassium iodide, saturated solution of potassium iodide (SSKI)
  - Antithyroid medication blocks production of T3, T4
    - Propylthiouracil (PTU), Tapazole (methimazole)

Interventions

- Monitor the vital signs.
- Follow a diet high in carbohydrates, protein, calories, vitamins, and minerals.
- Create a cool environment.
- Place the patient in a semi-Fowler's position (after surgery).
- Support the head and neck with pillows (after surgery).
- Monitor the incision for frank hemorrhage and a purulent, foul-smelling drainage (after surgery).
- Monitor for laryngeal edema (hoarseness or inability to speak clearly after surgery).
- Keep oxygen, suction, and a tracheotomy set near the bed (after surgery).
- Monitor for Trousseau's sign (inflate blood pressure cuff on the arm and muscles contract), and if positive, administer intravenous (IV) calcium (after surgery).
- Monitor for Chvostek's sign (tapping of the facial nerve causes twitching of the facial muscles), and if positive, administer IV calcium (after surgery).
- Monitor for tetany (muscle spasms and tremors), and if positive administer calcium gluconate.
- Monitor for hypocalcemia (tingling of hands and fingers), and if positive, administer calcium gluconate.
- Instruct the patient:
  - To use dark glasses and artificial tears (exophthalmos)

7.4 Simple Goiter

Simple goiter is an enlarged thyroid gland caused by insufficient iodine or by ingesting a large quantity of goitrogenic medication or goitrogenic foods that decrease production of thyroxine (goitrogenic). Goitrogenic foods include peas, peaches, spinach, strawberries, peanuts, and cabbage. Simple goiter is less common today because of the addition of iodine in table salt.

Signs and Symptoms

- Enlarged thyroid gland
- Dysphagia
- Coughing
- Respiratory distress

Medical Tests

- Ultrasound shows size of thyroid gland
- Radioactive iodine uptake test (RAIU) uptake increased or normal
- Blood test
  - Increased TSH
  - Decreased or normal T4

Treatment

- Administer:
  - If TSH is increased, then use hormone replacement

- Synthroid (levothyroxine), Cytomel (liothyronine), desiccated thyroid
  - o If overactive thyroid gland:
    - Lugol's solution, potassium iodide
  - o Thyroidectomy if not reduced by medication

Interventions

- No goitrogenic foods (peas, peaches, spinach, strawberries, peanuts, and cabbage)
- No goitrogenic medication
- Instruct the patient:
  - o About lifetime hormone replacement in the morning
  - o To use iodized salt

7.5   Hypopituitarism

Decreased secretion of pituitary hormones by the pituitary gland with a primary cause by infection, decreased blood supply to the pituitary gland, pituitary tumor, radiation of the pituitary gland, surgery of the pituitary gland. Secondary cause is disorder of the hypothalamus.

Signs and Symptoms

- Lethargy
- Fatigue
- Stunted growth
- Decreased appetite
- Diminished cognition
- Infertility
- Sensitivity to cold

Medical Tests

- Blood test:
  - o Decreased ACTH
  - o Decreased TSH
  - o Decreased prolactin
- Magnetic resonance imaging (MRI) shows pituitary tumor

Treatment

- Administer:
  - o Replacement hormones
    - Corticosteroids, estrogen, testosterone, thyroid hormone, growth hormone
- Surgical removal of the pituitary tumor (if a tumor exists)

Interventions

- Monitor the intake and output.
- Take daily weights
- Instruct the patient:
    - About lifetime hormone replacement in the morning

7.6   Hyperpituitarism (Acromegaly and Gigantism)

This is increased production of GH from the pituitary gland resulting from a pituitary gland tumor. Physical changes that occur before treatment are permanent.

1. Gigantism: Hyperpituitarism occurs before epiphyseal closure, resulting in overgrowth of all tissues.
2. Acromegaly: Hyperpituitarism occurs after epiphyseal closure, resulting in visceromegaly (enlarged organs), bone thickening, and transverse growth.

Signs and Symptoms

- Abnormal increase in body size

Medical Tests

- Blood test
    - Increased serum GH
    - Increased prolactin
    - Increased glucose

Treatment

- Administer:
    - Dopamine agonists decrease tumor
        - Bromocriptine, cabergoline
- Surgical removal of the pituitary tumor

Interventions

- Range-of-motion exercise
- Emotional support
- Instruct the patient:
    - Not to stop taking hormone replacement suddenly

7.7   Hyperprolactinemia

Overproduction of the prolactin hormone from a pituitary tumor, chronic kidney disease, hypothyroidism, or medication affecting the pituitary gland resulting in excessive lactation

Signs and Symptoms

- Decreased fertility
  - Males
    - Decreased libido
    - Erectile dysfunction
    - Mood changes
    - Headache
    - Gynecomastia
  - Females
    - Galactorrhea
    - Mood changes
    - Decreased or absent menstruation
    - Headache

Medical Tests

- MRI shows pituitary tumor
- Blood test
  - Increased
    - TSH
    - Blood urea nitrogen (BUN)
    - Creatinine
    - Aspartate aminotransferase (AST)
    - Alanine aminotransferase (ALT)
    - Total bilirubin
  - Decreased
    - FSH
    - LH
    - Estradiol
    - Prolactin
    - Testosterone
  - Positive human chorionic gonadotropin (HGC)

Treatment

- Radiation therapy reduces the pituitary tumor
- Surgical removal of the pituitary tumor
- Administer:
  - Dopamine agonists:
    - Bromocriptine, cabergoline
  - Discontinue medications that cause overproduction of prolactin
    - Amphetamines, estrogens, methyldopa, narcotics, protease inhibitors, risperidone, selective serotonin inhibitors, tricyclic inhibitors, verapamil

Interventions

- Monitor serum hormone levels.

7.8 Diabetes Insipidus

Kidneys have decreased ability to concentrate urine caused by a decrease in the production of antidiuretic hormone (ADH) by the hypothalamus or increased production of ADH by the pituitary gland, resulting in an increase in a large amount of diluted urine.

Signs and Symptoms

- Increased urination
- Increased thirst

Medical Tests

- MRI shows tumor of the pituitary gland or hypothalamus gland.
- Desmopressin stimulation test
- Urine specific gravity increase and urine output decrease indicate that the pituitary gland is the underlying cause.
- Urine specific gravity decrease and urine output remaining unchanged indicate that the kidneys are the underlying cause.
- Blood test:
  - Normal blood glucose
  - Increased BUN
  - Increased sodium
  - Increased chloride
- Urine analysis
  - Low specific gravity

Treatment

- Administer:
  - Replacement ADH hormone until condition resolves
    - Desmopressin
  - Diuretic to decrease urination
    - Hydrochlorothiazide

Interventions

- Increased fluid intake until condition resolves
- Monitor the intake and output.
- Weigh daily.

- Instruct the patient:
  - To follow a low-salt diet
  - To take medication daily

7.9   Syndrome of Inappropriate Antidiuretic Hormone Secretion (SIADH)

The pituitary gland is secreting too much ADH caused by disorders of the pituitary gland or the hypothalamus, lung cancer, inflammation of the brain, and medication (cyclophosphamides, selective serotonin receptor inhibitors [SSRIs], chlorpropamide, carbamazepine).

Signs and Symptoms

- Confusion
- Nausea
- Vomiting
- Personality change
- Headaches

Medical Tests

- Blood test
  - Low sodium (hyponatremia)

Treatment

- Administer:
  - IV normal saline
- Treat underlying cause

Interventions

- Weigh daily.
- Monitor the intake and output.
- Monitor sodium levels.
- Instruct the patient:
  - To limit fluid to prevent decrease in sodium

7.10   Addison's Disease

Addison's disease is damage to the adrenal cortex, which results in decreased secretion of corticosteroids (cortisol and aldosterone). This can be caused by an autoimmune reaction to the adrenal gland or by tuberculosis. An Addisonian crisis is a stressful event, such as surgery or infection, that causes decreased production of corticosteroids, resulting in a medical emergency.

Signs and Symptoms

- Orthostatic hypotension
- Bronze skin tone
- Weight loss
- Fatigue

Medical Tests

- Computed tomography (CT) scan shows abnormal adrenal glands
- Blood test:
  - Increased potassium
  - Increased BUN
  - Decreased glucose
  - Decreased cortisol
- 24-Hour urine aldosterone level positive
- ACTH stimulation test positive

Treatment

- Administer:
  - Replacement corticosteroids
  - Cortisone, hydrocortisone, fludrocortisone

Interventions

- Maintain fluid balance.
- Monitor the intake and output.
- Weigh daily.
- Instruct the patient:
  - To take medication daily

7.11 Cushing's Syndrome

Cushing's syndrome is excess secretion of glucocorticoids by the adrenal cortex or excess secretion of ACTH by the pituitary gland caused by glucocorticoid therapy or a tumor in the adrenal glands or pituitary gland.

Signs and Symptoms

- Buffalo hump
- Moon face
- Altered mental status
- Osteoporosis
- Amenorrhea

Medical Tests

- CT scan shows adrenal gland or pituitary tumor
- Dexamethasone suppression test
  - Cortisol suppression indicates that the pituitary gland is the underlying cause.
  - If cortisol is not suppressed, either the adrenal gland or an ectopic tumor is the cause.
- Blood test
  - Increased blood glucose
  - Increased sodium
  - Decreased potassium

Treatment

- Surgical removal of the tumor

Interventions

- Schedule rest periods.
- Monitor the intake and output.
- Weigh daily.
- Monitor for increased glucose and acetone in urine.
- Employ bone densitometry to assess for osteoporosis.
- Instruct the patient:
  - To maintain a high-calorie, high-calcium diet
  - To avoid skin injuries caused by a delay in wound healing

7.12　Primary Aldosteronism (Conn's Syndrome)

Primary aldosteronism is excessive production of aldosterone by the adrenal cortex as a result of an adrenal tumor, adrenal cortex disorder, or medications (calcium channel blockers).

Signs and Symptoms

- Polydipsia
- Polyuria
- Headache
- Hypertension
- Muscle weakness

Medical Tests

- 24-Hour urine analysis shows increased levels of aldosterone, creatinine, and cortisol
- CT scan shows adrenal tumor
- Blood test
  - Decreased potassium

Treatment

- Surgically remove tumor
- Administer:
  - Diuretics to control hypertension
    - Spironolactone
  - Antialdosterone medication
    - Eplerenone

Interventions

- Monitor the intake and output.
- Weigh daily.
- Restrict sodium intake.
- Instruct the patient:
  - To use ice chips and sips of water when thirsty.

7.13 Pheochromocytoma

Pheochromocytoma is a tumor on the adrenal medulla that secretes excessive amounts of epinephrine and norepinephrine.

Signs and Symptoms

- Dilated pupils
- Tachycardia
- Uncontrollable hypertension
- Headaches

Medical Tests

- CT scan shows adrenal tumor
- Blood test
  - Positive for catecholamines
- 24-Hour urine collection
  - Increase
    - Catecholamines
    - Metanephrines
    - Vanillylmandelic acid (VMA)

Treatment

- Surgical removal of the adrenal tumor
- Administer:
  - Beta-blockers
    - Nifedipine

- Nicardipine
- Propranolol

Interventions

- Monitor vital signs
- Instruct the patient:
  - To decrease stress
  - To stop smoking
  - to avoid caffeine

7.14   Hypoparathyroidism

Hypoparathyroidism is decreased secretion of PTH by the parathyroid gland, resulting in hypocalcemia caused by an autoimmune reaction to the parathyroid gland.

Signs and Symptoms

- Cataracts
- Convulsions
- Tetany
- Lethargy
- Tingling of periorbital, hands, feet

Medical Tests

- Positive Chvostek's sign
- Positive Trousseau's sign
- Blood test
  - Decreased calcium
  - Increased phosphate
  - Decreased parathyroid hormone PTH
- Urinalysis
  - Decreased calcium

Treatment

- Follow seizure precautions.
- Place a tracheostomy set at the bedside.
- Administer:
  - Calcium replacement
    - Calcium gluconate, lactate, carbonate
  - Vitamin D
    - Calciferol

     o Antiphosphatase medication

        ▪ Amphojel (aluminum hydroxide gel), Basaljel (aluminum carbonate gel, basic)

Interventions

- Monitor calcium levels.
- Instruct the patient:
  - o To take calcium replacements and vitamin D

7.15   Hyperparathyroidism

Hyperparathyroidism is excess production of PTH by the parathyroid gland caused by a parathyroid gland tumor, resulting in hypercalcemia, hypophosphatemia, and kidney stones.

Signs and Symptoms

- Asymptomatic
- Bone pain
- Bone fracture
- Kidney stone
- Frequent urination

Medical Tests

- Ultrasound shows parathyroid gland tumor
- Fine-needle biopsy identifies parathyroid gland tumor
- Blood test
  - o Increased calcium
  - o Increased PTH
  - o Decreased phosphate
- Urinalysis
  - o Increased calcium

Treatment

- Surgical removal of the parathyroid tumor
- Administer:
  - o Bisphosphonates to increase calcium absorption in bone
  - o IV normal saline
  - o Diuretic
    - ▪ Furosemide to excrete excess calcium

Interventions

- Monitor the intake and output.
- Monitor the electrolyte balance.

- Place the patient on a low-calcium and high-phosphorus diet.
- Instruct the patient:
  - o To drink acid-ash juices such as cranberry juice
  - o To abstain from nonprescribed calcium supplements
  - o To strain the urine for kidney stones

7.16 Diabetes Mellitus

Either none or an insufficient amount of insulin is secreted by the pancreas, resulting in increased blood glucose levels. There are three types of diabetes mellitus:

1. Type 1: Insulin-dependent diabetes mellitus (IDDM). An autoimmune process destroys beta cells in the pancreas or beta cells are destroyed by a pancreatic disorder such as pancreatic cancer.
2. Type 2: Noninsulin-dependent diabetes mellitus (NIDDM). Beta cells in the pancreas produce insufficient insulin resulting from pancreatic disorder.
3. Gestational diabetes mellitus: Beta cells in the pancreas produce insufficient insulin during pregnancy. Normal insulin production returns following birth; however, the patient is at risk for type 2 diabetes mellitus later in life.

Signs and Symptoms

- Type 1
  - o Polyphagia
  - o Polydipsia
  - o Polyuria
  - o Delayed healing
  - o Weight loss
  - o Frequent infections
  - o Fast onset
- Type 2
  - o Polydipsia
  - o Polyuria
  - o Candidal infection
  - o Delayed healing
  - o Slow onset
- Gestational
  - o Asymptomatic

Medical Tests

- Blood test
  - o Fasting plasma blood glucose test positive
  - o Oral glucose tolerance test (OGTT) positive

    ○ Random plasma glucose positive

    ○ Glycosylated hemoglobin A1C positive

- Urinalysis

    ○ Glucosuria

Treatment

- Type 1

    ○ Administer:

        ■ Insulin (Table 7.1)

- Type 2

    ○ Administer:

        ■ Oral sulfonylureas (Table 7.2)

        ■ Oral biguanides to reduce blood glucose production by the liver

          – Metformin

        ■ Thiazolidinediones to sensitize peripheral tissues to insulin

          – Rosiglitazone, pioglitazone

        ■ Meglitinide analogs to stimulate section of insulin from the pancreas

          – Repaglinide

        ■ D-Phenylalanine derivative to stimulate insulin production

          – Nateglinide

        ■ Alpha-glucosidase inhibitors to delay absorption of carbohydrates in the intestine

          – Acarbose, miglitol

    ○ Administer:

        ■ Dipeptidyl peptidase 4 (DPP4) inhibitors to slow the inactivation of incretin hormones, GLP-I that assist insulin product in the pancreas

          – Sitagliptin

    ○ Administer:

        ■ Incretin mimetics to assist insulin production in the pancreas and help regulate liver production of glucose

          – Amylin analog that causes glucose to enter the bloodstream slowly and can cause weight loss

    ○ Pramlintide

- Gestational

    ○ Diet

    ○ Exercise

    ○ Administer:

        ■ Insulin if blood glucose levels not controlled by diet and exercise

Interventions

- Monitor blood glucose
- Reduce stress
- Diet
- Exercise (type 2 and gestational)
- Instruct the patient:
  - To stop smoking
  - How to monitor glucose
  - How to inject insulin (type 1)
  - How to identify hypoglycemia (sweating, lethargy, confusion, hunger, dizziness, weakness) and respond to hypoglycemia (glucose tablets, or 4 oz fruit juice, several hard candies, or a small amount of a carbohydrate)
  - How to identify hyperglycemia (blurred vision, polyphagia, polydipsia, polyuria) and how to respond to hyperglycemia (meal planning, exercise, consult with health care provider).
  - How to examine feet.

TABLE 7.1 **Insulin Guide**

			INSULIN			
DRUG	SYNONYM	APPEARANCE	ONSET	PEAK	DURATION	COMPATIBILITY
Rapid acting	Regular	Clear	$\frac{1}{2}$–1 hr	2–4 hr	6–8 hr lente	All insulin except
Intermediate acting	NPH	Cloudy	1–1$\frac{1}{2}$ hr	8–12 hr	18–24 hr	Regular insulin
Long acting	Ultralente	Cloudy	4–6 hr	16–20 hr	30–36 hr	Regular

TABLE 7.2 **Oral Hypoglycemic Agents**

		ORAL HYPOGLYCEMIC AGENTS		
DRUG	ONSET	PEAK	DURATION	COMMENTS
Oral sulfonylureas				
Dymelor	1 hr	4–6 hr	12–24 hr	
Diabinese	1 hr	4–6 hr	40–60 hr	
Micronase, DiaBeta	$\frac{1}{4}$ min–1 hr	2–8 hr	10–24 hr	
Oral biguanides				
Glucophage	2–2$\frac{1}{2}$ hr		10–16 hr	Decreases glucose production in liver, decreases intestinal absorption of glucose, and improves insulin sensitivity

(Continued)

TABLE 7.2 **Oral Hypoglycemic Agents** (*continued*)

	ORAL HYPOGLYCEMIC AGENTS			
DRUG	ONSET	PEAK	DURATION	COMMENTS
Oral alpha-glucosidase				Delays glucose absorption and
Inhibitor	1 hr			digestion of carbohydrates,
Precose	2–3 hr			lowers blood sugar, reduces
Glyset	2–3 hr			plasma glucose and insulin
Rapid				

7.17 Metabolic Syndrome (Syndrome X/Dysmetabolic Syndrome)

A group of symptoms (hypertension, hyperglycemia, increased triglycerides, obesity), leading to insulin resistance and cardiovascular disease.

Signs and Symptoms

- Abdominal obesity
- Hypertension
- Hyperglycemia

Medical Tests

- Blood test:
  - Low-density lipoprotein (LDL) increase
  - High-density lipoprotein (HDL) decrease
  - Triglycerides increase
  - Fasting plasma blood glucose test positive

Treatment

- Administer:
  - Statin to lower LDL
  - Niacin to raise HDL
  - Fibrates to lower triglycerides
  - Ace inhibitors to lower blood pressure
  - Angiotensin receptor blockers to lower blood pressure
  - Insulin sensitizers to includes the effectiveness of insulin

Interventions

- Monitor blood glucose
- Instruct the patient:
  - To maintain a balanced diet
  - To exercise

Solved Problems

7.1   What is a myxedema?

Myxedema is little presence or absence of thyroid hormone as a result of decreased production of TSH hormone.

7.2   What is Hashimoto's thyroiditis?

Hashimoto's thyroiditis occurs when the thyroid is attacked by antibodies.

7.3   What medication is administered for hypothyroidism?

Synthroid (levothyroxine) is the medication administered for hypothyroidism.

7.4   What are the signs of thyrotoxicosis?

The signs of thyrotoxicosis are nausea, vomiting, diarrhea, sweating, and tachycardia.

7.5   What is Graves' disease?

Graves' disease is hyperthyroidism, which is overproduction of the thyroid hormone by the thyroid gland.

7.6   What treatment would you expect for a patient who has Graves' disease and is experiencing difficulty swallowing?

Treatment for a patient who has Graves' disease and is experiencing difficulty swallowing would be surgical reduction or removal of the thyroid if it complicates breathing or swallowing.

7.7   What is Chvostek's sign?

Chvostek's sign is tapping of the facial nerve, which causes twitching of the facial muscles.

7.8   What is tetany?

Tetany is muscle spasms and tremors.

7.9   What is Trousseau's sign?

Trousseau's sign occurs when the blood pressure cuff is inflated on the arm and the muscles contract.

7.10   What would cause a positive Trousseau's sign and Chvostek's sign?

Hypocalcemia would cause a positive Trousseau's sign and Chvostek's sign.

7.11   What is a simple goiter?

A simple goiter is an enlarged thyroid gland caused by insufficient iodine or by ingesting a large quantity of goitrogenic medication or goitrogenic food, which decreases production of thyroxine (goitrogenic).

7.12   What medication is administered to a patient with an overactive thyroid gland?

Lugol's solution and potassium iodide are administered to a patient with an overactive thyroid gland.

7.13   What are examples of goitrogenic foods?

Some examples of goitrogenic foods are peas, peaches, spinach, strawberries, peanuts, and cabbage.

7.14   What is hypopituitarism?

Hypopituitarism is decreased secretion of pituitary hormones by the pituitary gland.

7.15   What are the primary causes of hypopituitarism?

The primary causes of hypopituitarism are infection, decreased blood supply to the pituitary gland, pituitary tumor, radiation of the pituitary gland, and surgery of the pituitary gland.

7.16   What is gigantism?

Gigantism is hyperpituitarism that occurs before epiphyseal closure, resulting in overgrowth of all tissues.

7.17   What is acromegaly?

Acromegaly is hyperpituitarism that occurs after epiphyseal closure, resulting in visceromegaly (enlarged organs), bone thickening, and transverse growth.

7.18   What is hyperprolactinemia?

Hyperprolactinemia is overproduction of the prolactin hormone.

7.19   What is diabetes insipidus?

In diabetes insipidus the kidneys have a decreased ability to concentrate urine because of a decrease in the production of ADH by the hypothalamus or increased production of ADH by the pituitary gland, resulting in an increase in a large amount of diluted urine.

7.20   What is SIADH?

SIADH is the syndrome of inappropriate antidiuretic hormone secretion. The pituitary gland is secreting too much ADH caused by disorders of the pituitary gland or the hypothalamus, lung cancer, or inflammation of the brain and medication (cyclophosphamides, SSRIs, chlorpropamide, carbamazepine).

7.21   What is Addison's disease?

Addison's disease is damage to the adrenal cortex that results in decreased secretion of corticosteroids (cortisol and aldosterone). This can be caused by an autoimmune reaction to the adrenal gland or tuberculosis.

7.22   What is Addisonian crisis?

Addisonian crisis is a stressful event, such as surgery or infection, that causes decreased production of corticosteroids, resulting in a medical emergency.

7.23   What is Cushing's syndrome?

Cushing's syndrome is excess secretion of glucocorticoids by the adrenal cortex or excess secretion of ACTH by the pituitary gland caused by glucocorticoid therapy or a tumor in the adrenal glands or pituitary gland.

7.24   What is Conn's syndrome?

Conn's syndrome is excessive production of aldosterone by the adrenal cortex as a result of an adrenal tumor, adrenal cortex disorder, or medications (calcium channel blockers).

7.25   What is hyperparathyroidism?

Hyperparathyroidism is excess production of PTH by the parathyroid gland caused by a parathyroid gland tumor, resulting in hypercalcemia, hypophosphatemia, and kidney stones.

CHAPTER 8

Gastrointestinal System

8.1 Definition

The gastrointestinal system converts food into nutrients. Food is ingested. Nutrients are removed from the food and absorbed by the intestines then metabolized by the liver. Waste products are excreted.

Upper Gastrointestinal Tract

- Mouth
- Esophagus: A muscular tube through which food passes from the pharynx traveling via peristalsis to the stomach
- Stomach: A muscular pouch

Lower Gastrointestinal Tract

- Small intestine
  - Duodenum: The first section of the small intestine consisting of a hollow tube about 12 in. long connecting the stomach to the jejunum, where digestive enzymes from the pancreas and liver enter to assist in digestion
  - Jejunum: Connects the duodenum to the ileum
  - Ileum: Connects the jejunum to the cecum
  - The ileocecal valve separates the ileum from the large intestine.
- Large intestine:
  - Cecum: The first section of the large intestine connecting the ileum to the colon
  - Colon:
    - Ascending colon
    - Transverse colon
    - Descending colon
    - Sigmoid flexure
  - Rectum
  - Anus

Digestion

- Digestion is the process of breaking down food to be absorbed into the bloodstream.
- Glands along the mucosal lining of the mouth, stomach, and small intestine produce fluid that helps digest food.
- Smooth muscles along with the gastrointestinal tract help move and break down food.
- Food is mechanically broken down by mastication and chemically broken down by saliva in the mouth.
- Salivary glands produce saliva that contains enzymes that digest starches. Food is pushed into the esophagus by swallowing.
- Food travels along the esophagus via peristalsis to the stomach.
- The upper part of the stomach relaxes to accept swallowed food and liquid.
- Food and liquid are mixed by muscle action in the lower stomach with digestive juices produced by the stomach.
- Glands in the stomach lining produce hydrochloric acid and an enzyme that digests protein.
- The mucosal layer of the stomach protects the stomach from hydrochloric acid.
- This mixture is called *chyme*.
- Chyme empties from the stomach into the first part of the small intestine (duodenum) based on the contents of the chyme.
- Carbohydrates leave the stomach quickly.
- Protein remains in the stomach longer.
- Fat remains the longest.
- Digestive juices from the pancreas enter the duodenum to further digest carbohydrates, fats, and protein.
- The liver produces bile, which is stored in the gallbladder.
- When chyme enters the duodenum, bile is excreted from the gallbladder through the bile duct and into the duodenum, where bile acids in bile dissolve fat into watery liquid, which is then digested by pancreatic enzymes.
- Microvilli along the surface of the small intestine absorb nutrients and transport nutrients to the bloodstream, where nutrients are distributed throughout the body.
- Undigested chyme called *fiber* is moved into the large intestine, where fluid is removed.
- The remaining undigested chyme is called *feces* and is expelled during defecation.

Hormonal Control

- Hormones are chemical messengers that control the digestive function.
- Hormones are produced and released by the mucosa of the stomach and small intestine.
- Hormones are absorbed and transferred to the bloodstream, where hormones travel throughout the body to stimulate digestive juices and organs.
- Major digestive hormones are:
  - Gastrin: Signals the stomach to produce hydrochloric acid and mucosal cell growth.
  - Secretin: Signals the pancreas to produce bicarbonate digestive juices that neutralize hydrochloric acid in chyme before chyme enters the duodenum.
  - Secretin also signals the liver to produce bile and signals the stomach to produce the pepsin needed to digest protein.

- Ghrelin: Produced by the stomach and duodenum when no food is in the digestive tract to stimulate appetite.

- Cholecystokinin (CCK): Signals the pancreas to produce pancreatic enzymes and signals the gallbladder to excrete bile.

- Peptide YY: Produced by the digestive tract when food is present in the digestive tract to inhibit appetite.

Neural Control

- Extrinsic nerves:
  - Innervate the central nervous system with digestive organs.
  - Release acetylcholine: Causes contraction of smooth muscles of the digestive tract, production of digestive juices by the pancreas and stomach.
  - Release adrenaline: Causes relaxation of smooth muscles of the digestive tract, stopping digestion and decreasing blood flow to the digestive organs.
- Intrinsic nerves:
  - Nerves in the digestive system.
  - Triggered when food stretches digestive organs to increase digestion.

8.2 Appendicitis

An obstruction in the vermiform appendix leads to secretion of fluid by the mucosal lining of the appendix, increased pressure and decreased blood flow to the appendix, resulting in gangrene and possibly perforation (rupture) within 36 to 48 hours.

Signs and Symptoms

- Guarding of the abdomen
- Abdominal pain from periumbilical to right lower quadrant
- Abdominal rigidity
- Rebound pain
- Right lower quadrant abdominal pain that decreases with right hip flexing indicates perforation
- Loss of appetite
- Fever
- Nausea and vomiting

Medical Tests

- Ultrasound shows enlarged appendix
- Computed tomography (CT) scan shows enlarged appendix
- Blood test
  - Increased white blood cells (WBC)

Treatment

- Appendectomy

- Administer:
  - o Analgesics for pain
    - Meperidine
  - o Antibiotics

Interventions

- Maintain patient nothing by mouth (NPO).
- Monitor the vital signs.
- Monitor the intake and output.
- Monitor the bowel sounds.
- Assess the pain level.
- Instruct the patient:
  - o That he or she can return to a normal lifestyle after treatment

8.3 Cholecystitis

Cholecystitis is acute or chronic inflammation of the gallbladder related to cholelithiasis (gallstones). Acute cholecystitis occurs when blood flow to the gallbladder decreases, commonly from a blocked cystic duct by a gallstone leading to difficulty filling and emptying the gallbladder. The gallbladder becomes inflamed, bile is retained, and the gallbladder becomes distended. Chronic cholecystitis occurs when there are recurrent episodes of cholecystitis resulting in chronic inflammation of the gallbladder, leading to obstructive jaundice and an increased risk of gangrene and perforation.

Signs and Symptoms

- Pain in the upper right quadrant of the abdomen or epigastric area radiating to the right shoulder
- Positive Murphy's sign (upper right quadrant abdominal pain increases with palpation on inspiration, resulting in the patient being unable to take a deep breath)
- Increased flatulence
- Increased eructation (belching)
- Clay-colored stool
- Foamy, dark urine
- Nausea and vomiting after ingestion of fatty foods
- Decreased appetite
- Fever
- Icterus
- Pruritus (itching)
- Jaundice

Medical Tests

- Blood test
  - o Bilirubin direct (conjugated) increased.

- o Increased indirect (unconjugated)
- o Increased WBCs
- o Increased alkaline phosphatase, aspartate aminotransferase (AST)
- o Increased lactate dehydrogenase (LDH)
- CT scan shows inflammation of the gallbladder or gallstones.
- Ultrasound shows inflammation of the gallbladder or gallstones.
- Hepatic iminodiacetic acid (HIDA) scan shows blocked cystic duct.

Treatment

- Aspirate gallstone
- Surgical removal of gallbladder
  - o Laparoscopic cholecystectomy, open cholecystectomy
- Insert stent into gallbladder if surgery is not an option
- Administer:
  - o Antiemetics for nausea and vomiting
    - Prochlorperazine, trimethobenzamide
- Replace fat soluble vitamins
  - o Vitamins A, D, E, K
- Analgesics for pain
  - o Meperidine, no morphine
- Antibiotics

Interventions

- Maintain a low-fat diet.
- Monitor the vital signs.
- Monitor bowel sounds.
- Assess pain level.
- Instruct the patient:
  - o To eat a low-fat diet

8.4 Cirrhosis

Cirrhosis is chronic inflammation of the liver and necrosis of liver tissue leading to fibrosis and nodule formation, resulting in blockage of blood vessels and the bile duct, causing increased portal vein pressure, backup of venous blood to the spleen, enlarged liver and spleen, and decreased liver function. Common causes are chronic alcohol use, hepatitis, fatty liver (steatohepatitis), metabolic disorders (hemochromatosis), or cystic fibrosis.

Signs and Symptoms

- Asymptomatic
- Fatigue

- Weight loss
- Ecchymosis (bruises) related to decrease vitamin K absorption
- Petechiae
- Muscle cramps
- Nausea
- Pruritus (itching)
- Spider veins
- Peripheral edema
- Portal hypertension
- Jaundice
- Hepatomegaly (enlarged liver)
- Palmar erythema (red palms)
- Impotence
- Ascites
- Dyspnea
- Glossitis (inflammation of the tongue)
- Encephalopathy (asterixis, tremors, delirium, drowsiness, dysarthria, coma)

Medical Tests

- Blood test
  - Increased
    - AST
    - Alanine aminotransferase (ALT)
    - LDH
    - Bilirubin direct (conjugated)
    - Indirect (unconjugated)
    - Mean cell volume (MCV)
    - Mean cell hemoglobin (MCH)
    - Ammonia
    - Prothrombin time (PT)
  - Decreased
    - Protein
    - Albumin
    - WBC count
    - Platelet count
- Urinalysis
  - Increased bilirubin
- Fecal analysis
  - Decreased urobilinogen

- X-ray shows hepatomegaly.
- CT scan shows hepatomegaly and ascites.
- Ultrasound shows hepatomegaly, ascites, portal vein blood flow.
- Esophagogastroduodenoscopy (EGD) shows esophageal varices.
- Liver biopsy shows fibrosis and regenerative nodules.

Treatment

- Paracentesis to remove ascitic fluid
- Insertion of shunt to drain ascitic fluid and divert blood flow
- Gastric lavage
- Esophagogastric balloon tamponade to control esophageal varices bleeding
- Sclerotherapy to control esophageal variceal bleeding
- Administer:
  - Vitamins
    - Folate acid, thiamine, multivitamin
  - Diuretics to excrete fluids
    - Furosemide, spironolactone
  - Lactulose to remove ammonia
  - Antibiotics to kill flora that produce ammonia
    - Neomycin sulfate, metronidazole

Interventions

- Elevate head of bed 30° or greater.
- Elevate the feet.
- Monitor for signs of bleeding.
- Monitor mental status.
- Restrict fluid intake.
- Monitor the intake and output.
- Monitor the vital signs.
- Weigh daily.
- Measure abdominal girth.
- Monitor electrolytes for imbalance.
- Monitor PT, partial thromboplastin time (PTT), international normalized ratio (INR).
- Monitor for peripheral edema.
- Monitor heart and lung sounds for excess fluid.
- Instruct the patient:
  - To eat a low-sodium diet
  - Not to consume alcohol

8.5   Crohn's Disease

Crohn's disease is characterized by periods of inflammation of the gastrointestinal tract commonly affecting the intestine (terminal ileum and ascending colon), resulting in transmural inflammation (below the superficial mucosal layer) leading to strictures and fistulas.

Signs and Symptoms

- Nonbloody diarrhea
- Fatigue
- Weight loss
- Postprandial bloating (after meals)
- Borborygmi (loud, frequent bowel sounds)
- Abdominal cramping
- Pain in the right lower quadrant of the abdomen
- Fever
- Abdominal mass
- Fistula formation

Medical Tests

- Blood test
  - o Decreased red blood cells (RBCs)
  - o Decreased albumin
  - o Increased erythrocyte sedimentation rate (during exacerbations)
  - o Decreased electrolytes
- CT scan shows thickening of bowel and abscess formation
- Barium X-ray shows fistula formation, stricture formation

Treatment

- Surgical repair of stricture and fistulas
- Administer:
  - o Vitamins:
    - B_{12}, folic acid
  - o Aminosalicylates
    - Mesalamine, sulfasalazine, olsalazine, balsalazide
  - o Glucocorticoids
    - Hydrocortisone, budesonide
    - Purine
    - Azathioprine, 6-mercaptopurine
    - Methotrexate
  - o Antidiarrheal medications
  - o Diphenoxylate hydrochloride and atropine sulfate

Interventions

- Observe dietary restrictions.
- Monitor the intake and output.
- Monitor the vital signs.
- Instruct the patient:
  o About the proper skin care if bowel-skin fistula
  o About the importance of dietary restrictions
  o About the importance of nutritional supplements

8.6 Diverticulitis Disease

In diverticulitis disease, undigested food becomes trapped in outpouches (diverticula) along the intestinal tract, commonly in the large intestine, leading to bacterial growth, and resulting in inflammation of the intestine and risk for bleeding, intestinal perforation, and fistula formation within the abdomen.

Signs and Symptoms

- Asymptomatic
- Bloating
- Rectal bleeding
- Change in bowel habits
- Abdominal pain
- Fever
- Nausea
- Vomiting

Medical Tests

- Blood test
  o Increased WBC count
- CT scan show thickening intestinal wall
- Barium enema shows diverticula (not performed during acute inflammation, in which there is a risk of perforation)
- Colonoscopy shows diverticula (not performed during acute inflammation, in which there is a risk of perforation)

Treatment

- Surgical repair of intestine
- Administer:
  o Antibiotics
    ▪ Ciprofloxacin, metronidazole, trimethoprim-sulfamethoxazole

Interventions

- Keep the patient NPO.
- Monitor the vital signs.
- Monitor the intake and output.
- Assess the abdomen for bowel sounds and distention.
- Instruct the patient:
  - To eat a high-fiber diet when asymptomatic
  - To eat a low-residue diet during acute during acute inflammation
  - Not to eat seeds or nuts
  - Not to lift during acute during acute inflammation
  - Not to take laxatives
  - Not to take enemas

8.7 Gastroenteritis

Gastroenteritis is inflammation of the gastric/intestinal mucosa, commonly caused by a viral (common), bacterial, parasitic, or protozoal infection or as an allergic response to toxin exposure.

Signs and Symptoms

- Diarrhea
- Abdominal pain
- Nausea and vomiting
- Fever
- Malaise
- Headache
- Dehydration
- Abdominal distention

Medical Tests

- Blood test
  - Increased BUN
  - Increased creatinine
  - Electrolyte imbalance
  - Increased eosinophil count
  - Increased WBC count
- Stool sample
  - Positive for parasitic infection

Treatment

- Administer:
    - o Intravenous IV fluids for dehydration
    - o Antiemetic medication
        - Prochlorperazine, trimethobenzamide
    - o Antidiarrheal medications
        - Loperamide, diphenoxylate, kaolin-pectin, bismuth subsalicylate
    - o Antimicrobials
        - Ciprofloxacin, metronidazole

Interventions

- Monitor the vital signs.
- Monitor the intake and output.
- Assess for dehydration.
- Replace fluids.
- Instruct the patient:
    - o That vomiting and diarrhea are the mechanisms that the body uses to remove the infecting microorganism.

8.8   Gastroesophageal Reflux Disease (GERD)

In gastroesophageal reflux disease (GERD), contents (acid) of the stomach enter into the esophagus causing pain (heartburn) because the lining of the esophagus is unprotected. Pain worsens after eating and when lying down. Scarring may occur, leading to formation of strictures and resulting in difficulty swallowing. Barrett's esophagus is a premalignant esophageal growth resulting from chronic GERD.

Signs and Symptoms

- Sour taste
- Hoarseness
- Epigastric burning
- Burping (eructation)
- Cough
- Nausea
- Bloating

Medical Tests

- Barium X-ray shows reflux.
- Endoscopy shows irritation.
- Esophageal manometry indicates decreased lower esophageal sphincter tone.

Treatment

- Surgery to strengthen lower esophageal sphincter tone
- Administer:
  - Antacids
    - Maalox, Mylanta, Tums, Gaviscon
  - H_2 (histamine type 2) blockers
    - Ranitidine, famotidine, nizatidine, cimetidine
  - Proton pump inhibitors
    - Omeprazole, esomeprazole, pantoprazole, rabeprazole, lansoprazole

Interventions

- Monitor the vital signs.
- Elevate the head of the bed.
- Instruct the patient:
  - To eat six small meals daily
  - Not to eat acidic foods (citrus, vinegar, tomato) or peppermint or drink caffeine or alcohol
  - Not to lie down after eating
  - Not to wear tight clothing at the waist

8.9 Gastrointestinal Bleeding

This is bleeding from the upper or lower gastrointestinal tract leading to substantial blood loss. Common causes of upper gastrointestinal bleeding are neoplasms, ulcers, Mallory-Weiss tears related to vomiting, and esophageal varices. Common causes of lower gastrointestinal bleeding are ulcerations, polyps, diverticulitis, fissure formation, colon cancer, and hemorrhoids.

Signs and Symptoms

- Pallor
- Lightheadedness
- Diaphoresis
- Orthostatic blood pressure
- Black, tarry stool (melena)
- Red or maroon rectal bleeding (hematochezia)
- Vomiting maroon, coffee-ground blood (hematemesis)
- Nausea
- Tachycardia

Medical Tests

- Fecal occult blood test is positive.
- Colonoscopy shows site of bleeding.

- Arteriography shows site of bleeding.
- Blood test
  - Decreased hemoglobin
  - Decreased hematocrit
  - Decreased RBCs

Treatment

- Endoscopy to stop bleeding
- Tamponade with Blakemore-Sengstaken tube for esophageal varices
- Administer:
  - Isotonic IV fluids
  - Normal saline
  - Transfuse packed RBCs
  - Fresh-frozen plasma
  - Albumin

Interventions

- Monitor the vital signs.
- Monitor the intake and output.
- Maintain large-bore IV tube (14- to 18-gauge) access.
- Instruct the patient:
  - That treatment will stop the bleeding

8.10 Gastritis

Gastritis is inflammation of the stomach lining leading to malnutrition, gastric cancer, or lymphoma.

- Erosive gastritis: Caused by stress or medication (NSAIDs)
- Atrophic gastritis: Caused by *Helicobacter pylori* bacteria, pernicious anemia, and alcohol use.

Signs and Symptoms

- Vomiting maroon, coffee-ground blood (hematemesis)
- Nausea
- Black, tarry stool (melena)
- Epigastric tenderness
- Anorexia
- Anemia

Medical Tests

- Endoscopy shows inflammation.

- Fecal occult blood test is positive.
- Blood test
  - Decreased hemoglobin
  - Decreased hematocrit
  - Decreased RBCs
  - *H. pylori* positive

Treatment

- Administer:
  - Antacids
    - Maalox, Mylanta, Tums, Gaviscon
  - Sucralfate
  - H_2 blockers
    - Ranitidine, famotidine, nizatidine, cimetidine
  - Proton pump inhibitors
    - Omeprazole, esomeprazole, pantoprazole, rabeprazole, lansoprazole

Interventions

- Monitor stool for occult blood.
- Monitor the vital signs.
- Monitor the intake and output.
- Instruct the patient:
  - Not to ingest alcohol, caffeine, or acidic foods
  - Not to take NSAIDs
  - Not to smoke

8.11 Hepatitis

Hepatitis is inflammation of the liver commonly caused by a viral infection or exposure to drugs and toxins.

Types of hepatitis:

- Hepatitis A: Transmitted orally related to contaminated water or poor sanitation. Can be prevented by vaccine.
- Hepatitis B: Transmitted percutaneously related to sexual contact, IV drug use, mother-to-neonate transmission, and transfusion. Can be prevented by vaccine.
- Hepatitis C: Transmitted percutaneously, related to IV drug use and sexual contact (less common). No vaccine available.
- Hepatitis D: Transmitted percutaneously. Needs hepatitis B to spread. No vaccine available.
- Hepatitis E: Transmitted orally related to water contamination. Acute. No vaccine available.
- Hepatitis G: Transmitted percutaneously. Associated with chronic infection but not liver disease.

Signs and Symptoms

- Acute hepatitis
  - o Tenderness in right upper quadrant of abdomen
  - o Jaundice
  - o Dark urine
  - o Hepatomegaly
  - o Diarrhea
  - o Constipation
  - o Malaise
  - o Nausea and vomiting
  - o Low-grade fever
- Chronic hepatitis
  - o Asymptomatic
  - o Bleeding
  - o Enlarged spleen
  - o Cirrhosis
  - o Ascites
  - o Esophageal varices
  - o Encephalopathy
  - o Same as acute hepatitis

Medical Tests

- Liver biopsy shows hepatocellular necrosis.
- Urinalysis shows protein and bilirubin.
- Blood test
  - o Increased AST
  - o Increased ALT
  - o WBC count normal to low
  - o Immunoglobulin G (IgG) anti-hepatitis B core (HBc) shows convalescent or past infection with hepatitis B.
  - o Immunoglobulin M (IgM) anti-HBc shows acute or recent infection with hepatitis B.
  - o Hepatitis B surface antigen (HBsAg) shows current or past infection with hepatitis B.
  - o IgM anti-hepatitis A virus (HAV) shows acute or early convalescent stage of hepatitis A.
  - o IgG anti-HAV shows later convalescent stage of hepatitis A.
  - o Hepatitis Be antigen (HBeAg) shows current viral replication of hepatitis B and infectivity.
  - o Hepatitis B virus (HBV) DNA shows presence of hepatitis B DNA (most sensitive).
  - o Anti-hepatitis C virus (HCV) shows hepatitis C infection.
  - o Hepatitis C virus (HCV) RNA shows hepatitis C infection.
  - o Anti-hepatitis D virus (HDV) shows hepatitis D infection.

Treatment

- Liver transplantation
- Administer:
  - Interferon or lamivudine (chronic hepatitis B)
  - Interferon and ribavirin (hepatitis C)
  - Prednisone (autoimmune hepatitis)

Interventions

- Remove drug to toxin.
- Allow activity as tolerated.
- Monitor the intake and output.
- Monitor the vital signs.
- Schedule rest periods (acute).
- Instruct the patient:
  - Not to smoke (including second-hand smoke)
  - To eat a high-calorie diet
  - To eat more at breakfast (best tolerated meal)
  - Not to take medications metabolized in the liver (acetaminophen)
  - Not to drink alcohol

8.12   Hiatal Hernia (Diaphragmatic Hernia)

A hiatal hernia is the protrusion of a portion of the stomach through the diaphragm into the chest near the esophagus.

- Sliding hiatal hernia: The upper portion of the stomach and the lower esophageal sphincter moves throughout the diaphragm (GERD).
- Rolling hiatal hernia: The upper portion of the stomach but not the lower esophageal sphincter moves throughout the diaphragm (no GERD).

Signs and Symptoms

- Rolling hernia
  - Chest pain
  - Fullness after eating
  - Difficulty breathing after eating
- Sliding hernia
  - Chest pain
  - Heartburn
  - Eructation (burping)
  - Dysphagia (difficulty swallowing)
  - Burping (eructation)

Medical Tests

- Barium X-ray shows hiatal hernia.

Treatment

- Administer:
  - Antacids for patients
    - Maalox, Mylanta, Tums, Gaviscon
  - H_2 blockers
    - Ranitidine, nizatidine, famotidine, cimetidine
  - Proton pump inhibitors to reduce the production of acid
    - Omeprazole, esomeprazole, pantoprazole, rabeprazole, lansoprazole

Interventions

- Elevate the head of the bed.
- Monitor the vital signs.
- Instruct the patient:
  - To eat small, frequent meals
  - Not to lie down after eating
  - Not to wear tight clothes at the waist
  - Not to eat acidic foods (citrus, vinegar, tomato) or peppermint or to drink caffeine or alcohol
  - Not to smoke

8.13   Intestinal Obstruction and Paralytic Ileus

Intestinal obstruction is when motility through the intestine is blocked because of a mechanical obstruction such as fecal impaction, tumor, or adhesion or caused by a paralytic ileus such as sepsis, diabetic ketoacidosis, or medication.

Signs and Symptoms

- Paralytic ileus
  - Diminished or absent bowel sounds
  - Vomiting
  - Constant abdominal pain
  - Abdominal distention
- Obstruction
  - Vomiting
  - Constipation
  - High-pitched bowel sounds
  - Abdominal tenderness
  - Abdominal cramping
  - Intermittent or constant abdominal pain
  - Abdominal distention

Medical Tests

- Abdominal x-ray shows small bowel dilation.

Treatment

- Administer:
  - Antiemetics after nasogastric (NG) tube insertion
    - Prochlorperazine, trimethobenzamide
  - IV fluid replacement
    - Isotonic solution

Interventions

- Keep the patient NPO.
- Insert an NG tube to suction to remove stomach contents.
- Administer parenteral nutrition and vitamin supplements.
- Monitor the vital signs.
- Monitor the intake and output.
- Assess for abdomen tenderness.
- Assess bowel sounds.
- Instruct the patient:
  - That his or her normal lifestyle will return after intestinal motility is restored

8.14   Pancreatitis

Pancreatitis is inflammation of the pancreas as a result of chronic alcohol use, elevated cholesterol, blockage of the pancreatic duct by gallstones, or surgical or abdominal trauma.

- Acute: Autodigestion of the pancreas by pancreatic enzymes and development of fibrosis. Life threatening and a risk for pleural effusion
- Chronic: Fibrosis resulting in decrease in pancreatic function

Signs and Symptoms

- Cullen's sign (bluish gray discoloration of periumbilical area and abdomen)
- Turner's sign (bluish gray discoloration of flank areas)
- Abdominal pain
  - Acute: Radiate to back or left shoulder
  - Chronic: Gnawing, continuous pain
- Epigastric pain
- Knee-chest position reduces pain
- Nausea
- Vomiting

- Fatigue
- Hyperglycemia
- Ascites
- Weight loss

Medical Tests

- CT scan shows inflammation.
- Blood test
  - Increased
    - Amylase
    - Lipase
    - WBC
    - Cholesterol
    - Glucose
    - Bilirubin

Treatment

- Surgical removal of abscess or pseudocyst
- Administer
  - Morphine because it prevents spasm of the sphincter of Oddi
  - IV fluids
  - Total parenteral nutrition
  - Vitamin supplements
  - Patient controlled or transdermal analgesia
  - Insulin (chronic)

Interventions

- Keep the patient NPO (acute).
- Insert an NG tube to suction to remove stomach contents if the patient is vomiting.
- Monitor the intake and output.
- Monitor the vital signs.
- Monitor the blood glucose.
- Monitor the lung sounds for pleural effusion.
- Assess the abdomen for bowel sounds, tenderness, masses, and ascites.
- Instruct the patient:
  - To schedule rest periods
  - To take pancreatic enzymes with meals
  - Not to drink alcohol
  - Not to drink caffeine
  - To eat a bland, low-fat, high-protein, high-calorie diet

- o To eat small, frequent meals
- o To monitor the blood glucose

8.15   Peritonitis

Peritonitis is an acute inflammation of the peritoneum (lining of the abdominal cavity) commonly caused by bacterial infection. It is a life-threatening disease that may lead to septicemia if infection enters the bloodstream.

Signs and Symptoms

- Abdominal rebound pain
- Abdominal distention
- Rigid abdomen
- Decreased bowel sounds
- Fever
- Tachycardia
- Nausea
- Vomiting
- Decreased urine output
- Decreased appetite

Medical Tests

- Abdominal X-rays show free air.
- Ultrasound shows underlying cause.
- CT scan shows underlying cause.
- Peritoneal lavage culture and sensitivity identify microorganism.
- Blood test:
  - o Increased WBC count
  - o Blood cultures to identify microorganism

Treatment

- Surgery to correct underlying cause
- Administer:
  - o Broad-spectrum antibiotics
  - o IV fluids

Interventions

- Keep the patient NPO.
- Elevate the head of the bed.
- Monitor the vital signs.

- Monitor the intake and output.
- Weigh daily.
- Instruct the patient:
  - That a normal lifestyle will return after the inflammation is resolved.

8.16 Peptic Ulcer Disease (PUD)

Peptic ulcer disease (PUD) is erosion of the mucosal layer of the stomach or duodenum allowing stomach acid to contact epithelial tissues commonly caused by *H. pylori* bacteria or stress leading to bleeding, perforation, peritonitis, paralytic ileus, septicemia, shock, ischemia, or ulcerate.

- Gastric ulcer: Mucosal layer of the stomach is eroded, lessening the curvature of the stomach.
- Duodenal ulcer: Mucosal layer of the duodenal is eroded, resulting in penetration to the muscular layer.

Signs and Symptoms

- Epigastric pain
  - Worse after eating (gastric ulcer)
  - Worse 1 to 2 hours after eating or at night (duodenal ulcer)
- Weight change
  - Loss (gastric ulcer)
  - Gain (duodenal ulcer)
- Bleeding
  - Vomiting red, maroon blood (hematemesis) (gastric ulcer)
  - Coffee-ground emesis (gastric ulcer)
  - Tarry stool (melena) (duodenal ulcer)
- Perforation
  - Sudden, sharp pain relieved with knee-chest position
  - Tender, rigid abdomen
  - Hypovolemic shock

Medical Tests

- Blood test
  - Decreased RBC
  - Decreased hemoglobin
  - Decreased hematocrit
- Barium X-ray shows ulceration.
- Abdominal X-ray shows free air if perforated.
- Endoscopy shows ulceration.
- Stool occult blood is positive.
- *H. pylori* test is positive.

Treatment

- Administer
  - Antacids
    - Maalox, Mylanta, Amphojel
  - H_2 blockers
    - Famotidine, ranitidine, nizatidine
  - Proton pump inhibitors
    - Omeprazole, lansoprazole, rabeprazole, esomeprazole, pantoprazole
  - Mucosal barrier fortifiers
    - Sucralfate
  - Prostaglandin analog
    - Misoprostol
  - *H. pylori* medication
    - Proton pump inhibitor plus clarithromycin plus amoxicillin, proton pump inhibitor plus metronidazole plus clarithromycin, bismuth subsalicylate plus metronidazole plus tetracycline

Interventions

- Monitor the intake and output.
- Monitor the vital signs.
- Monitor the bowel sounds.
- Monitor abdomen tenderness and rigidity.
- Instruct the patient:
  - To eat small frequent meals
  - Not to drink caffeine
  - Not to drink alcohol
  - Not to eat acidic foods
  - Not to take NSAID medication
  - Not to smoke

8.17 Ulcerative Colitis

Ulcerative colitis is inflammation of the mucosal layer of the large intestine beginning with the colon and rectum and spreading to adjacent tissues, leading to ulcerations and abscess formation. Periods of exacerbations and remissions. Symptoms increase with each exacerbation. Risk for malabsorption, toxic megacolon, and perforation.

Signs and Symptoms

- Chronic bloody diarrhea with pus
- Tenesmus (spasms of the anal sphincter)
- Weight loss
- Abdominal pain

Medical Tests

- Double-contrast barium X-ray shows ulceration and inflammation.
- Colonoscopy shows ulcerations and bleeding.
- Blood test
  o Decreased RBC count
  o Decreased hemoglobin
  o Decreased hematocrit
  o Increased erythrocyte sedimentation rate

Treatment

- Surgical resection of affected area
- Administer
  o Antidiarrheal medications
    ▪ Loperamide, diphenoxylate hydrochloride, and atropine
  o Salicylate medications
    ▪ Sulfasalazine, mesalamine, olsalazine, balsalazide
  o Corticosteroids during exacerbations
    ▪ Prednisone, hydrocortisone
  o Anticholinergics
    ▪ Dicyclomine

Interventions

- Patient must be NPO during exacerbations.
- Monitor the intake and output.
- Monitor the stool output.
- Weigh daily.
- Monitor for toxic megacolon (distended, tender abdomen, fever, distended colon).
- Instruct the patient:
  o To keep a stool diary to identify irritating foods
  o To eat a low-fiber, high-protein, high-calorie diet
  o About perianal skin care area
    ▪ Sitz bath
    ▪ A&D ointment
    ▪ Apply barrier cream to skin
    ▪ Apply witch hazel to soothe sensitive skin
    ▪ Do not use fragranced products

Solved Problems

8.1   What is appendicitis?

Appendicitis is an obstruction in the vermiform appendix that leads to secretion of fluid by the mucosal lining of the appendix, increased pressure and decreased blood flow to the appendix, resulting in gangrene and possibly perforation (rupture) within 36 to 48 hours.

8.2   What is cholecystitis?

Cholecystitis is acute or chronic inflammation of the gallbladder related to cholelithiasis (gallstones).

8.3   What is acute cholecystitis?

Acute cholecystitis occurs when blood flow to the gallbladder decreases, commonly from a blocked cystic duct by a gallstone leading to difficulty filling and emptying the gallbladder. The gallbladder becomes inflamed, bile is retained, and the gallbladder becomes distended.

8.4   What is chronic cholecystitis?

Chronic cholecystitis occurs when there are recurrent episodes of cholecystitis resulting in chronic inflammation of the gallbladder and leading to obstructive jaundice and an increased risk of gangrene and perforation.

8.5   What is Murphy's sign?

Murphy's sign occurs when upper right quadrant abdominal pain increases with palpation on inspiration, resulting in the patient being unable to take a deep breath.

8.6   What is cirrhosis?

Cirrhosis is chronic inflammation and necrosis of the liver tissue, leading to fibrosis and nodule formation, and resulting in blockage of blood vessels and the bile duct, causing increased portal vein pressure, backup of venous blood to the spleen, enlarged liver and enlarged spleen, and decreased liver function.

8.7   What are common causes of cirrhosis?

Common causes of cirrhosis are chronic alcohol use, hepatitis, fatty liver (steatohepatitis), metabolic disorders (hemochromatosis), or cystic fibrosis.

8.8   Why would a patient with cirrhosis have bruising?

A patient with cirrhosis would have bruising because of decreased vitamin K absorption.

8.9   What are signs of encephalopathy?

Signs of encephalopathy are asterixis, tremors, delirium, drowsiness, dysarthria, and coma.

8.10 What is Crohn's disease?

Crohn's disease is characterized by periods of inflammation of the gastrointestinal tract commonly affecting the intestine (terminal ileum and ascending colon), resulting in transmural inflammation (below the superficial mucosal layer), and leading to strictures and fistulas.

8.11 What are signs of Crohn's disease?

Signs of Crohn's disease are nonbloody diarrhea, fatigue, weight loss, postprandial bloating (after meals), borborygmi (loud, frequent bowel sounds), abdominal cramping, pain in the right lower quadrant of the abdomen, fever, abdominal mass, and fistula formation.

8.12   About what should you instruct the patient who has Crohn's disease?

The patient who has Crohn's disease should be instructed about proper skin care if he or she has a bowel-skin fistula, the importance of dietary restrictions, and the importance of nutritional supplements.

8.13   What is diverticulitis disease?

Diverticulitis disease occurs when undigested food becomes trapped in outpouches (diverticula) along the intestinal tract, commonly in the large intestine, leading the bacterial growth, and resulting in inflammation of the intestine and risk for bleeding, intestinal perforation, and formation of a fistula within the abdomen.

8.14   What should not be performed during an acute inflammation of diverticulitis disease?

A barium enema and colonoscopy should not be performed during an acute inflammation of diverticulitis disease.

8.15   What instructions should be given to a patient who has diverticulitis disease?

The instructions that should be given to a patient who has diverticulitis disease are:

- To eat a high-fiber diet when asymptomatic
- To eat a low-residue diet during acute during acute inflammation
- Not to eat seeds or nuts
- Not to lift during acute during acute inflammation
- Not to use laxatives
- Not to take enemas

8.16   What is gastroenteritis?

Gastroenteritis is inflammation of the gastric/intestinal mucosa.

8.17   What is a common cause of gastroenteritis?

A common cause of gastroenteritis is a virus.

8.18   What would you tell a patient who has gastroenteritis regarding vomiting and diarrhea?

Vomiting and diarrhea are the mechanisms the body uses to remove the infecting microorganism.

8.19   What is GERD?

GERD is contents (acid) of the stomach entering the esophagus and causing pain (heartburn) because the lining of the esophagus is unprotected.

8.20   What is Barrett's esophagus?

Barrett's esophagus is a premalignant esophageal growth resulting from chronic GERD.

8.21   What instruction would you give a patient who has GERD?

The instructions that should be given to a patient who has GERD are:

- Eat six small meals daily.
- Do not eat acidic foods, such as citrus, vinegar, tomato, or peppermint or drink caffeine or alcohol.
- Do not lie down after eating.
- Do not wear clothing that is tight at the waist.

8.22   What is gastritis?

Gastritis is inflammation of the stomach lining leading to malnutrition, gastric cancer, or lymphoma.

8.23   To what is a Mallory-Weiss tear related?

A Mallory-Weiss tear is related to vomiting.

8.24   What is erosive gastritis?

Erosive gastritis is gastritis caused by stress or medication (NSAIDs).

8.25   What is ulcerative colitis?

Ulcerative colitis is inflammation of the mucosal layer of the large intestine beginning with the colon and rectum and spreading to adjacent tissues, leading to ulcerations and abscess formation. There are periods of exacerbations and remissions. Symptoms increase with each exacerbation. There is risk for malabsorption, toxic megacolon, and perforation.

CHAPTER 9

OB-GYN

9.1 Definition

Female Reproductive Organs

- Vagina: A canal joining the outside of the body to the lower part of the uterus (cervix)
- Uterus:
  - Corpus: The womb where the fetus develops
  - Cervix: Lower part of the uterus connecting the uterus to the vagina
- Ovaries: Produce eggs and hormones; located on the sides of the uterus
- Fallopian tubes: Connect the upper part of the uterus to the ovaries. The site of fertilization. The fertilized ova moves from the fallopian tube to the lining of the uterus, where it implants into the lining.

Menstruation Cycle (28 Days)

- Follicular phase (first day)
  - The brain releases follicle stimulating hormone (FSH) and luteinizing hormone (LH) into the bloodstream.
  - FSH and LH reach the ovaries, stimulating the growth of 20 eggs, and stimulate increased production of estrogen.
  - Each egg has a shell called a *follicle*.
  - Estrogen reaches a level that stops production of FSH, limiting the number of eggs that grow.
  - One follicle in an ovary fully matures, resulting in suppression of other follicles. One follicle matures.
- Ovulatory phase (14th day)
  - LH levels increase, resulting in release of the egg from the ovary in a process called *ovulation*.
  - The egg leaves the ovary and is caught by fimbriae (fingerlike projections on the end of the fallopian tube), and the egg is brought into the fallopian tube.
  - The endometrium (lining of the uterus) thickens to capture, nourish, and move sperm toward the egg for fertilization.

- Luteal phase (immediately after ovulation)
    - The empty follicle that released the egg forms the corpus luteum.
    - The corpus luteum secretes progesterone, which prepares the uterus for implantation of the fertilized egg.
    - If conception occurs, the embryo moves through the fallopian tube and implants into the uterus. The patient is pregnant.
    - If conception does not occur, the egg moves through the uterus. Muscle contractions decrease the blood supply to the endometrium and force the endometrium out through the vagina.

9.2   Breast Cancer

Breast cancer is a malignant tumor formed of breast cells typically in cells in the lining of the small tubes (ducts) that carry breast milk from glands (lobules) to the nipple. Cancer cells spread (metastasis) through the body via the lymph system. Malignant breast cells can spread to the axillary nodes under the arm, leading to the swelling of the node and commonly metastasize to the lung.

- Ductal cancer: A malignant tumor formed by cells from the lining of the ducts
- Lobular cancer: A malignant tumor formed by cells from the lobules
- Benign breast tumor: Abnormal growths caused by cysts (fluid-filled sacs) or fibrosis (scarlike tissue) that remain within the breast and are not life threatening. Most breast lumps are benign breast tumors.

Signs and Symptoms

- Nipple inversion
- Nipple drainage
- Painless lump in breast

Medical Tests

- Mammography: Shows mass
- Ultrasound: Shows mass
- Biopsy: Confirms breast cancer
- Magnetic resonance imaging (MRI): Shows mass
- Computed tomography (CT) scan: Shows metastasis

Treatment

- Lumpectomy: To remove a small tumor.
- Mastectomy: To remove a large tumor.
- Radiation therapy: To reduce the tumor size.
- Prophylactic bilateral mastectomy: For patient with *BRCA1* or *BRCA2* genes
- Administer:
    - Chemotherapy
        - Cyclophosphamide, methotrexate, fluorouracil, doxorubicin, epirubicin, vincristine, paclitaxel, docetaxel
    - Hormonal therapy
        - Tamoxifen, anastrozole

Interventions

- Monitor incision site if surgery is performed.
- Monitor for infection if surgery is performed.
- Explain chemotherapy and hormonal therapy if ordered.
- Instruct the patient:
  - That most breast lumps are benign
  - That breast cancer is diagnosed with a biopsy
  - To eat a low-fat diet
  - To have regular mammograms

9.3   Cervical Cancer

Abnormal growth of cells on the lining of the cervix, typically in the transformation zone. The transformation zone is the place where squamous cells and glandular cells meet. Squamous cells are located in the part of the cervix that is close to the vagina (exocervix). Glandular cells are located in the part of the cervix that is close to the uterus (endocervix).

- Precancerous: Cells in the lining of the cervix gradually change and can be detected with a Papanicolaou (Pap) test and then treated before cancer develops. This change is referred to as *precancerous* and is categorized as:
  - CIN: Cervical intraepithelial neoplasia
  - SIL: Squamous intraepithelial lesion
  - Dysplasia

Signs and Symptoms

- Pelvic pain
- Vaginal bleeding
- Postcoital bleeding (bleeding after sex)

Medical Tests

- Pap smear: Shows precancerous cells
- Biopsy: Confirms cervical cancer

Treatment

- Cryotherapy: Freezes cells to remove the lesion
- Cone biopsy: Removes dysplasia
- Hysterectomy: Removes the uterus
- Radiation: Removes the lesion
- Administer:
  - Chemotherapy
    - Cisplatin, 5-fluorouracil

Interventions

- Monitor the vital signs.
- Monitor the intake and output.
- Assess the abdomen.
- Assess the bowel sounds.
- Monitor for vaginal bleeding.
- Administer the human papillomavirus (HPV) vaccine.
- Instruct the patient:
  - To have an annual Pap test
  - On the difference between precancer and cervical cancer

9.4   Dysmenorrhea

Dysmenorrhea is menstrual pain that limits activities of daily living or requires medication. The endometrium thickens during ovulation, after which uterine muscles contract, releasing prostaglandins and causing constriction of the blood supply and deoxygenation of endometrium tissues and surrounding tissues, which lead to cramps (pain). Deoxygenation destroys endometrial cells. Uterine muscle contraction squeezes the destroyed cells through the cervix and out the vagina.

Signs and Symptoms

- Cramps
- Headache
- Nausea

Medical Tests

- Pelvic exam: Normal
- Blood test
  - Decreased hemoglobin
  - Decreased hematocrit

Treatment

- Administer:
  - Nonsteroidal anti-inflammatory drugs (NSAIDs)
    - Ibuprofen, naproxen, nabumetone
  - Oral contraceptives

Interventions

- Schedule a rest period during menstruation.
- Instruct the patient:
  - To exercise

9.5 Ectopic Pregnancy

A fertilized egg implants outside the uterus, typically in the fallopian tube, increasing the risk that the fallopian tube will burst, and results in hemorrhage if the fertilized egg continues to grow. There is a high risk of maternal death.

Signs and Symptoms

- Sharp, darting pain in the lower pelvis
- Backache
- Vaginal bleeding
- Absence of menstruation (amenorrhea)

Medical Tests

- Urine pregnancy test: Positive
- Blood test
  - Beta human chorionic gonadotropin (hCG): Elevated but lower than if pregnant
- Ultrasound: Shows empty uterus

Treatment

- Surgical removal of the fertilized egg
- Surgical removal of partial or complete fallopian tube (salpingectomy)

Interventions

- Monitor the vital signs.
- Monitor the bowel sounds.
- Monitor abdominal distention.
- Monitor vaginal bleeding.
- Instruct the patient:
  - That there is an increased risk of future ectopic pregnancies

9.6 Endometrial Cancer

Endometrial cancer is abnormal hyperplasia tissue growth (endometrial carcinomas) in the endometrium, influenced by elevated estrogen; it most commonly appears in postmenopausal patients.

Signs and Symptoms

- Abnormal vaginal bleeding

Medical Tests

- Pap test: Positive
- Blood test:
  - Cancer antigen 125 (CA-125) Positive
- Endometrial biopsy: Positive
- Endocervical curettage: Positive

Treatment

- Hysterectomy (bilateral salpingo-oophorectomy)
- Biopsy of the nodes
- Radiation to reduce tumor size
- Administer:
  - Hormone therapy
    - Progestins
  - Chemotherapy
    - Doxorubicin, cisplatin, iphosphamide

Interventions

- Monitor the vital signs.
- Monitor the intake and output.
- Monitor vaginal bleeding.
- Assess bowel sounds.
- Assess for abdominal distention.
- Instruct the patient:
  - To ambulate after surgery

9.7   Uterine Fibroids (Leiomyomas)

These are noncancerous growths of the smooth muscles of the uterus that are common during the childbearing years. They do not increase risk of uterine cancer. The size changes with menses and decreases with menopause.

Signs and Symptoms

- Asymptomatic
- Vaginal bleeding
- Uterine pressure
- Uterine pain

Medical Tests

- Ultrasound: shows tumor
- MRI: Shows tumor
- CT scan: Shows tumor
- Blood test:
    o Decreased hematocrit (if bleeding)
    o Decreased hemoglobin (if bleeding)

Treatments

- No treatment if asymptomatic
- Myomectomy: Surgical removal of tumor
- Hormone therapy: To reduce tumor size

Interventions

- Monitor the vital signs.
- Monitor uterine pain.
- Instruct the patient:
    o That these tumors are noncancerous
    o That the condition does increase risk of uterine cancer

9.8 Infertility

Infertility is the inability to become pregnant during 1 year of unprotected intercourse while in the reproductive age. Common causes are:

- Blocked fallopian tube
- Failure to ovulate
- Endometriosis
- Decreased secretion of hormones from the anterior pituitary gland
- Frequent exercise
- Radiation exposure
- Poor sperm motility

Signs and Symptoms

- No conception during reproductive years after 1 year of unprotected intercourse

Medical Tests

- Blood test:
    o Progesterone, LH, follicle-stimulating hormone (FSH), TSH low levels
- Sonogram: Shows abnormal uterine lining

- Hysterosalpingogram: Shows obstruction in uterus or fallopian tubes
- Endometrial biopsy: Uterine lining unable to support conception
- Postcoital test—cervix: Shows cervical patency and thin mucus for sperm to penetrate
- Semen analysis

Treatments

- Structural obstruction:
  - Myomectomy: Surgical removal of obstruction
  - Surgical repair of fallopian tube
  - In vitro fertilization
- For anovulation:
  - Administer:
    - LH/FSH, clomiphene to stimulate ovulation
    - Bromocriptine to stimulate thymus gland

Interventions

- Explain reasons for infertility
- Instruct the patient:
  - To maintain a menstrual diary

9.9   Ovarian Cancer

Ovarian cancer is an abnormal growth of cells in or on one or both ovaries. There is a genetic risk. Types of ovarian cancer are:

- Ovarian epithelial cancer (most common): Abnormal growth of cells on the surface of the ovary
- Ovarian germ cell tumor: Abnormal growth of cells in the ovaries
- Ovarian low malignant potential tumors: Abnormal growth of cells on the tissue covering the ovaries. Typically this is noncancerous.

Signs and Symptoms

- Asymptomatic in early stage
- Bloating
- Pelvic mass

Medical Tests

- No screening for ovarian cancer
- Ultrasound: Shows tumor
- Blood test:
  - Elevated CA-125

Treatment

- Complete abdominal hysterectomy, with bilateral salpingo-oophorectomy
- Omentectomy
- Node dissection
- Metastasis—debulking
- Radiation: Reduces tumor size
- Administer:
  - Chemotherapy
    - Cisplatin, carboplatin, paclitaxel

Interventions

- Monitor vaginal bleeding.
- Monitor the bowel sounds.
- Monitor abdominal distention.
- Monitor the vital signs.
- Instruct the patient:
  - To ambulate after surgery

9.10 Ovarian Cysts

Ovarian cysts are fluid-filled sacs that form on the ovary, many of which are self-resolving. A follicle forms inside the ovary during ovulation and then ruptures, releasing the egg. A corpus luteum forms in the ruptured follicle and dissolves if there is no conception. Abnormal dissolving of the corpus luteum results in formation of a cyst.

Types of ovarian cysts:

- Endometrioma: Forms when uterus lining tissue attaches to the ovaries
- Dermoid: Cysts containing hair, skin, and other tissue
- Polycystic ovarian disease: A buildup of follicles resulting in enlarged ovaries with a thick outer covering, leading to decreased or no ovulation. This may occur because of an imbalance of estrogen and progesterone.
- Functional: Self-resolving within three menstrual cycles
- Cystadenoma: Developed from the surface of the ovaries

Signs and Symptoms

- Asymptomatic
- Menstruation changes
- Pelvic pain (unilateral, sharp)

Medical Tests

- Ultrasound: Shows cyst

Treatment

- No treatment. Self-resolving
- Administer:
  - o Oral contraceptives
- Surgical removal of the cyst

Interventions

- Explain why menstrual pain worsens during ovulation
- Instruct the patient:
  - o That most cysts are self-resolving

9.11   Pelvic Inflammatory Disease

Pelvic inflammatory disease is inflammation of the uterus, fallopian tubes, or other reproductive organs resulting from sexually transmitted disease and leading to ectopic pregnancy, abscess, chronic pelvic pain, and infertility.
Common causes are:

- *Chlamydia trachomatis*
- *Neisseria gonorrhoeae*
- *Escherichia coli*
- *Bacteroides spp.*

Signs and Symptoms

- Vaginal discharge
- Fever
- Painful sexual intercourse (dyspareunia)
- Cervical motion tenderness

Medical Tests

- Chandelier sign positive
- Blood test:
  - o Chlamydia test positive
  - o Gonorrhea test positive
  - o Venereal Disease Research Laboratory (VDRL) test positive
  - o Rapid plasma reagent (RPR) test positive
  - o White blood cell (WBC) count elevated

Treatment

- Administer:
  - o Antibiotics
    - Ofloxacin and metronidazole, ceftriaxone and doxycycline, azithromycin and metronidazole, clindamycin and gentamicin

Interventions

- All sexual partners must be treated.
- Instruct the patient:
  - o To take all prescribed antibiotics

9.12 Trophoblastic Disease

Trophoblastic disease is the abnormal growth of cells inside the uterus between the embryo and the endometrium. These cells would normally develop in the placenta. The cells form villi projections that grow into the uterine lining. Most of these cells are benign. Types are:

- Hydatidiform mole (most common): Called *molar pregnancy*. Villi swollen with fluid form a grapelike shape. There are two types:
  - o Complete: Sperm fertilize an egg that does not contain a nucleus or DNA. No fetal tissue is formed.
  - o Partial: Sperm fertilize a normal egg. Some fetal tissue is formed, but the fetus is not formed.
- Invasive mole: Called *chorioadenoma destruens*. This is a hydatidiform mole that grows into the muscle layer of the uterus (myometrium). It can develop from both types of hydatidiform mole.
- Choriocarcinoma: A malignant growth that spreads to other organs and develops typically from a complete hydatidiform mole.
- Placental site trophoblastic tumor (rare): Develops where the uterus attaches to the placenta.

Signs and Symptoms

- Vaginal bleeding
- Grapelike tissue passing from vagina
- Pregnancy signs with no fetal heart beat
- Enlarged uterus

Medical Tests

- Blood pressure: Elevated
- Blood test:
  - o Abnormally elevated hCG value
  - o Liver function tests to assess for liver metastasis
- Ultrasound: Shows abnormal growth
- Pelvic examination: Enlarged pelvis

Treatment

- Dilatation and curettage (D&C): Remove trophoblastic cells
- Total abdominal hysterectomy
- Administer
  - Chemotherapy until normal hCG levels return
    - Methotrexate, actinomycin-D
  - Contraception for a full year

Interventions

- Monitor the grieving process.
- Instruct the patient:
  - To use contraceptives for 1 year

9.13   Rh Incompatibility

If the mother is Rh negative and the fetus is Rh positive, then the mother's immune system creates antibodies against the fetal blood cells, treating fetal blood cells as a foreign substance. Anti-Rh antibodies might cross the placenta into the fetal blood system, destroying fetal RBCs. The first-born child is usually not affected by the antibodies because the fetus is born by the time the buildup of antibodies occurs. The second-born infant is usually affected by the antibodies if the fetus is Rh positive.

Signs and Symptoms

- Blood test is administered to identify Rh incompatibility before signs and symptoms develop.

Medical Tests

- Blood test:
  - Indirect/direct Coombs', test: Positive

Treatment

- Administer:
  - Rh Immunoglobulin G (IgG)
    - RhoGAM

Interventions

- Administer an antibody titer.
- Instruct the patient:
  - That RhoAM prevents against the negative effects of Rh incompatibility

9.14   Preeclampsia and Eclampsia

Preeclampsia (toxemia): High blood pressure, elevated urine protein, swollen hands and feet in second or third trimester
Eclampsia: Untreated preeclampsia leading to seizures, coma, and death during or after birth

Signs and Symptoms

- Preeclampsia:
  - Asymptomatic
  - Blood pressure: >140/90
  - Headache
  - Weight gain (rapid)
  - Nausea and vomiting
  - Edema
  - Urine output decreased
- Eclampsia:
  - Seizure
  - Asymptomatic
  - Blood pressure: >140/90
  - Headache
  - Weight gain (rapid)
  - Nausea and vomiting
  - Edema
  - Urine output decreased

Medical Tests

- Blood test:
  - Creatinine elevated
  - Platelet: Decreased
  - Red blood cells: Decreased
  - Hemoglobin: Decreased
- Urinalysis
  - Proteinuria >300 mg/24 hr
  - Creatinine elevated

Treatment

- Deliver the infant.
- Administer:

- o Antihypertensive medication
  - ▪ Hydralazine, labetalol, methyldopa, nifedipine
- o Antiseizure medication
  - ▪ Magnesium sulfate

Interventions

- Put the patient on bed rest.
- Monitor the vital signs.
- Monitor the intake and output.
- Instruct the patient:
  - o To eat a low-salt diet

Solved Problems

9.1   Where do breast cancer cells typically form?

Breast cancer cells typically form in the lining of the small tubes (ducts) that carry breast milk from glands (lobules) to the nipple.

9.2   What is lobular breast cancer?

Lobular breast cancer is a malignant tumor formed by cells from the lobules.

9.3   What is a benign breast tumor?

A benign breast tumor is an abnormal growth caused by cysts or fibrosis.

9.4   What are the signs of breast cancer?

The signs of breast cancer are nipple inversion, nipple drainage, and a painless lump in the breast.

9.5   What is a lumpectomy?

A lumpectomy is the removal of a small tumor.

9.6   What is the purpose of radiation therapy?

The purpose of radiation therapy is to reduce the tumor's size.

9.7   What is cervical cancer?

Cervical cancer is abnormal growth of cells on the lining of the cervix.

9.8   What is the transformation zone?

The transformation zone is the place where squamous cells and glandular cells meet in the cervix.

9.9   Why is the transformation zone important?

The transformation zone is important because cervical cancer typically forms there.

9.10   What is precancerous cervical cancer?

Precancerous cervical cancer occurs when cells in the lining of the cervix gradually change. These can be detected by a Pap test and treated before cancer develops.

9.11   What are the signs of cervical cancer?

The signs of cervical cancer are pelvic pain, vaginal bleeding, and postcoital bleeding (bleeding after sex).

9.12   What is dysmenorrhea?

Dysmenorrhea is menstrual pain that limits activities of daily living or requires medication.

9.13   What leads to dysmenorrhea?

The endometrium thickens during ovulation, after which uterine muscles contract, releasing prostaglandins and causing constriction of the blood supply and deoxygenation of endometrium tissues and surrounding tissues, which leads to cramps (pain).

9.14   What destroys excess endometrial cells?

Deoxygenation destroys endometrial cells.

9.15   What is an ectopic pregnancy?

An ectopic pregnancy occurs when a fertilized egg implants outside the uterus.

9.16   Where does an ectopic pregnancy typically occur?

An ectopic pregnancy typically occurs in the fallopian tube.

9.17   What is a major complication of an ectopic pregnancy?

A major complication of an ectopic pregnancy is the risk that the fallopian tube will burst, resulting in hemorrhage if the fertilized egg continues to grow.

9.18   What are the signs of an ectopic pregnancy?

The signs of an ectopic pregnancy are a sharp and darting pain in the lower pelvic region, backache, vaginal bleeding, and the absence of menstruation (amenorrhea).

9.19   What is endometrial cancer?

Endometrial cancer is abnormal hyperplasia tissue growth (endometrial carcinomas) in the endometrium influenced by elevated estrogen.

9.20   What patients have an increased risk of endometrial cancer?

Postmenopausal patients have an increased risk of endometrial cancer.

9.21   What are leiomyomas?

Leiomyomas are noncancerous growths of the smooth muscles of the uterus.

9.22   What causes the size of leiomyomas to change?

Menses and menopause cause the size of leiomyomas to change. Menopause causes a decrease in size.

9.23   What would you say if a patient who is diagnosed with uterine fibroids asks whether she has an
increased risk of uterine cancer?

Uterine fibroids do not increase the risk for uterine cancer.

9.24   What is ovarian epithelial cancer?

Ovarian epithelial cancer is abnormal growth of cells on the surface of the ovary. This is the most
common form of ovarian cancer.

9.25   What is preeclampsia?

Preeclampsia is high blood pressure, elevated urine protein, and swollen hands and feet in the second
or third trimester of pregnancy.

CHAPTER 10

Integumentary System

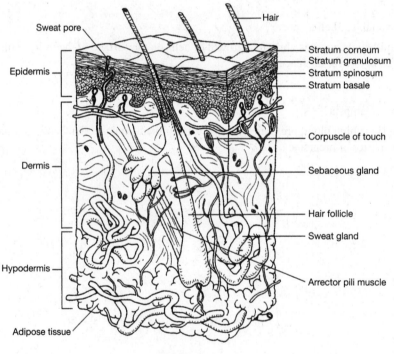

Figure 10.1

10.1 Definition

- Skin: Divided into three layers
  - Epidermis: Outermost layer consisting of epithelial tissue. Consists of four layers:
    - Stratum corneum: Makes skin waterproof; consists of dead cells and keratinized cells
    - Stratum granulosum: Can reproduce cells
    - Stratum lucidum: Can reproduce cells
    - Stratum Spinosum Can reproduce cells

- o Dermis: Between epidermis and subcutaneous layer. Contains blood supply, sweat glands, collagen fibers, and hair roots.
    - Sweat glands: Collect water and waste products from bloodstream that are excreted from the pores in the form of sweat
    - Hair: Hair cells that reach outside the epidermis are dead.
    - Collagen fibers: Connective tissues that give elasticity and strength to the skin
  - o Subcutaneous: Deepest layer of skin composed of adipose tissue. Provides cushioning and insulates the body to control body temperature.

Function of Skin

- Sensation: Pressure, pain, touch, hot, cold, vibration
- Thermoregulation: Evaporation of sweat cools the body and regulation of blood flow to dermis increases temperature.
- Healing: Lower skin layers grow upward to repair skin breakage.
- Protection: Skin prevents microorganisms from entering the body.

10.2   Burns

Burns are damage to skin and body tissue resulting from heat, friction, radiation, chemicals, or cold. The categories of burn are:

- First degree: Damage to the epidermis resulting in pain, swelling, and redness areas with no break in skin
- Second degree: Damage to the epidermis and dermis resulting in pain, swelling, white and reddened areas
- Third degree: Damage to all layers of the skin and underlying tissue resulting in no pain because of nerve damage; blackened (eschar) or reddened area.

Medical Tests

- Rule of nines: Measurement to estimate the total body surface area burned: Head, 9%; anterior torso, 18%; posterior torso, 18%; each leg, 18%; each arm, 9%; perineum, 1%.
- Pulse oximetry: 95 to 100%
- Pulmonary function test: Shows whether lungs are affected by burn

Treatment

- Administer:
  - o Topical antibiotic ointment if skin is broken
    - Silvadene:
  - o Pain medication before dressing change
    - Ibuprofen, acetaminophen, oxycodone, morphine

Interventions

- Isolate the patient if a large area of skin is missing.
- Flush a chemical burn to remove the chemical.

- Apply cold water to decrease burning sensation.
- Cover the burn with dry gauze.
- Débride eschar (third-degree burns) to encourage the growth of new tissue.
- Cover with a moist sterile saline gauze (third-degree burns).
- Maintain fluids because fluid loss is common.
- Assist the patient in range-of-motion exercises.
- Instruct the patient:
  o To encourage family visits
  o That the patient may require assistance in activities of daily living
  o That range-of-motion exercises are painful but necessary to prevent contracture

10.3 Dermatitis

Dermatitis is inflammation of the skin resulting from contact with an irritant.

Signs and Symptoms

- Rash
- Pruritus
- Erythema
- Edema
- Vesicles
- Hyperpigmentation

Medical Tests

- Radioallergosorbent assay test (RAST) testing: Positive for allergens
- Patch testing: Positive for allergens

Treatment

- Administer:
  o Antihistamines for pruritus
  o Topical corticosteroid cream to decrease inflammation

Interventions

- Remove and avoid irritants.
- Use mild soap.
- Keep the skin moist.
- Apply cool compresses.
- Instruct the patient:

- o   To wash hands often
- o   Not to take hot showers
- o   To apply moisturizers

10.4   Skin Cancers

Skin cancer is the abnormal growth of skin cells. Types:

- Basal cell (common): Directly related to sun-exposed areas. Sun interrupts the process of newer cells pushing older cells to the surface for shedding, resulting in abnormal cell growth.
- Squamous cells: Because of sun exposure. Difficult to distinguish from normal skin changes. Spreads rapidly.
- Melanoma (fastest growing): Occurs on face or upper back. Most deadly form.

Signs and Symptoms

- Basal cell: Pearly white, waxy appearing papule or a flat, brown patch
- Squamous cell: Firm red nodule; a flat scaly lesion; a change in a scar
- Melanoma: A mole that is new, has changed, or meets any of the ABCDE criteria:
  - o   A—Asymmetrical shape
  - o   B—Borders that are irregular
  - o   C—Change in color
  - o   D—Diameter larger than a pencil eraser
  - o   E—Ever changing.

Medical Tests

- Biopsy: Confirms abnormal cell growth

Treatment

- Surgical: Removes tissue.
- Cryosurgery: Cells killed by freezing with liquid nitrogen
- Mohs' surgery: Tumor removed layer by layer, checking each surface area by microscopic evaluation to ascertain that no cancer cells remain in the tissue
- Laser: Vaporizes the cancer cells
- Radiation: Kills cancer cells in melanoma
- Chemotherapy: Kills melanoma cells

Interventions

- Routine skin examination
- Instruct the patient:
  - o   To wear sunscreen
  - o   Not to go to tanning salons
  - o   To wear sun protective clothing

10.5 Cellulitis

Cellulitis is a skin infection, commonly affecting the legs, that is caused by bacteria.

Signs and Symptoms

- Skin area is hot and red
- Swollen skin area
- Painful skin area

Medical Tests

- Complete blood cell count (CBC): Elevated white blood cells (WBCs)
- Culture and sensitivity: Identify microorganism and medication
- Ultrasound: Rule out a deep-vein thrombosis in leg

Treatment

- Administer:
  - Antibiotics
    - Cephalexin
    - Dicloxacillin
    - Levofloxacin

Interventions

- Monitor the vital signs.
- Elevate the legs.
- Wash the affected area daily.
- Instruct the patient:
  - To use moisturizer daily
  - To examine the legs and feet for skin lesions

10.6 Pressure Ulcers

Pressure ulcers are characterized by impaired circulation caused by pressure, typically over a bony prominence, which leads to ulceration of the skin. This is commonly related to lack of mobility. The ulcerated skin loses integrity by the friction of shear force from linens.

Signs and Symptoms

- Stage I:
  - Firm, warm areas of skin from poor circulation
  - Spongy, reddened tissue from increased pressure
- Stage II:
  - Opening in the skin with surrounding erythema from pressure

- Stage III:
  - o The ulcer is deep, down to the dermis, with a red base and some drainage.
- Stage IV:
  - o This is a deep ulcer involving muscle and bone, with visible signs of tissue death.

Medical Tests

- Blood test:
- CBC:
  - o Decreased hemoglobin
  - o Decreased hematocrit
  - o Decreased albumin
  - o Decreased prealbumin

Treatment

- Débridement: Remove necrosis with a topical enzyme cream.
- Clean with saline, water, and soap.
- Give whirlpool treatments.
- Administer:
  - o Hydrocolloids to keep skin moist
  - o Semipermeable nonadherent bulk dressing: Enables gas to escape but impermeable to liquids

Interventions

- Sleep on a specialized mattress.
- Use specialized wheelchair cushions.
- Perform daily skin inspection.
- Reposition the patient every 2 hours.
- Maintain proper nutrition.
- Maintain adequate fluid.
- Instruct the patient:
  - o To stop smoking
  - o To use pillows to reduce pressure

10.7   Wounds

Wounds are any break in the skin resulting in inflammation.

Signs and Symptoms

- Pain
- Bleeding
- Drainage

Medical Tests

- Blood test: CBC shows elevated WBC count, indicating infection.

Treatment

- Irrigate the wound with saline.
- Keep a dirty wound open during healing.
- Close a clean wound with Steri-Strips, sutures, or dressing.
- Administer antibiotics.
- Administer tetanus.
- Assess circulation if the wound is in a limb. Check the distal pulses.

Interventions

- Monitor the vital signs.
- Maintain nutrition.
- Maintain hydration.
- Change the dressing frequently.
- Monitor the patient for signs of infection.
- Explain the disease process to the patient.
- Instruct the patient:
  - To rest
  - To decrease activities

Solved Problems

10.1 What is a first-degree burn?

A first-degree burn is damage to the epidermis resulting in pain, swelling, and areas of redness with no break in the skin.

10.2 What is a second-degree burn?

A second-degree burn is damage to the epidermis and dermis resulting in pain, swelling, and white and reddened areas.

10.3 What is a third-degree burn?

A third-degree burn is damage to all layers of the skin and underlying tissue.

10.4 How much pain will a patient typically experience in a third-degree burn?

During a third-degree burn, a patient will experience no pain because the nerves are damaged.

10.5 What is blackened skin called in a third-degree burn?

Blackened skin during a third-degree burn is called *eschar*.

10.6   What is the rule of nines?

The rule of nines is the measurement to estimate the total body surface area burned: head, 9%; anterior torso, 18%; posterior torso, 18%; each leg, 18%; each arm, 9%; perineum, 1%.

10.7   Why might a pulmonary function test be ordered for a burn patient?

A pulmonary function test might be ordered for a burn patient to determine whether the lungs have been affected by the burn.

10.8   What is the primary treatment for any burn?

The primary treatment for any burn is to keep the burned area clean.

10.9   What is Silvadene?

Silvadene is a topical antibiotic ointment administered to a burn.

10.10   What is the first treatment in a chemical burn?

The first treatment in a chemical burn is to flush the chemical.

10.11   Why are range-of-motion exercises important for a burn patient?

Range-of-motion exercises are painful but necessary to prevent contracture.

10.12   What is dermatitis?

Dermatitis is inflammation of the skin.

10.13   What causes dermatitis?

An irritant causes dermatitis.

10.14   What are the signs and symptoms of dermatitis?

The signs and symptoms of dermatitis are rash, pruritus, erythema, edema, vesicles, and hyperpigmentation.

10.15   What is the purpose of RAST testing?

The purpose of RAST testing is to identify the allergen that is causing dermatitis.

10.16   Why administer antihistamines to a patient who has dermatitis?

Antihistamines should be administered to a patient who has dermatitis to reduce pruritus.

10.17   What is the primary treatment of dermatitis?

The primary treatment of dermatitis is to remove the irritant.

10.18   What causes basal cell skin cancer?

Basal cell skin cancer is directly related to sun-exposed areas. Sun interrupts the process of newer cells pushing older cells to the surface for shedding, which results in abnormal cell growth.

10.19   What are signs and symptoms of melanoma?

The signs and symptoms of melanoma are a mole that is new, has changed, or meets any of the ABCDE criteria:

- A—Asymmetrical shape
- B—Borders that are irregular

- C—Change in color
- D—Diameter larger than a pencil eraser
- E—Ever changing

10.20 What is cryosurgery?

Cryosurgery is the killing of cells by freezing with liquid nitrogen.

10.21 What is Mohs' surgery?

Mohs' surgery is the removal of a tumor layer by layer, checking each surface area by microscopic evaluation to ascertain that no cancer cells remain in the tissue.

10.22 How does a laser kill skin cancer cells?

A laser kills skin cancer cells by vaporizing them.

10.23 What is cellulitis?

Cellulitis is a skin infection, commonly affecting the legs, caused by bacteria.

10.24 What are pressure ulcers?

Impaired circulation caused by pressure typically over bony prominence leads to ulceration of the skin commonly related to lack of mobility. The ulcerated skin loses integrity by the friction shear force from linens.

10.25 What are the stages of pressure ulcers?

- Stage I:
  - Firm warm areas of skin from poor circulation
  - Spongy, reddened tissue from increased pressure
- Stage II:
  - Opening in the skin with surrounding erythema from pressure
- Stage III:
  - The ulcer is deep, down to the dermis, with a red base and some drainage.
- Stage IV:
  - This is a deep ulcer involving muscle and bone, with visible signs of tissue death.

CHAPTER 11

Genitourinary System

11.1 Definition

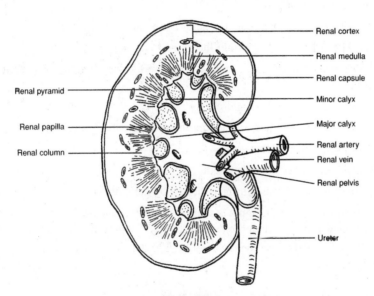

Figure 11.1

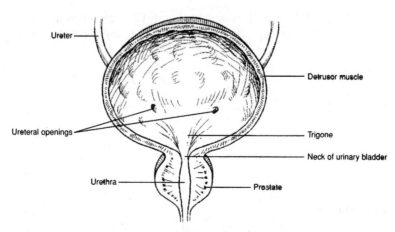

Figure 11.2

- Kidneys:
  - Each is located near the middle of the back alongside the spine and protected by the rib cage
  - Filters 200 quarts of blood daily
  - Extracts 2 quarts of waste products from blood daily
- Ureters
  - Tubes that connect the kidneys to the urinary bladder
- Nephrons
  - Each kidney has a million nephrons that filter blood and contain glomerulus.
  - Glomerulus: Tiny capillaries that intertwine the tubule and filter blood by retaining proteins and extracting fluid and wastes.
  - Tubules: Receive waste material and electrolytes (sodium, phosphorus, and potassium). If the body has an oversupply of an electrolyte, that electrolyte is extracted from the blood and released into the urine. If the body has an undersupply of an electrolyte, that electrolyte is retained.
- Hormones: The kidney releases three hormones:
  - Erythropoietin (EPO): Stimulates bone marrow to make red blood cells
  - Renin: Regulates blood pressure
  - Calcitriol: Active form of vitamin D that helps maintain calcium levels
- Renal function: The efficient kidneys filter the blood
  - Estimated glomerular filtration rate (eGFR): Measures kidney function as percentage of kidney function available
    - 100%: Both kidneys are filtering properly
    - 60%: Considered a small decrease that probably is not noticeable
    - 25%: Serious health problems occur
    - 15%: Dialysis or kidney transplant required
- Urinary bladder: Stores and releases urine collected by the kidneys
- As the urinary bladder expands, a signal is sent to the brain indicating the need to urinate. The brain signals muscles in the urinary bladder to contract. Urine flows from the urinary bladder through the urethra and urine is excreted.

11.2   Benign Prostatic Hypertrophy (BPH)

Benign prostatic hypertrophy (BPH) occurs when an enlarged prostate gland presses against the urethra, causing narrowing of the urethra. This leads to urinary retention, hydronephrosis, and dilation of the renal pelvis and ureter.

Signs and Symptoms

- Urinary hesitancy
- Urinary frequency
- Urinary urgency
- Nocturia
- Hematuria
- Decreased urinary stream
- Intermittent urinary stream

Medical Tests

- Digital rectal exam: Loss of median sulcus and full prostate
- Prostate-specific antigen test (PSA): Elevated
- Urography: Shows increase post void residual urine
- Prostate ultrasound: Shows prostate hypertrophy

Treatment

- Administer:
  - Alpha$_1$-blockers for symptom relief
    - Doxazosin
    - Tamsulosin
    - Terazosin
- Administer finasteride to shrink prostate gland
- Surgical removal of portion of prostate

Interventions

- Monitor vital signs
- Monitor renal function
- Monitor intake and output
- Instruct the patient:
  - Not to drink caffeine
  - Not to drink alcohol
  - Not to take decongestants
  - Not to take anticholinergics
  - To monitor for signs of urinary tract infection

11.3 Bladder Cancer

Bladder cancer is abnormal growth of the transitional cell layer or deeper layer of the bladder.

Signs and Symptoms

- Fatigue
- Hematuria
- Change in color, frequency, or amount of urine

Medical Tests

- Urinalysis: Shows red blood cells (RBCs) in urine
- Cystoscopy: To obtain biopsy for diagnosis
- Computed tomography (CT) scan: Shows metastasis

Treatment

- Surgical removal of tumor
- Instillation of bacillus Calmette-Guérin into bladder
- Radiation therapy
- Chemotherapy

Interventions

- Monitor vital signs.
- Monitor intake and output.
- Monitor the color of urine.
- Instruct the patient:
    - About self-catheterization of ileal reservoir, if necessary
    - On proper skin care (postoperatively)

11.4 Acute Glomerulonephritis

Acute glomerulonephritis is a kidney infection known as acute nephritic syndrome, which results from an ascending urinary infection or infection from elsewhere in the body.

Signs and Symptoms

- Oliguria
- Hematuria
- Peripheral edema
- Blood pressure: Elevated

Medical Tests

- Elevated blood urea nitrogen (BUN)
- Decreased albumin
- Decreased glomerular filtration rate
- 24-Hour urine: Elevated protein
- Urinalysis: Shows RBC casts
- Renal biopsy: Identifies cause of infection

Treatment

- Administer:
    - Diuretic
        - Plasmapheresis: If cause is an autoimmune disorder

Interventions

- Monitor the vital signs.
- Monitor the intake and output.
- Weigh daily.
- Monitor extremities for edema.
- Instruct the patient:
  - To decrease fluid intake

11.5   Kidney Cancer

Kidney cancer is abnormal cell growth within the kidney.

Signs and Symptoms

- Flank pain
- Elevated blood pressure
- Weight loss
- Anemia
- Hematuria

Medical Tests

- Blood test:
  - Complete blood cell (CBC) count: Low RBC count, low hemoglobin
  - Elevated erythrocyte sedimentation rate
- Urinalysis: Shows presence of red blood cells
- Ultrasound: Shows renal mass
- CT scan with contrast: Shows renal mass
- Magnetic resonance imaging (MRI): Shows renal mass

Treatment

- Nephrectomy: Surgical removal of the kidney
- Radiofrequency ablation: Destroys tumor ablation
- Chemotherapy

Interventions

- Monitor the vital signs.
- Monitor the intake and output.
- Monitor the hemoglobin and hematocrit.
- Instruct the patient:
  - That he or she can live a healthy life with one kidney

11.6   Kidney Stones

Kidney stones are also known as *renal calculi* and *nephrolithiasis*. Slow urine flow enables crystals to form from calcium, uric acid, cystine, or struvite in the kidneys or the urinary tract. The crystal may block the ureter, causing hydronephrosis and swelling. There is a genetic predisposition to kidney stones.

Signs and Symptoms

- Unilateral extreme flank pain (renal colic) may radiate to lower abdomen, groin, scrotum, or labia.
- Hematuria
- Blood pressure elevated with pain
- Nausea
- Vomiting

Medical Tests

- Urinalysis: Shows leukocytosis
- Ultrasound: Shows stones
- X-ray of kidneys, ureters, and bladder (KUB): Shows stones
- CT scan: Shows stones
- MRI: Shows stones

Treatment

- Lithotripsy: Shock waves break the stone into pieces so the stone can pass
- Surgical removal of the stone
- Surgical insertion of stent
- Administer:
  - Narcotics
    - Morphine
  - Nonsteroidal anti-inflammatory drugs (NSAIDs)
    - Ketorolac

Interventions

- Monitor the intake and output.
- Strain the urine.
- Instruct the patient:
  - To increase fluid intake
  - About dietary modification based on the makeup of the stone

11.7   Prostate Cancer

Prostate cancer is abnormal malignant growth of prostate tissue.

Signs and Symptoms

- Back pain
- Urinary hesitancy
- Urinary frequency
- Urinary urgency
- Urinary retention
- Nocturia
- Hematuria

Medical Tests

- PSA: Elevated
- Digital rectal exam: Palpable nodule
- Transrectal ultrasound: Identify and stage cancer
- MRI: Identify prostate lesions
- Biopsy: Identify cell type
- Alkaline phosphatase: Elevated with metastasis to bone

Treatment

- Watchful waiting: Monitor PSA and ultrasound
- Radiation therapy: External beam or brachytherapy (insertion of radioactive substance into prostate)
- Radical prostatectomy: Surgical removal of the prostate
- Chemotherapy
- Cryosurgery: Freezing of tissue
- Administer:
  - Hormonal treatment to suppress natural androgen production
    - Leuprolide, goserelin, estrogen
- Orchiectomy: Reduce natural androgen production

Interventions

- Monitor the vital signs.
- Monitor the intake and output.
- Monitor for signs of bladder distention.
- Assess for pain in the back.
- Instruct the patient:
  - On the side effects of treatment.

11.8 Pyelonephritis

Infection of the kidneys commonly from *Escherichia coli, Klebsiella spp., Enterobacter spp., Proteus spp.*, or *Pseudomonas spp., Staphylococcus saprophyticus* related to ascending urinary tract infection.

Signs and Symptoms

- Flank pain
- Fever
- Chills
- Urinary frequency
- Urinary urgency
- Costovertebral angle tenderness
- Nausea
- Vomiting
- Diarrhea

Medical Tests

- Urinalysis: Shows RBCs
- Urine culture and sensitivity: Identifies organism and medication to treat the illness
- CBC: Shows leukocytosis

Treatment

- Administer:
  - Antibiotics
    - Nitrofurantoin, ciprofloxacin, levofloxacin, ofloxacin, trimethoprim-sulfamethoxazole, ampicillin, amoxicillin
  - Antipyretics
  - Phenazopyridine

Interventions

- Monitor the vital signs.
- Monitor the intake and output.
- Increase the fluid intake.
- Instruct the patient:
  - That phenazopyridine will cause orange urine

11.9   Renal Failure

- Decreased renal function.
  - Acute: Sudden decrease in renal function
    - Prerenal: Caused by diminished renal perfusion
    - Hypovolemia: Caused by blood or fluid loss
    - Postrenal: Caused by urinary tract obstruction
  - Chronic: Progressive decrease in renal function caused by irreversible renal disease

Signs and Symptoms

- Decreased urinary output
- Peripheral edema
- Abdominal bruit
- Weight loss
- Uremic pruritus

Medical Tests

- Blood test:
  - Elevated BUN
  - Elevated creatinine
  - Decreased creatinine clearance
  - Decreased RBCs
  - Decreased hemoglobin
- Urinalysis: Shows proteinuria
- GFR: Decreased
- Renal ultrasound: Shows decrease in renal size

Treatment

- Administer dialysis treatment.
- Place a stent or catheter to allow for the drainage of urine.
- Administer phosphate binders to reduce phosphate levels.
- Administer sodium polystyrene sulfonate to reduce potassium levels.
- Administer EPO to treat anemia.
- Administer antibiotics for pyelonephritis.

Interventions

- Monitor the vital signs.
- Monitor the intake and output.
- Monitor the electrolyte levels.
- Monitor the blood glucose levels.
- Do not use contrast dye tests.
- Do not administer nephrotoxic medication.
- Instruct the patient:
  - To restrict potassium, phosphate, sodium, and protein in the diet

11.10 Testicular Cancer

Testicular cancer is an abnormal tissue growth in the testicle occurring in males who are in their teens or twenties.

Signs and Symptoms

- Painless enlargement of the testis
- Palpable mass on surface of testis
- Unilateral feeling of heaviness in the scrotum

Medical Tests

- Scrotal ultrasound: Shows mass on testis
- CT scan: Shows mass on testis
- Blood test:
  - Elevated human chorionic gonadotropin (hCG)
  - Elevated alpha-fetoprotein (AFP)
  - Elevated lactate dehydrogenase (LDH)

Treatment

- Orchiectomy
- Chemotherapy
- Radiation therapy

Interventions

- Monitor tumor markers periodically.
- Monitor the vital signs.
- Monitor the intake and output.
- Instruct the patient:
  - To perform self-exams
  - How to bank sperm

11.11   Urinary Tract Infection

An infection of the urinary tract typically is caused by a gram-negative bacteria such as *E. coli* found on the skin of the genital area or introduced by an invasive procedure.

Signs and Symptoms

- Dysuria
- Low back pain
- Feeling of fullness in suprapubic area
- Urinary frequency
- Urinary urgency

Medical Tests

- Urinalysis: Shows leukocytes, nitrites, RBCs
- Urine culture and sensitivity: Identifies microorganism and medication to treat microorganism.

Treatment

- Administer:
    o Antibiotics
        ▪ Nitrofurantoin, ciprofloxacin, levofloxacin, ofloxacin, trimethoprim-sulfamethoxazole, ampicillin, amoxicillin
    o Phenazopyridine

Interventions

- Increase the fluid intake.
- Monitor the intake and output.
- Monitor the vital signs.
- Instruct the patient:
    o That phenazopyridine will cause orange-colored urine
    o To drink cranberry juice to acidify the urine

Solved Problems

11.1   What is BPH?

BPH is benign prostatic hypertrophy.

11.2   What is the effect of BPH?

The effect of BPH is an enlarged prostate gland, which pressures the urethra and causes the narrowing of the urethra. This leads to urinary retention, hydronephrosis, and dilation of the renal pelvis and ureter.

11.3   What are the signs and symptoms of BPH?

The signs and symptoms of BPH are urinary hesitancy, urinary frequency, urinary urgency, nocturia, hematuria, decreased urinary stream, and an intermittent urinary stream.

11.4   What test is commonly administered to detect BPH?

The PSA test is commonly administered to detect BPH.

11.5   What instructions should you give to a patient diagnosed with BPH?

A patient with BPH should be instructed to intake no caffeine, no alcohol, no decongestants, and no anticholinergics and to monitor for signs of urinary tract infection.

11.6   What is bladder cancer?

Bladder cancer is abnormal growth of the transitional cell layer or deeper layer of the bladder.

11.7   How is bladder cancer diagnosed?

Bladder cancer is diagnosed with cystoscopy to obtain a biopsy for diagnosis.

11.8   What is acute glomerulonephritis?

Acute glomerulonephritis is a kidney infection known as acute nephritic syndrome, resulting from an ascending urinary infection or infection from elsewhere in the body.

11.9   What are signs and symptoms of acute glomerulonephritis?

The signs and symptoms of acute glomerulonephritis are oliguria, hematuria, peripheral edema, and elevated blood pressure.

11.10   What is kidney cancer?

Kidney cancer is abnormal cell growth within the kidney.

11.11   What are signs and symptoms of kidney cancer?

The signs and symptoms of kidney cancer are flank pain, elevated blood pressure, weight loss, anemia, and hematuria.

11.12   What is a nephrectomy?

Nephrectomy is surgical removal of a kidney.

11.13   What are renal calculi?

Renal calculi are kidney stones.

11.14   What is a kidney stone?

A kidney stone is a slow urine flow that enables crystals to form from calcium, uric acid, cystine, or struvite in the kidneys or the urinary tract. The crystal may block the ureter, causing hydronephrosis and swelling. There is a genetic predisposition to kidney stones.

11.15   What are signs and symptoms of a kidney stone?

The signs and symptoms of a kidney stone are unilateral extreme flank pain (renal colic), which may radiate to lower abdomen, groin, scrotum, or labia; hematuria; elevated blood pressure with pain, nausea, and vomiting.

11.16   What KUB?

KUB is an X-ray of the kidneys, ureters, and bladder.

11.17   What is lithotripsy?

Lithotripsy occurs when shock waves break the stone into pieces so the stone can pass.

11.18   What instruction should you give to a patient who has kidney stones?

A patient with kidney stones should be instructed to increase fluid intake and make appropriate dietary modifications.

11.19   How do you know whether the kidney stone has passed?

One can tell whether the kidney stone has passed by straining the urine.

11.20   What is brachytherapy?

Brachytherapy is insertion of a radioactive substance into the prostate.

11.21 What is the purpose of hormonal treatment in prostate cancer?

The purpose of hormonal treatment in prostate cancer is to suppress natural androgen production.

11.22 What is pyelonephritis?

Pyelonephritis is infection of the kidneys.

11.23 What should you tell the patient about phenazopyridine?

The patient should be informed that phenazopyridine will turn the urine orange.

11.24 What is prerenal acute renal failure?

Prerenal acute renal failure is acute renal failure caused by diminished renal perfusion.

11.25 What is a urinary tract infection?

A urinary tract infection is an infection of the urinary tract typically by a gram-negative bacteria such as *E. coli* found on the skin of the genital area or introduced by an invasive procedure.

CHAPTER 12

Fluids and Electrolytes

12.1   Definition

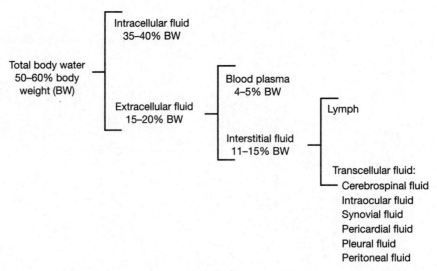

Figure 12.1

- Fluids are:
  - Intracellular: Within the cells
  - Extracellular: Outside the cells
  - Interstitial space (third space): Within the tissue spaces
  - Fluid balance is maintained by osmotic pressure.
- Electrolytes are substances that conduct electricity. These are:
  - Sodium
  - Potassium
  - Calcium
  - Magnesium
  - Chloride
  - Phosphate

Osmolarity

- *Osmolarity* is a measure of solute concentration of a fluid. A *solute* is a substance contained in a fluid.
- Osmolarity of plasma is 270 to 300 mOsm/L and prevents fluid from shifting into the interstitial space. This is referred to as an *isotonic (normotonic) solution.*
- Hypertonic solution has an osmolarity >300 mOsm/L and causes increased pressure, resulting in fluid moving from an isotonic solution to a hypertonic area solution to equalize osmolarity.
- Hypertonic solution has an osmolarity <270 mOsm/L and causes less pressure, resulting in fluid moving from a hypotonic solution to an isotonic solution to equalize osmolarity.
- Osmotic pressure is pressure that prevents fluid from moving across (diffusion) a semipermeable membrane (cell wall). The concentration of fluids and electrolytes maintains osmotic pressure.
- Edema occurs when fluid enters the interstitial space. Higher hydrostatic (fluid) pressure in blood vessels causes fluid to leave blood vessels and enter into the interstitial space.
- Hypotonic solutions have a concentration of <270 mOsm/L and exert less pressure, which allows water to be pulled from the hypotonic area into the isotonic area.

Fluid Regulation

- Water follows sodium.
- Aldosterone is a hormone secreted by the adrenal cortex to control sodium and potassium levels in plasma. Increase aldosterone causes tubules within the nephrons in the kidneys to reabsorb sodium and water. Increased aldosterone increases plasma osmolarity, resulting in fluid retention.
- Renin is a hormone secreted by the kidneys to control sodium and fluid volume. Renin causes the plasma protein angiotensinogen to convert to angiotensin I. Angiotensin I converts to angiotensin II. Angiotensin causes vascular constriction and aldosterone secretion.
- Antidiuretic hormone (ADH) is stored in the posterior pituitary gland. ADH causes the renal tubules to reabsorb water resulting in decreased plasma osmolarity. ADH stops releasing when the osmolarity is too low, resulting in increased urination.
- Natriuretic peptides are secreted when blood pressure and blood volume increase, causing the kidney to stop reabsorbing sodium, and increasing the glomerular filtration rate (GFR), resulting in increased urination and decreased plasma osmolarity.

Acid-Base Balance

- Acid-base balance is an environment in which physiology activity can flourish, which is between (acid) 7.35 and 7.45 (base) on the pH scale.
- pH scale is used to measure the acid-base balance.
- Bicarbonate is a chemical that is a base.
- Carbon dioxide is a chemical that is an acid.
- Lungs and kidneys control the acid-base balance. When blood becomes acidic, the lungs excrete carbon dioxide. When blood becomes alkaline (base), the kidneys excrete bicarbonate.
- Acidosis occurs when the blood is too acidic.
- Respiratory acidosis occurs because of a buildup of carbon dioxide.
- Metabolic acidosis occurs because of an overexcretion of bicarbonate.
- Alkalosis occurs when the blood is too alkaline.
- Respiratory alkalosis occurs because of excretion of carbon dioxide by the lungs.
- Metabolic alkalosis occurs because of a buildup of bicarbonate by the kidneys.

12.2   Hyponatremia

Hyponatremia is an abnormally low amount of sodium in blood commonly caused by diuretics, diarrhea, vomiting, hypothyroidism, water imbalance, renal failure, excess secretion of sodium, and intake of Ecstasy and can lead to seizures and death.

Signs and Symptoms

- Orthostatic hypotension
- Increased gastrointestinal motility
- Diarrhea
- Increased bowel sounds
- Nausea
- Decreased deep-tendon reflexes
- Muscle weakness
- Excessive activity
- Malaise
- Altered level of consciousness

Medical Tests

- Blood test:
  - Sodium level <135 mEq/L
- Urinalysis: Low sodium

Treatment

- Treat the underlying cause.
- Administer:
  - Intravenous (IV) saline solution

Interventions

- Restrict water.
- Monitor the intake and output.
- Monitor the vital signs.
- Weigh the patient daily.
- Instruct the patient:
  - To restrict fluid
  - To increase the sodium in his or her diet

12.3   Hypernatremia

Hypernatremia is an abnormally high amount of sodium in the blood. It is commonly caused by insufficient water intake, corticosteroids, renal failure, hormone imbalance, dehydration, increased sodium intake, sweating, vomiting, diarrhea, and treatment for hyponatremia.

Signs and Symptoms

- Increased blood pressure
- Increased thirst
- Distended neck veins
- Muscle twitching
- Muscle weakness
- Restlessness
- Agitation
- Weight gain
- Irritability

Medical Tests

- Blood test:
  - Sodium level >145 mEq/L
- Urinalysis: High sodium

Treatment

- Administer:
  - IV hypotonic
    - 0.225% Sodium chloride, 0.33% sodium chloride, 0.45% sodium chloride
  - Diuretics
    - Furosemide; bumetanide

Interventions

- Monitor the vital signs.
- Weigh the patient daily.
- Monitor the intake and output.
- Instruct the patient:
  - About proper oral hygiene
  - To restrict fluid
  - To restrict sodium in diet

12.4 Hypocalcemia

Hypocalcemia is an abnormally low level of calcium in the blood commonly caused by an endocrine disorder, excess loss of calcium related to renal disorder, alcoholism, burns, diuretics, vitamin D deficiency or malabsorption, sepsis, hyperphosphatemia, or decreased albumin. It can lead to cardiac arrhythmias and seizures.

Signs and Symptoms

- Muscle spasm
- Cramping

- Tetany
- Positive Chvostek's sign
- Positive Trousseau's sign
- Irritability
- Abdominal pain
- Cardiac arrhythmias
- Paresthesia of lips

Medical Tests

- Blood test:
  - Calcium level <9 mg/dL

Treatment

- Administer:
  - Vitamin D
    - Ergocalciferol (vitamin D_2)
  - IV calcium gluconate 10%
  - IV calcium chloride

Interventions

- Monitor the vital signs.
- Monitor the intake and output.
- Monitor the neurologic status.
- Monitor for signs of hypercalcemia.
- Instruct the patient:
  - To eat a high-calcium diet
  - To restrict the use of antacids
  - Not to use laxatives

12.5   Hypercalcemia

This is an abnormally high amount of calcium in the blood, commonly caused by thiazide diuretics, immobility, hyperthyroidism, lithium, hyperparathyroidism, glucocorticoids, renal failure, excess intake of antacids, dehydration, and bone metastasis leading to cardiac, muscle, and neural excitability and cardiac arrest.

Signs and Symptoms

- Nausea
- Vomiting
- Kidney stones

- Constipation
- Dehydration
- Muscle weakness
- Cardiac arrhythmias
- Shallow respirations
- Bounding peripheral pulses
- Increased heart rate
- Bradycardia (later sign)

Medical Tests

- Blood test:
  - Calcium level >10.5 mEq/L
- Urinalysis: High calcium
- Electrocordiogram (ECG): Shows shortened ST segment and widened T waves

Treatment

- Administer:
  - 0.9% IV normal saline solution
  - Loop diuretics
    - Furosemide
  - Plicamycin to bind to calcium
  - Calcitonin
  - Phosphorus
  - Bisphosphonates to reabsorb calcium into bone

Interventions

- Monitor the vital signs.
- Monitor the intake and output.
- Assess the muscle strength.
- Assess the abdomen.
- Perform range-of-motion exercises.
- Strain the urine for stones.
- Instruct the patient:
  - To eat a low-calcium diet
  - Not to take calcium-based antacids
  - To perform weight-bearing exercises
  - That mobilization is encouraged

12.6   Hypokalemia

Hypokalemia is a lower than normal level of potassium in the blood commonly caused by endocrine disorders, low magnesium levels, diuretics, diarrhea, fluid loss, and decreased dietary intake of potassium, leading to cardiac arrhythmia.

Signs and Symptoms

- Lethargy
- Palpitations
- Constipation
- Decreased deep-tendon reflex
- Muscle cramps
- Muscle weakness
- Anorexia

Medical Tests

- Blood test:
  - Potassium level <3.5 mEq/L
- ECG: Shows depressed ST segment and presence of U wave

Treatment

- Treat the underlying cause.
- Administer:
  - IV potassium
    - Potassium concentration of no more than 40 mEq/L in peripheral lines
- No glucose

Interventions

- Monitor the vital signs.
- Monitor the intake and output.
- Instruct the patient:
  - To eat a high-potassium diet

12.7   Hyperkalemia

Hyperkalemia is an elevated level of potassium in the blood, commonly caused by the intake of potassium, angiotensin receptor blockers, angiotensin-converting enzyme (ACE) inhibitors, nonsteroidal anti-inflammatory drugs (NSAIDs), potassium-sparing diuretics, hemolysis, low insulin levels, acidosis, digoxin overdose, beta-blockers, and rhabdomyolysis and leading to cardiac arrhythmias and cardiac arrest.

Signs and Symptoms

- Diarrhea
- Palpitations
- Nausea
- Vomiting
- Dizziness
- Weakness
- Abdominal distention

Medical Tests

- Blood test:
  - Potassium level >5 mEq/L
- ECG: Shows widened QRS complex and peaked T waves

Treatment

- Dialysis for critically high levels
- Administer:
  - IV insulin and glucose
  - IV calcium gluconate
  - IV sodium bicarbonate
  - Diuretics
  - Kayexalate to remove potassium using gastrointestinal tract

Interventions

- Monitor the vital signs.
- Monitor the abdomen.
- Instruct the patient:
  - To eat a low-potassium diet
  - Not to use salt substitutes

12.8   Hypomagnesemia

Hypomagnesemia is a low magnesium level in the blood commonly caused by vomiting, diarrhea, malnutrition, Crohn's disease, celiac disease, diuretics, renal disorder, aminoglycoside antibiotics, ascites, hyperglycemia, and chronic alcohol intake, and leading to cardiac arrhythmias and seizures.

Signs and Symptoms

- Positive Chvostek's sign
- Positive Trousseau's sign

- Headaches
- Irritability
- Decreased bowel sounds
- Decreased appetite
- Nausea
- Muscle twitching
- Hyperactive deep tendon reflexes
- Constipation
- Paresthesia
- Confusion
- Mood changes
- Arrhythmia

Medical Tests

- Blood test:
  - Magnesium level <1.5 mEq/L
- ECG: Shows depressed ST segment and tall T waves

Treatment

- Administer:
  - IV magnesium sulfate

Interventions

- Monitor the vital signs.
- Monitor the intake and output.
- Monitor the cardiac rhythm.
- Instruct the patient:
  - To increase magnesium in the diet
  - Not to take laxatives

12.9   Hypermagnesemia

Hypermagnesemia is a high level of magnesium in the blood commonly caused by decreased renal function and increased use of medication that contains magnesium, leading to cardiac risk.

Signs and Symptoms

- Urinary retention
- Confusion
- Drowsiness
- Bradycardia

- Hypotension
- Lethargy
- Weakness
- Decreased deep tendon reflexes

Medical Tests

- Blood test:
  - Magnesium level >2.5 mEq/L
  - Elevated blood urea nitrogen (BUN) (renal insufficiency)
- ECG: Shows widened QRS complex and prolonged PR interval

Treatment

- Dialysis
- Administer:
  - IV magnesium antagonist
    - Calcium chloride
  - Loop diuretic
    - Furosemide

Interventions

- Monitor the vital signs.
- Monitor the intake and output.
- Instruct the patient:
  - To decrease magnesium in the diet
  - To increase fluid intake

12.10   Metabolic Acidosis

Arterial blood pH is <7.35, commonly caused by diabetic ketoacidosis, renal failure, diarrhea, seizure, fever, starvation, high alcohol intake, or excess intake of aspirin.

Signs and Symptoms

- Muscle weakness
- Hyperventilation
- Hypotension
- Lethargy
- Muscle weakness
- Tachycardia (initially)
- Bradycardia (later)

Medical Tests

- Arterial blood gas:
  - pH <7.35
  - Bicarbonate <22 mEq/L
  - Partial pressure of carbon dioxide in arterial gas ($Paco_2$) normal
- Urinalysis: Positive for ketones

Treatment

- Treat the underlying cause.
- Hemodialysis

Interventions

- Monitor the vital signs.
- Monitor the intake and output.
- Instruct the patient:
  - That he or she will return to activities of normal living once the electrolyte balance is restored

12.11   Metabolic Alkalosis

In metabolic acidosis, arterial blood pH >7.45, commonly caused by decreased levels of calcium, potassium, parenteral nutrition, nasogastric suctioning, increased use of antacids, aldosterone, Cushing's disease, thiazide diuretics, and prolonged vomiting.

Signs and Symptoms

- Positive Chvostek's sign
- Positive Trousseau's sign
- Irritability
- Tetany
- Muscle weakness
- Muscle cramping
- Anxiety

Medical Tests

- Arterial blood gas:
  - pH >7.45
- Bicarbonate >28 mEq/L
  - Elevated $Paco_2$

Treatment

- Treat the underlying cause.
- Instruct the patient:
  - o That he or she will return to activities of normal living once the electrolyte balance is restored

Interventions

- Monitor the vital signs.
- Monitor the intake and output.
- Monitor the neurological signs.

12.12 Hypophosphatemia

Hypophosphatemia is a low amount of phosphorus in the blood and is commonly caused by corticosteroids, chronic obstructive pulmonary disease, diuretics, beta-adrenergic agonists, hyperparathyroidism, or vitamin D deficiency, and leading to electrolyte imbalance.

Signs and Symptoms

- Paresthesia
- Petechiae
- Hemolytic anemia
- Muscle weakness
- Rhabdomyolysis
- Irritability
- Confusion
- Disorientation
- Hypotension

Medical Tests

- Blood test:
  - o Phosphorus level <1.7 mEq/L
  - o Increased parathyroid hormone (PTH)
  - o Decrease hemoglobin
  - o Decreased hematocrit
  - o Increased creatine kinase
- Urinalysis: Shows decreased phosphate

Treatment

- Treat the underlying cause.
- Administer:
  - Potassium phosphate

Interventions

- Monitor the vital signs.
- Monitor the intake and output.
- Advise a diet high in phosphorus for chronic hypophosphatemia.
- Instruct the patient:
  - To increase phosphorus in his or her diet

12.13 Hyperphosphatemia

Hyperphosphatemia is a high amount of phosphorus in the blood commonly caused by excessive vitamin D, laxatives, enemas, renal insufficiency, hypoparathyroidism, and rhabdomyolysis.

Signs and Symptoms

- Asymptomatic

Medical Tests

- Blood test:
  - Phosphorus level >4.6 mEq/L

Treatment

- Treat the underlying cause.
- Administer medication to bind the phosphate.
  - Calcium acetate; aluminum hydroxide; lanthanum
- Dialysis

Interventions

- Monitor the vital signs.
- Monitor the intake and output.
- Instruct the patient:
  - To decrease phosphorus in his or her diet
  - Not to take laxatives
  - Not to take enemas

12.14   Dehydration

Dehydration is less than a normal volume of body fluid commonly caused by a shift of fluid from circulation to interstitial tissue, lack of hydration, or loss of fluid.

Signs and Symptoms

- Decreased urinary output
- Hypotension
- Poor skin turgor
- Increased thirst
- Tachycardia
- Tachypnea

Medical Tests

- Blood test:
  - Elevated BUN
  - Elevated hemoglobin
  - Elevated hematocrit

Treatment

- Treat the underlying cause.
- Replace fluid orally or intravenously.

Interventions

- Monitor the vital signs.
- Monitor the intake and output.
- Assess the skin and mucus membranes.
- Instruct the patient:
  - To increase fluids in his or her diet
  - To increase mouth care

Solved Problems

12.1   What is hyponatremia?

Hyponatremia is a low amount of sodium in the blood.

12.2   What are underlying causes of hyponatremia?

The underlying causes of hyponatremia are diuretics, diarrhea, vomiting, hypothyroidism, water imbalance, renal failure, excess secretion of sodium, and intake of Ecstasy.

12.3   What are signs and symptoms of hyponatremia?

Signs and symptoms of hyponatremia are orthostatic hypotension, increased gastrointestinal motility, diarrhea, increased bowel sounds, nausea, decreased deep-tendon reflexes, muscle weakness, excessive activity, malaise, and altered level of consciousness.

12.4   What is the key test for hyponatremia?

The key test for hyponatremia is the test for blood sodium level (results would be <135 mEq/L).

12.5   What is a treatment for hyponatremia?

A treatment for hyponatremia is to administer saline solution intravenously.

12.6   What interventions should be taken with a patient who is diagnosed with hyponatremia?

The interventions that should be taken with a patient who is diagnosed with hyponatremia are water restriction, monitoring intake and output, monitor of the vital signs, and weighing the patient daily.

12.7   What are signs and symptoms of hypernatremia?

The signs and symptoms of hypernatremia are increased blood pressure, increased thirst, distended neck veins, muscle twitching, muscle weakness, restlessness, agitation, weight gain, and irritability.

12.8   What test result would you expect in a patient who is diagnosed with hypernatremia?

The test result expected in a patient who is diagnosed with hypernatremia is a blood sodium level of >145 mEq/L.

12.9   What treatment should be given to a patient with hypernatremia?

The treatment that should be given to a patient with hypernatremia is to administer intravenous (IV) hypotonic (0.225% sodium chloride, 0.33%, sodium chloride, or 0.45% sodium chloride) and diuretics (furosemide, bumetanide).

12.10   What can a patient do when diagnosed with hypernatremia?

When diagnosed with hypernatremia, a patient can decrease sodium in the diet.

12.11   What is hypocalcemia?

Hypocalcemia is an abnormally low level of calcium in the blood.

12.12   What can cause hypocalcemia?

The causes of hypocalcemia are endocrine disorder, excess loss of calcium related to renal disorder, alcoholism, burns, diuretics, vitamin D deficiency or malabsorption, sepsis, hyperphosphatemia, or decreased albumin.

12.13   What can happen to a patient who has hypocalcemia if it goes untreated?

If hypocalcemia goes untreated, a patient can experience cardiac arrhythmias and seizures.

12.14　What are the signs and symptoms of hypocalcemia?

The signs and symptoms of hypocalcemia are muscle spasm, cramping, tetany, Chvostek's sign (positive), Trousseau's sign (positive), irritability, abdominal pain, cardiac arrhythmias, and paresthesia of lips.

12.15　What blood test result would you expect to find in a patient who has hypocalcemia?

The blood test result expected in a patient who has hypocalcemia would be a calcium level that is <9 mg/dL.

12.16　What is the treatment for hypocalcemia?

The treatment for hypocalcemia is to administer vitamin D (ergocalciferol, vitamin D_2), IV calcium gluconate 10%, and IV calcium chloride.

12.17　What should a patient do who is diagnosed with hypocalcemia?

A patient diagnosed with hypocalcemia should consume a diet high in calcium, restrict the use of antacids, and avoid laxatives.

12.18　What can cause hypomagnesemia?

The causes of hypomagnesemia are vomiting, diarrhea, malnutrition, Crohn's disease, celiac disease, diuretics, renal disorder, aminoglycoside antibiotics, ascites, hyperglycemia, and chronic alcohol intake.

12.19　What is metabolic alkalosis?

Metabolic alkalosis is an arterial blood gas test with a pH >7.45, bicarbonate >28 mEq/L, and an elevated $Paco_2$.

12.20　What can cause metabolic acidosis?

The causes of metabolic acidosis are diabetic ketoacidosis, renal failure, diarrhea, seizure, fever, starvation, high alcohol intake, or excess intake of aspirin.

12.21　What can cause hypophosphatemia?

The causes of hypophosphatemia are corticosteroids, chronic obstructive pulmonary disease, diuretics, beta-adrenergic agonists, hyperparathyroidism, or vitamin D deficiency.

12.22　What can cause dehydration?

Dehydration can be caused by a shift of fluid from circulation to interstitial tissue, lack of hydration, or loss of fluid.

12.23　What are signs and symptoms of dehydration?

The signs and symptoms of dehydration are decreased urinary output, hypotension, poor skin turgor, increased thirst, tachycardia, and tachypnea.

12.24 What are the blood test results for dehydration?

The blood test results for dehydration are:

- Elevated BUN
- Elevated hemoglobin
- Elevated hematocrit

12.25 What is the treatment for dehydration?

The treatment for dehydration is to:

- Treat the underlying cause
- Replace fluid orally or through an IV

CHAPTER 13

Perioperative Period

13.1 Definition

Perioperative is the period from when the patient enters the health care facility for surgery until discharge. The perioperative period is divided into:

- Preoperative: Period before surgery
- Intraoperative: Period during surgery
- Postoperative: Period after surgery ending with recovery

Classification

Surgical procedures are classified based on:

- Risk: Risk of doing or not doing the surgery
- Urgency: Emergent (emergency), urgent (relatively soon), elective (patient's choice)
- Surgery location: Thoracic, heart, lung, vascular, and brain surgery have a high risk. Surgery on the extremities has a low risk.
- Extent of the surgery: Extensive surgeries pose a high risk because a longer duration of anesthesia is required that increases stress on the patient.
- Reason: Diagnostic (required to determine a diagnosis), restorative (restore function), curative (remove the disease), palliative (for comfort), or cosmetic (for aesthetics).
- Age: Surgery on elderly and very young patients is risky.
- Health: Surgery on a patient who has multiple comorbidities is risky.

13.2 Preoperative Period

The preoperative period is the period before surgery when the patient is physically and psychologically prepared for surgery. Patient receives vitamin B_{12}, vitamin C, folic acid, and iron supplements to increase red blood cell production.

Clearance

Assess the patient's health to determine medical risk of surgery.

- Assess:
  - Current health
  - Health history
  - Prior surgeries
  - Family history
  - Current medications
  - Allergies
  - Herbal supplements usage
  - Alcohol usage
  - Illegal drug usage
  - Smoking history
- Diagnostic studies:
  - Complete blood cell count (CBC): To identify infection, anemia, and risk for bleeding
  - Prothrombin time (PT)/partial thromboplastin time (PTT)/international normalized ratio (INR): To identify blood clotting status
  - Chemistry panel: To assess liver and renal function, electrolyte balance, and glucose level.
  - Urinalysis: To identify infection, glucose level and protein
  - Electrocardiogram (ECG): To identify cardiac abnormality
  - Chest X-ray: To identify pulmonary and cardiac abnormalities
  - Pulmonary function test: To identify pulmonary abnormalities

Informed Consent

Informed consent is a written agreement from the patient consenting to an invasive or dangerous procedure.

- The informed consent contains:
  - Type of surgery
  - Reason for surgery
  - Risk associated with the surgery
  - Benefits of undergoing the surgery
  - Types of alternative treatments
  - Benefits of alternative treatments
  - Risks of alternative treatments
  - Benefits of anesthesia
  - Risks of anesthesia
- Requirements:
  - Contents of the informed consent are explained to the patient by the physician.
  - Consent must be witnessed by the nurse or other responsible party.
  - Patient must be a competent adult and not medicated in such a way to alter the patient's ability to reason.

Teaching

- Explain to the patient and his or her family:
  - Preoperative routine
    - Medical clearance
    - Informed consent
    - Not allowed to eat or drink anything (NPO)
    - Insertion of intravenous (IV) lines
    - Insertion of tubes
    - Anesthesia
    - Timeline from admission to facility to surgery and recovery
    - Introduction to health care providers who will visit the patient before surgery
    - How to use the incentive spirometer
    - Discharge plan and follow-up care
    - Scarring
    - Dressing care
    - Pain and pain medication
    - Preoperative skin preparation including removal of hair
    - Bowel preparation
  - Surgical procedures
    - Experience of being transported to surgery
    - Type of incision
    - Reason for surgery
    - Duration of surgery
    - Where family members can wait during the surgery
    - When family members will know the results of the surgery
    - When family members can visit the patient
  - Postoperative routine
    - Drains
    - Tubes
    - IV
    - Anesthetic side effect
    - Timeline from recovery to discharge
    - When the patient will be expected to return to normal urination and bowel movement
    - How to use the incentive spirometer
    - Discharge plan and follow-up care
    - When and how to return to normal activities of daily living
    - Dressing care
    - Scarring
    - Pain and pain medication

- NPO until gag reflex returns and bowl sounds return
- Step up diet
- Administering medication for existing conditions (i.e., diabetes)
- How to use patient-controlled analgesia (PCA) for pain management

Transfer

Move the patient from his or her room or the preoperative area to surgery.

- Be sure to:
  - Verify patient's identity
  - Verify informed consent has been signed
  - Verify preoperative skin preparation is completed
  - Verify markings on surgery site
  - Verify preoperative lab tests are completed
  - Ensure that the patient's chart accompanies the patient to surgery
  - Ensure that supplies needed for surgery (i.e., fresh frozen plasma) accompany the patient to surgery
  - Reassure the patient about the surgery by explaining what it is and what will be taking place
  - Explain to the patient where he or she will be moved to after the surgery (i.e., recovery room and then back to the patient's room).
  - Introduce the patient to each staff member involved in the transfer
  - Assist the patient transferring from the bed to the gurney
  - Make sure that the patient is properly covered during transportation both for comfort and modesty

13.3   Intraoperative Period

The intraoperative period is the time during the surgical procedure.
- Dress according to asepsis protocol:
  - Scrub suits
  - Surgical cap
  - Shoe cover
- Surgical team:
  - Surgeon: The health care provider who performs the surgery
  - Surgical assistant: Another surgeon, surgical resident, physician assistant, or registered nurse (RN) first assistant
  - Anesthesiologist: A physician or certified RN anesthetist (CRNA) who administers anesthesia and monitors the patient's vital signs during the surgery
  - Circulating nurse: An RN who prepares the operating table, positions the patient, ensures surgical supplies are available, ensures that diagnostic studies are completed, ensures that the patient's skin is prepared, advocates for the patient, and counts sponges and instruments before, during, and after surgery

- o Scrub nurse/surgical tech: Drapes the patient, gathers instruments for the surgery, hands the surgeon instruments during the surgery, and counts sponges and instruments before, during, and after surgery

  o Holding area nurse: Receives the patient from the floor nurse and cares for the patient in the holding area before the patient is taken into surgery

- Surgical routine:

  o Surgical team member applies face mask or goggles before entering the surgery.

  o Surgical team members scrub (i.e., clean) from the fingertips to 2 in. above the elbow before entering the surgery. The skin is clean and not sterile.

  o The skin is dried with a sterile towel.

  o Sterile gown and gloves are applied in the surgery by the circulating nurse to the surgical team. The front of the gown is sterile from 2 in. below the neck to the waist and from the elbow to the wrist.

- Risk:

  o Positioning the patient for maximal access to operative site can form pressure ulcers over bony prominences and nerve damage. Padding is used to decrease pressure on the patient's skin.

  o The patient can lose heat during surgery because of the cool temperature in the surgery related to the higher air exchange rate in the room and the patient's lack of clothes and exposure caused by the surgical incision. Warmers are used to maintain the patient's body temperature.

- Closure:

  o The incision is closed with absorbable or nonabsorbable (removed during postoperative period) sutures, skin closure tape, or staples.

  o Drain tubes are inserted into the wound before the wound in closed to drain the wound during the postoperative period. The drainage occurs either through gravity or a self-suctioning ball. The drain site is covered with sterile dressing.

- Anesthesia:

  o General anesthesia: The patient is unconscious and unable to breathe. The patient is intubated and mechanically ventilated during the surgery.

  o Regional anesthesia:

    - Nerve block: An anesthetic agent is injected into a nerve bundle, blocking nerve impulses.

    - Epidural: An anesthetic agent is injected into the epidural space surrounding the lower lumbar area of the spinal column, resulting in a nerve blockage affecting the area of the body supplied by these nerves.

13.4 Postoperative Period

The postoperative period is the period immediately after the operative period.

- Postanesthesia care unit (PACU): The patient is transferred to the PACU once he or she is stabilized after surgery. The patient remains in the PACU until he or she regains consciousness, regains the gag reflex, and is stabilized. Patients who are unable to be stabilized are transferred to the intensive care unit (ICU).

- Assessment:

  o Airway

  o Breathing

- o Circulation
- o Pulse oximeter
- o Signs of edema
- o Signs of bronchospasm
- o Vital signs every 15 minutes
- o Wound for drainage and bleeding
- o Drains for patency and output
- o Level of consciousness
- Progression of return to consciousness:
  - o Muscular irritability
  - o Restlessness
  - o Pain recognition
  - o Reasoning returns
  - o Ability to control behavior
  - o Pupil response bilaterally equal response to light
  - o Purposeful response to painful stimuli
  - o Purposeful response to commands
- Pain management:
  - o Begins when patient has purposeful response to commands
  - o Assess patient's level of pain
  - o Fully conscious patient can respond to pain scale
  - o Semiconscious patient: Elevated pulse, elevated blood pressure, moaning, changes in movement
- Assess gastrointestinal state:
  - o Nausea (reaction to anesthesia)
  - o Vomiting (reaction to anesthesia)
  - o Abdominal distention
  - o Presence of bowel sounds
  - o Monitor drainage from nasogastric tube
- Assess lab results:
  - o Hemoglobin
  - o Hematocrit
  - o Electrolytes
  - o Arterial blood gas (ABG)

13.5   Cardiovascular Complications

Cardiovascular complications result from:

- Physiologic stress related to surgery
- Preexisting medical conditions

- Effects of anesthesia
- Hypotension
- Myocardial infarction (MI)
- Cardiac arrhythmias
- Deep-vein thrombosis (DVT) related to decreased mobility

Signs and Symptoms

- Lower-extremity pain (DVT)
- Shortness of breath
- Hypotension
- Dizziness
- Chest pain
- Pain radiates to back, neck, jaw, or arm
- Palpitations
- Cardiac arrhythmias
- Lower-extremity edema (DVT)

Medical Tests

- Decreased blood pressure
- ECG:
  - Elevated ST wave
  - Inverted T wave
  - Rhythm: arrhythmia
- Doppler ultrasound: Positive blood clot in extremities
- Blood test:
  - Elevated troponin

Treatment

- Administer (if needed):
  - Anticoagulants
    - Heparin, lovenox, warfarin

Intervention

- Monitor the vital signs.
- Monitor cardiovascular status.
- Assess for peripheral edema.
- Assess for DVT.
- Administer elastic stocking.

- Instruct the patient:
  - Sit on the side of bed side for 2 minutes before standing.
  - Ambulate as soon as permitted.
  - Perform leg exercises while in bed.

13.6   Respiratory Complications

Decreased mobility and pain medication lead to:

- Decreased diaphragmatic movement
- Decreased gas exchange
- Collapse of alveolar sacs
- Atelectasis
- Reduce respiratory drive
- Increased respiratory secretions
- Decreased airflow into lungs
- Increased inflammatory process
- Pneumonia
- Pulmonary embolism

Signs and Symptoms

- Sudden shortness of breath and sudden chest pain (pulmonary embolism)
- Productive cough (pneumonia)
- Fever (infection)
- Shortness of breath (decreased oxygenation)
- Chest pain (atelectasis)
- Decrease pulse oximetry (decreased oxygenation)

Medical Tests

- Pulse oximetry: Shows decreased oxygenation
- Chest X-ray: Shows collapsed lung, infiltrate (pneumonia), or wedge infiltrate (pulmonary embolism)
- Computed tomography (CT) scan: Shows collapsed lung, infiltrate (pneumonia)
- Spiral CT: Shows pulmonary embolism
- Helical CT: Shows pulmonary embolism
- Blood test:
  - White blood cell (WBC) count: Elevated (bacterial pneumonia)

Treatment

- Administer:
  - Antibiotics (pneumonia)

- Macrolides, fluoroquinolones
  - Anticoagulants (pulmonary embolism)
    - Heparin, Lovenox, warfarin

Intervention

- Administer oxygen.
- Monitor the vital signs.
- Monitor respiratory status.
- Monitor pulse oximeter level.
- Instruct the patient:
  - To cough and perform deep breathing exercises
  - To use incentive spirometer
  - To ambulate as soon as permitted

13.7 Infection

Disruption of the skin during surgery interrupts the body's first line of defense against infection, exposing the body to microorganisms resulting in an inflammatory response. This includes:

- Bacteria called flora is on the skin surface entering the wound during healing.
- Nosocomial infection is caused by bacteria transmitted throughout the health care facility.

Signs and Symptoms

- Fever
- Redness at wound site
- Change in color and odor of drainage
- Pain
- Swelling caused by inflammation

Medical Tests

- Blood test:
  - Elevated WBCs count
  - Elevated erythrocyte sedimentation rate
- Culture and sensitivity test: Identifies microorganisms and which medication to be used for treatment

Treatment

- Administer:
  - Antibiotics according to results of the sensitivity test

Intervention

- Monitor the vital signs.
- Assess the wound.
- Assess the pain.
- Instruct the patient:
  - To keep the wound site clean and dry
  - To change the dressing per instructions

13.8 Gastrointestinal Complications

Motility of the gastrointestinal tract is reduced because of anesthesia and pain medication. Medications can act on the chemoreceptor trigger zone, located within the medulla. The patient may experience:

- Nausea from anesthesia and pain medication
- Vomiting from anesthesia and pain medication and direct visceral afferent stimulation
- Constipation resulting from slowing of peristaltic activity
- Paralytic ileus (paralysis of the intestinal muscles)

Signs and Symptoms

- Nausea
- Vomiting
- Abdominal distention (paralytic ileus)
- Reduced bowel sounds (constipation)
- No bowel sounds (paralytic ileus)

Medical Tests

- Abdominal X-ray: Shows stool (constipation) or gas-filled intestine (paralytic ileus)

Treatment

- Administer:
  - Antiemetics for vomiting
  - Total parenteral nutrition to maintain nutrition
- Nasogastric (NG) tube to suction (paralytic ileus)

Intervention

- Monitor the vital signs.
- Monitor for flatus and bowel movement.
- Assess the abdomen.
- Assess for dehydration.

- Do not allow oral intake (because of paralytic ileus, nausea, and vomiting).
- Monitor the intake and output.
- Monitor secretions drained from the NG tube.
- Instruct the patient:
  - To intake no fluid or food until the he or she passes flatus or has a bowel movement and nausea and vomiting stop.

Solved Problems

13.1   What is the preoperative period?

The preoperative period is the period before surgery.

13.2   What is the intraoperative period?

The intraoperative period is the period during surgery.

13.3   What is the postoperative period?

The postoperative period is the period after surgery, ending with recovery.

13.4   What is the perioperative period?

The perioperative period is the period from when the patient enters the health care facility for surgery until discharge.

13.5   How are surgical procedures classified?

Surgical procedures are classified by:

- Risk: Risk of doing or not doing the surgery
- Urgency: Emergent (emergency), urgent (relatively soon), elective (patient's choice)
- Surgery location: Thoracic, heart, lung, vascular, and brain surgery have a high risk. Surgery on extremities has a low risk.
- Extent of the surgery: Extensive surgeries pose high risk because a longer duration of anesthesia is required that increases the stress on the patient.
- Reason: Diagnostic (required to determine a diagnosis), restorative (restore function), curative (remove the disease), palliative (for comfort), or cosmetic (for aesthetics).
- Age: Surgery on elderly and very young patients is risky.
- Health: Surgery on a patient who has multiple comorbidities is risky.

13.6   What are reasons for performing surgery?

The reasons for performing surgery are diagnostic (required to determine a diagnosis), restorative (to restore function), curative (to remove the disease), palliative (for comfort), or cosmetic (for aesthetics).

13.7   What is the urgency of surgery?

The urgency of surgery is emergent (emergency), urgent (relatively soon), or elective (patient's choice).

13.8   What is the goal of the preoperative period?

The goal of the preoperative period is that the patient is physically and psychologically prepared for surgery.

13.9   What is medical clearance?

Medical clearance is an assessment of the patient's health to determine the medical risk of surgery.

13.10   What is assessed in clearance?

The items assessed in clearance are current health, health history, prior surgeries, family history, current medications, allergies, herbal supplements use, alcohol use, illegal drug use, and smoking history.

13.11   What are some diagnostic studies performed during the clearance?

Some diagnostic studies performed during the clearance are:

- CBC: To identify infection, anemia, and risk for bleeding
- PT/INR/PTT: To identify blood clotting status
- Chemistry panel: To assess liver and renal function, electrolyte balance, and glucose level
- Urinalysis: To identify infection, glucose level, and protein
- ECG: To identify cardiac abnormality
- Chest X-ray: To identify pulmonary and cardiac abnormalities
- Pulmonary function test: To identify pulmonary abnormalities

13.12   What is informed consent?

Informed consent is a written agreement from the patient consenting to an invasive or risky procedure.

13.13   What is contained in an informed consent?

The items contained in an informed consent are type of surgery, reason for surgery, risk associated with the surgery, benefits of undergoing the surgery, types of alternative treatments, benefits of alternative treatments, risks of alternative treatments, benefits of anesthesia, and risks of anesthesia.

13.14   What are the requirements of an informed consent?

The requirements of an informed consent are:

- Contents of the informed consent are explained to the patient by the physician.
- Consent is witnessed by a nurse or other responsible party.
- Patient must be a competent adult and not medicated in such a way to alter his or her ability to reason.

13.15   What preoperative routine would a health care provider teach a patient?

The preoperative routine that a health care provider would teach a patient is medical clearance, informed consent, NPO, insertion of IVs, insertion of tubes, anesthesia, timeline from admission to facility to surgery and recovery, introduction to health care providers who will visit the patient before surgery, how to use the incentive spirometer, discharge plan and follow-up care, scarring, dressing care, pain and pain medication, preoperative skin preparation (including removal of hair), and bowel preparation.

13.16 What preoperative surgical procedures would a health care provider teach the patient?

The preoperative surgical procedures that a health care provider would teach the patient are the experience of being transported to surgery, type of incision, reason for surgery, duration of surgery, where family members can wait during the surgery, when family members will know the results of the surgery, and when family members can visit the patient.

13.17 What should be done when transferring the patient to surgery?
- Verify patient's identity.
- Verify informed consent has been signed.
- Verify preoperative skin preparation is completed.
- Verify markings on surgery site.
- Verify preoperative labs are completed.
- Ensure that the patient's chart accompanies the patient to surgery.
- Be sure to include supplies needed for surgery (i.e., fresh frozen plasma) accompanies the patient to surgery.
- Reassure the patient about the surgery by explaining what it is and what will be taking place.
- Explain to the patient where he or she will be moved to after the surgery (i.e., recovery room and then back to the patient's room.)
- Introduce the patient to each staff member involved in the transfer.
- Assist the patient to transfer from the bed to the gurney.
- Make sure that the patient is properly covered during transportation for both comfort and modesty.

13.18 Who are members of the surgical team?

Members of the surgical team are the:
- Surgeon: The health care provider who performs the surgery
- Surgical assistant: Another surgeon, surgical resident, physician assistant, or RN first assistant
- Anesthesiologist: A physician or certified RN anesthetist (CRNA) who administers anesthesia and monitors the patient's vital signs during the surgery
- Circulating nurse: An RN who prepares the operating table, positions the patient, ensures surgical supplies are available, ensures diagnostic studies are completed, ensures the patient's skin is prepared, advocates for the patient, and counts sponges and instruments before, during, and after surgery
- Scrub nurse/surgical tech: Drapes the patient, gather instruments for the surgery, hands the surgeon instruments during the surgery, and counts sponges and instruments before, during, and after surgery
- Holding area nurse: Receives the patient from the floor nurse and cares for the patient in the holding area before the patient is taken into surgery

13.19 What are two common risks that a patient is exposed to during surgery?
- Positioning the patient for maximal access to operative site can form pressure ulcers over bony prominences and nerve damage. Padding is used to decrease pressure on the patient's skin.
- The patient can lose heat during surgery because of the cool temperature in the surgery related to the higher air exchange rate in the room and the patient's lack of clothes and exposure caused by the surgical incision. Warmers are used to maintain the patient's body temperature.

13.20   What is general anesthesia?

The patient is unconscious and unable to breathe. The patient is intubated and mechanically ventilated during the surgery.

13.21   What is a nerve block?

In a nerve block, an anesthetic agent is injected into a nerve bundle, blocking nerve impulses.

13.22   What is a PACU?

A PACU is a place where the patient is transferred once he or she is stabilized after surgery. The patient remains in the PACU until he or she regains consciousness, regains the gag reflex, and is stabilized. Patients who are unable to be stabilized are transferred to the ICU.

13.23   What assessments are performed in the PACU?

Assessments performed in the PACU are airway, breathing, circulation, pulse oximetry, signs of edema, signs of bronchospasm, vital signs every 15 minutes, wound for drainage and bleeding, drains for patency and output, and level of consciousness.

13.24   What are gastrointestinal complications?

Motility of the gastrointestinal tract is reduced, resulting from anesthesia and pain medication. Medications can act on the chemoreceptor trigger zone, located within the medulla.

CHAPTER 14

Mental Health

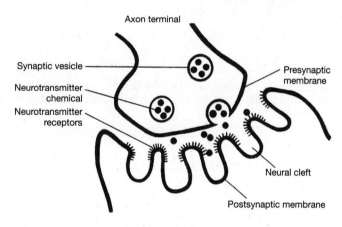

Figure 14.1

14.1   Definition

Mental health is a level of cognitive and emotional well-being, impulse control, through processes, and behavior based on the patient's age, social situation, culture, and environment. A mental health disorder is a disruption of a person's cognitive and emotional well-being at times caused by a chemical imbalance in the brain. Medical-surgical patients can have a mental health disorder comorbidly.

Mental health is assessed through a patient's history and current presentation. No laboratory or imaging tests are available to diagnose a mental disorder. Initial signs of a mental disorder are:

- Delusion
- Suicidal ideation
- Paranoid ideation
- Bizarre behavior
- Anxiety
- Depression
- Manic ideation
- Impaired judgment
- Self-neglect
- Low self-esteem
- Somatic complaints

Neurotransmitters

Neurons are nerve cells that transmit impulses to other neurons and muscles, glands, and other cells within the body. The junction between a neuron and another cell is called a *chemical synapse*. The space between the neuron and another cell is called the *synapse*.

An impulse is transmitted across the synapse when the neuron releases a neurotransmitter into the synapse. The receiving cell contains receptors designed to accept a specific neurotransmitter. Once the neurotransmitter is received, the reuptake pump sends the neurotransmitter back to the transmitting neuron.

Neurotransmitters care categorized into systems. These are:

- Noradrenaline: Arousal and reward
- Dopamine: Motor system, reward, cognition, endocrine, nausea
- Serotonin: Mood, emotion, satiety, body temperature, and sleep
- Cholinergic: Learning, short-term memory, arousal, reward

14.2 Anxiety

Anxiety is an unnatural and uncontrollable state of nervousness that can lead to a panic attack or compulsive behavior. Symptoms of anxiety occur when there are more neurotransmitter receptor sites than there are neurotransmitters.

Signs and Symptoms

- Restlessness
- Irritability
- Sleep disruption
- Fear
- Decreased concentration
- Headache
- Fatigue
- Palpitations
- Hypertension
- Tachycardia
- Tremors
- Sweating

Medical Tests

- Normal medical tests

Treatment

- Administer:
  - Anxiolytics
    - Alprazolam, clonazepam, clorazepate, diazepam, lorazepam, oxazepam, buspirone

Interventions

- Monitor the vital signs.
- Monitor the weight.
- Monitor sleep.
- Group therapy
- Family therapy
- Emotive therapy
- Psychotherapy
- Cognitive-behavioral therapy
- Relaxation techniques such as biofeedback
- Desensitization
- Instruct the patient:
    - To avoid alcohol

14.3 Panic Disorder

Panic disorder is increased anxiety with pronounced physical symptoms that has sudden onset and no predictable pattern, resulting in the patient restricting activities of daily living in anticipation of onset of an attack. There is a high risk of self-medication with alcohol and a risk of dependence on tranquilizers.

Signs and Symptoms

- Sense of doom
- Fear of losing control
- Dyspnea
- Palpitations
- Tachycardia
- Chest pain
- Diaphoresis
- Numbness
- Depersonalization

Medical Tests

- Normal medical tests

Treatment

- Administer:
    - Antidepressants:
        - Selective serotonin reuptake inhibitors (SSRIs)
        - Tricyclics
        - Monoamine oxidase inhibitors

  o Benzodiazepines
    ▪ Clonazepam, alprazolam, lorazepam

Interventions

- Monitor the vital signs.
- Provide reassurance.
- Provide a quiet environment.
- Cognitive-behavioral therapy
- Relaxation therapy
- Instruct the patient:
  o To focus on calming activities (i.e., hobbies, walks) at first sign of a panic attack and that the panic attack will pass within a few minutes

14.4   Depressive Disorder

A decrease in serotonin results in an increase in depression, leading to loss of interest in normal activities of daily living and an increased risk of suicide. The patient is unable to recover from depression without medication. Depressive disorder is different from a depressed mood that occurs as a result of psychosocial stressors such as a death or loss of job in that a depressed mood is relatively short and the patient can maintain activities of daily during the depressed mood.

Signs and Symptoms

- Hopelessness
- Anhedonia
- Isolation
- Decreased concentration
- Suicidal ideation
- Increased or decreased sleeping
- Increased or decreased eating
- Indecision

Medical Tests

- Normal medical tests

Treatment

- Administer:
  o Antidepressant
    ▪ SSRIs, venlafaxine, nefazodone, bupropion, mirtazapine, tricyclics, monoamine oxidase inhibitors
- Electroconvulsant therapy (ECT)

Interventions

- Develop trust with the patient.
- Monitor for suicidal ideation.
- Constantly observe the patient for suicidal ideation.
- Monitor the patient closely for risky behavior.
- Monitor the vital signs.
- Perform cognitive-behavioral therapy.
- Perform psychotherapy.
- Instruct the patient:
  - About the importance of restful sleep
  - Assure that medication can restore the patient to normal activities of daily living

14.5   Bipolar Disorder

Bipolar disorder is alternating episodes of clinical depression and mania.

- Classification:
  - Bipolar I: One manic disruption of activities of daily life and one depressive episode
  - Bipolar II: One hypomanic episode and one depressive episode
  - Bipolar not otherwise specified (NOS): Bipolar features without recent episodes

Signs and Symptoms

- Hopelessness
- Anhedonia
- Isolation
- Decreased concentration
- Suicidal ideation
- Increased or decreased sleeping
- Increased or decreased eating
- Indecision
- Hyperactivity
- Rapid speech
- Grandiosity
- Increased irritability
- Flight of ideas
- Easily distracted

Medical Tests

- Normal medical tests

Treatment

- Administer:
  - Mood stabilizers
    - Lithium, valproic acid, carbamazepine, lamotrigine
  - Antipsychotic medications
    - Olanzapine, risperidone, aripiprazole
- Psychotherapy
- Assess suicide risk
- Antidepressants

Interventions

- Develop trust with the patient.
- Monitor for suicidal ideation.
- Constantly observe the patient for suicidal ideation.
- Monitor the patient closely for risky behavior.
- Monitor the vital signs.
- Instruct the patient:
  - About the importance of restful sleep
  - That medication can restore the patient to the normal activities of daily living
  - About the importance of taking medication even when feeling good

14.6   Schizophrenia

Schizophrenia is a loss of contact with reality (psychosis), false perceptions (hallucinations), false beliefs (delusions), impaired reasoning (cognitive deficits), restricted range of emotions (flattened affect), and disorganized behavior for >6 months.

Signs and Symptoms

- Psychosis
- Hallucinations
- Delusions
- Flat affect
- Disorganized thought process
- Cognitive deficits

Medical Tests

- Normal medical tests

Treatment

- Administer:
  - o Antipsychotic medications
- Clozapine, aripiprazole, ziprasidone, loxapine, risperidone, olanzapine, quetiapine, thiothixene

Interventions

- Structured environment
- Psychotherapy
- Behavioral therapy
- Instruct the patient:
  - o About the importance of taking medication even when feeling good

14.7   Anorexia Nervosa

Anorexia nervosa is an alteration in normal eating behavior resulting from fear of gaining weight, leading to caloric restrictions. There is a risk of renal dysfunction and cardiovascular disorder.

Signs and Symptoms

- Amenorrhea
- Oligomenorrhea
- Abnormal eating behaviors
- Decreased body weight
- Dental caries
- Gastrointestinal abnormalities
- Hypotension
- Electrolyte imbalances
- Temporal wasting
- Disturbed self-perception

Medical Tests

- Blood test:
  - o Decreased red blood cells (RBCs)
  - o Decreased calcium
  - o Decreased magnesium
  - o Decreased phosphorus
  - o Increased blood urea nitrogen (BUN)
  - o Normal thyroid-stimulating hormone (TSH)
  - o Normal follicle-stimulating hormone (FSH)

- o Normal luteinizing hormone (LH)
- o Abnormal electrolytes
- o Increased amylase
- o Normal lipase

Treatment

- Administer:
    - o Antidepressant medications
        - SSRI

Interventions

- Monitor the vital signs.
- Monitor the intake and output.
- Monitor the weight.
- Perform psychotherapy.
- Perform cognitive-behavioral therapy.
- Instruct the patient:
    - o To focus attention away from food and body image

14.8   Bulimia Nervosa

Alteration in normal eating behavior leading to binge eating then purging to prevent weight gain. The patient prevents weight gain by excessive exercise, fasting, enemas, diuretic, and self-induced vomiting.

Signs and Symptoms

- Binge eating
- Excessive exercising
- Fasting
- Self-induced vomiting
- Laxative dependency
- Callous formation on knuckles
- Amenorrhea
- Oligomenorrhea
- Gastrointestinal disturbances
- Erosion of enamel on teeth

Medical Tests

- Blood test:
    - o Decreased calcium

- o   Decreased magnesium
- o   Decreased phosphorus
- o   Increased BUN
- o   Abnormal electrolytes
- o   Increased amylase
- o   Normal lipase

Treatment

- Administer:
  - o   Antidepressant medications
    - ▪ SSRI

Interventions

- Monitor the vital signs.
- Monitor the weight.
- Monitor the intake and output.
- Perform psychotherapy.
- Perform cognitive-behavioral therapy.
- Instruct the patient:
  - o   To focus attention away from food and body image

14.9   Delirium

Delirium is a debilitating disturbance in cognitive function caused by disruption of neurons in the cerebral cortex by disease or a chemical, leading to the patient losing the ability to focus attention and developing abnormal perceptions that can result in abnormal behavior.

Signs and Symptoms

- Disorientation
- Confusion
- Inappropriate behavior

Medical Tests

- Blood test:
  - o   Increased white blood cells WBCs
  - o   Abnormal glucose
  - o   Abnormal electrolytes
- Electrocardiography (ECG): Shows myocardial ischemia or infarction
- Computed tomography (CT) scan: Shows ischemia in brain
- Electroencephalography (EEG): Shows slowing

Treatment

- Treat the underlying cause.

Interventions

- Monitor the neurological status.
- Monitor the vital signs.
- Administer oxygen.
- Protect the patient from injury.
- Instruct the patient:
  - That delirium will normally resolve once the underlying cause is treated

Solved Problems

14.1 **What is mental health?**

Mental health is a level of cognitive and emotional well-being, impulse control, thought processes, and behavior based on the patient's age and social, cultural, and environmental status.

14.2 **Why are mental health disorders difficult to diagnose?**

Mental health disorders are difficult to diagnose because there are no laboratory or imaging tests available to diagnose a mental disorder.

14.3 **What are initial signs of mental health disorders?**

Initial signs of mental health disorders are delusion, suicidal ideation, paranoid ideation, bizarre behavior, anxiety, depression, mania, impaired judgment, self-neglect, low self-esteem, or somatic complaints.

14.4 **What is a neurotransmitter?**

A neurotransmitter is a chemical messenger that transmits an impulse across a synapse.

14.5 **What does the dopamine neurotransmitter system control?**

The dopamine neurotransmitter system controls the motor, reward, cognitive, and endocrine systems as well as nausea.

14.6 **What does the serotonin neurotransmitter system control?**

The serotonin neurotransmitter system controls mood, emotion, satiety, body temperature, and sleep.

14.7 **What does the cholinergic neurotransmitter system control?**

The cholinergic neurotransmitter system controls learning, short-term memory, arousal, and reward.

14.8 **What does the noradrenaline neurotransmitter system control?**

The noradrenaline neurotransmitter system controls arousal and reward.

14.9   What is anxiety?

Anxiety is an unnatural and uncontrollable state of nervousness that can lead to a panic attack or compulsive behavior.

14.10   What causes the symptoms of anxiety?

The symptoms of anxiety occur when there are more neurotransmitter receptor sites than there are neurotransmitters.

14.11   What are the symptoms of anxiety?

The symptoms of anxiety are restlessness, irritability, sleep disruption, fear, decreased concentration, headache, fatigue, palpitations, hypertension, tachycardia, tremors, and sweating.

14.12   What medications are prescribed for anxiety?

Anxiolytics (e.g., alprazolam, clonazepam, clorazepate, diazepam, lorazepam, oxazepam, and buspirone) are prescribed for anxiety.

14.13   What should a health care provider tell a patient who has anxiety?

A health care provider should tell a patient who has anxiety to avoid alcohol.

14.14   What is panic disorder?

Panic disorder is increased anxiety with pronounced physical symptoms that has sudden onset and no predictable pattern, resulting in the patient restricting activities of daily living in anticipation of onset of an attack.

14.15   What are the risks to a patient diagnosed with panic disorder?

The risks of a patient diagnosed with panic disorder are high risk of self-medication with alcohol and a risk of dependency on tranquilizers.

14.16   What are the signs and symptoms of a panic disorder?

The signs and symptoms of a panic disorder are sense of doom, fear of losing control, dyspnea, palpitations, tachycardia, chest pain, diaphoresis, numbness, and depersonalization.

14.17   What should a health care provider instruct a patient who has a panic attack?

A health care provider should instruct a patient who has had a panic attack to focus on calming activities (i.e., hobbies, walks) at the first sign of a panic attack and that the panic attack will pass within a few minutes.

14.18   What medications are prescribed for a patient who has a panic attack?

The medications that are prescribed for a patient who has a panic attack are antidepressants (SSRIs, tricyclics, monoamine oxidase inhibitors) and benzodiazepines (clonazepam, alprazolam, lorazepam).

14.19   What is depressive disorder?

Depressive disorder is a loss of interest in normal activities of daily living and an increased risk of suicide. The patient is unable to recover from depression without medication.

14.20   What causes depressive disorder?

Decrease in serotonin results in increased depression.

14.21   What is a depressive mood?

Depressive disorder is different from a depressed mood that occurs as a result of psychosocial stressors such as a death or loss of job. A depressed mood is relatively short and the patient can maintain activities of daily living during the depressed mood.

14.22   What are the signs of a depressive disorder?

The signs of a depressive disorder are hopelessness, anhedonia, isolation, decreased concentration, suicidal ideation, increased or decreased sleeping, increased or decreased eating, and indecision.

14.23   What is bipolar disorder?

Bipolar disorder is alternating episodes of clinical depression and mania.

14.24   What is delirium?

Delirium is a debilitating disturbance in cognitive function caused by disruption of neurons in the cerebral cortex by disease or a chemical, leading to the patient losing the ability to focus attention. The patient develops abnormal perceptions that can result in abnormal behavior.

14.25   What is bulimia nervosa?

Bulimia nervosa is an alteration in the normal eating behavior leading to binge eating and then purging to prevent weight gain. The patient prevents weight gain by excessive exercise, fasting, enemas, diuretics, and self-induced vomiting.

CHAPTER 15

Oncology

15.1 Definition

Oncology is the area of medicine that studies and treats cancer. Cancer is a disease in which abnormal cells grow uncontrollably, invading and destroying normal tissues and sometimes metastasizing throughout the body.

15.2 Normal Cell Proliferation

- Normal cells undergo the cell cycle in which the new cell is produced, grows, degenerates, and dies.
- New cells are generated when existing cells die.
- New cells are considered immature and undifferentiated, which means the new cells can become any type of cell. These are known as *stem cells*.
- New cells become differentiated when the new cell matures, which means the new cells have become a specific type of cell.
- Proto-oncogenes regulate cell growth.
- A new cell continues to grow until the boundary of the other cell is contacted, causing the new cell to stop growing. The new cell is then considered to be in the mature state.

Cancer Cell Proliferation

- Cancer cells are abnormal cells in which growth is unregulated.
- They do not stop growing when in contact with other cells.
- They will grow on top and between normal cells.
- They divide indiscriminately, sometimes producing two cells at the same time.
- They proliferate at the rate of normal cells from the same tissue where it originated, which is why some cancer cells proliferate slower or faster than other cancer cells.
- An abnormal growth of cells is called a neoplasia, commonly called a *tumor*.
- Neoplasia comprises both benign and malignant tumors.
- It is not clear what causes the unregulated growth of abnormal cells, which is why it is difficult to develop a cure for cancer.

15.3   Causes of Cancer

- Carcinogen: An agent that disables proto-oncogenes, enabling the cell to continue to grow
- Oncogenes: Genes present in the cell that enable the cell to continue to grow
- Oncogenic virus: A virus that either disables the proto-oncogenes or introduces the oncogenes

Carcinogenesis (Etiology)

The cause of cancer is unknown, but there are current theories:

- Environmental factors:
  o More than 80% of cancers are related to environmental carcinogens
- Types:
  o Physical:
    ▪ Radiation: X-rays, radium, nuclear explosion or waste, ultraviolet
    ▪ Trauma or chronic irritation
  o Chemical:
    ▪ Nitrites and food additives, polycyclic hydrocarbons, dyes, alkylating agents
    ▪ Drugs: Arsenicals, stilbestrol, urethane
    ▪ Cigarette smoke
    ▪ Hormones
  o Genetic:
    ▪ May be caused by inherited genetic defects
- Viral theory:
  o Oncoviruses: RNA-type viruses
  o Human T-cell leukemia virus type I (HTLV-I)
  o Epstein-Barr
  o Human papilloma virus (HPV)
- Immunologic factors:
  o The immune system fails to kill cancer cells

15.4   Cell Dysfunctions

Defective Cellular Proliferation (Growth)

- Stem cells mutate, causing the proto-oncogenes to become dysfunctional.
- The growth rate of cells increases.
- The survival time of cells increases.
- Cancer cells grow on top of each other, forming tumors.
- Double time: A measurement of the time necessary for a tumor to double in size.

Defective Cellular Differentiation

- Stem cells can become any type of cell.

- A stem cell is an undifferentiated cell and can mature to become any type of cell.
- *Anaplastic* means an undifferentiated cell.
- *Differentiation* is the degree from which a cancer cell is different from its originating cell.
- Cancer cells appear as fetal cells.
- A fetus has carcinoembryonic antigen (CEA) and alpha-fetoprotein (AFP).
- CEA and AFP stop producing shortly before birth.
- A fetus has CEA and AFP, which are present in the blood of cancer patients.

Spread (Metastasis)

- Normal cells bind together.
- Cancer cells lack adhesion to bind together.
- Lack of adhesion enables cancer cells to spread to other locations in the body.

15.5 Metastases

Common Sites of Metastases

- **Breast cancer** metastases to bone and lung
- **Lung cancer** metastases to brain
- **Colorectal cancer** metastases to liver
- **Prostate cancer** metastases to bone, spine, and legs
- **Brain tumors** metastases to the central nervous system

Routes of Metastasis

- Local seeding: Distribution occurs in the local area of the primary tumor.
- Blood-borne: Distribution is by blood.
- Lymphatic spread: Primary sites area rich in lymphatics.

15.6 Cancer Classification

- Neoplasm: Abnormal mass of tissue that results from excessive cell division

Clinical Evidence

- 1-cm tumor: Palpable and contains one billion cancer cells
- 0.5-cm tumor: Smallest tumor detected with magnetic resonance imaging (MRI)

Cancer Is Classified by Anatomic Site (Table 15.1)

- Benign (not cancerous):
  - Encapsulated
  - Does not metastasize
  - Does not recur

TABLE 15.1 Anatomic Site Classification of Cancer

SITE	BENIGN	MALIGNANT
Epithelial tissue	-oma	-carcinoma
Surface	Papilloma	Carcinoma
Glandular	Adenoma	Adenocarcinoma
Connective tissue	-oma	-sarcoma
Fibrous	Fibroma	Fibrosarcoma
Cartilage	Chondroma	Chondrosarcoma
Striated muscle	Rhabdomyoma	Rhabdomyosarcoma
Bone	Osteoma	Osteosarcoma
Nerve tissue	-oma	-oma
Meninges	Meningioma	Meningeal sarcoma
Nerve cells	Ganglioneuroma	Neuroblastoma
Hematopoietic tissues		
Lymphoid tissue		Hodgkin's disease, non-Hodgkin's lymphoma
Plasma cell		Multiple myeloma
Bone marrow		Lymphocytic and myelogenous leukemia

- o Normal cells
- o Grows by expansion
- o Differentiated: Reaches its specialized cell form
- o Vascularity (blood supply): Does not have its own blood supply
- Malignant (cancerous):
  - o Not encapsulated
  - o Does metastasize
  - o Does recur
  - o Abnormal cells
  - o Grows by infiltration
  - o Undifferentiated: Does not reach its specialized cell form
  - o Vascularity (blood supply): Has its own blood supply

15.7 Stages of Cancer

- Initiation stage:
  - o Carcinogen enters the body. Normally detoxified by the immune system.
  - o If fails, the carcinogen enters the cell, modifying the DNA.
  - o The cell becomes neoplastic.
  - o The genetic structure of the cell mutates and develops into a neoplastic cell.
- Promotion:
  - o Cancer cell divides (localized).
  - o The tumor is at the primary site.

- Progression:
  - Growth rate increases.
  - Neoplastic cells are invasive and metastasize.
  - The tumor is angiogenetic (i.e., it has its own blood vessels).
  - Hematogenous metastasis occurs.
- Neoplastic cells release metalloproteinase enzymes, enabling cells to penetrate blood vessels.
  - Neoplastic cells circulate and adhere to small blood vessels of distant organs.
  - Most neoplastic cells are killed by the immune system.
  - Neoplastic cells are protected from the immune system's platelets and fibrogen.
  - Neoplastic cells might be trapped in the lymph nodes.
  - Skip metastasis: Neoplastic cells may bypass regional lymph nodes and travel to distant lymph nodes.

Implantation

- Neoplastic cells embed on the surface of body organs.

15.8   Cancer Cells and the Immune System

- Every cell contains antigens on its surface used to identify the cell.
- Normal cells have antigens that identify the cell as a friendly cell.
- The immune system destroys cells that have "nonfriendly" antigens.
- The first lines of defense are cytotoxic T cells, natural killer cells, macrophages, and B lymphocytes that kill cells that have "nonfriendly" antigens.
- The second lines of defense are antibodies that develop once the immune system is sensitized to the "nonfriendly" antigen.
- When a normal cell becomes a cancer cell, the "friendly antigen" is changed to the tumor-associated antigen (TAA) and is destroyed by the immune system.
- Some cancer cells evade the immune system by:
  - Maintaining the "friendly antigen"
  - Suppressing T-cell production. T cells kill tumor cells.
  - Suppressing the immune system

15.9   Staging of Cancer

Staging is a process of measuring the status and growth of cancer cells.

Histologic Grading of Cancer Cells

- Dysplasia: Abnormality of growth
- Anaplasia: Loss of cellular differentiation and function
- Grade 1 = Cells differ slightly from normal cells (mild dysplasia); well differentiated
- Grade 2 = Cells are more abnormal (moderate dysplasia); moderately differentiated
- Grade 3 = Cells are very abnormal (severe dysplasia); poorly differentiated
- Grade 4 = Cells immature and primitive (anaplasia); differentiated

Clinical Staging

Carcinoma in situ: A lesion with all histologic signs of cancer except invasion. If left untreated, it will become invasive.

- Stage 0 = Cancer in situ
- Stage 1 = Tumor limited to the tissue of origin—localized tumor growth
- Stage 2 = Limited local spread
- Stage 3 = Extensive local and regional spread
- Stage 4 = Metastasis

TNM Classification Staging

Standard International used after biopsy:

- Primary tumor (T) = Tumor size:
  - T_0 = No evidence of primary tumor
  - T_{is} = Carcinoma in situ
  - T_{1-4} = Ascending degrees of increase in tumor size and involvement (T2 is between 2 and 5 cm)
- Regional lymph nodes (N) = Degree of spread:
  - N_0 = No evidence of disease in lymph nodes
  - N_1 = Spread to an ipsilateral (same side of body) movable node
  - N_2 = Metastasis to an ipsilateral axillary node (armpit) fixed to another node or structure
  - N_{1-4} = Ascending degree of nodal involvement
  - N_x = Regional lymph nodes unable to be assessed clinically
- Distant metastases (M):
  - M_0 = No evidence of distant metastases
  - M_{1-4} = Ascending degrees of metastatic involvement of the host, including distant nodes
  - Mx = Metastasis cannot be assessed

Karnofsky Functional Performance Scale

The Karnofsky Functional Performance Scale describes the status of the patient with cancer.

- 100 = Normal, no complaint, no evidence of cancer
- 90 = Ability to carry out normal activities, minor signs of disease
- 80 = Normal activity with effort
- 70 = Ability to carry out self-care, unable to carry out work and normal activities
- 60 = Occasional assistance necessary, able to care for most needs
- 50 = Considerable assistance, medical care necessary
- 40 = Disabled, special care and assistance needed
- 30 = Severely disabled, needs hospitalization, death not imminent
- 20 = Very sick, hospitalization, active support treatment
- 10 = Morbid fatal process progressing rapidly
- 0 = Dead

15.10   Cancer Prevention and Detection

- Prevention:
  - Avoid exposure to carcinogens.
  - Eat a balanced diet including vegetables, fresh fruits, whole grains, and fiber.
  - Reduce fats and preservatives.
  - Exercise regularly.
  - Sleep 6 to 8 hours per night.
  - Get regular examinations (Table 15.2)
  - Reduce stress and enhance coping.
  - Engage in regular periods of relaxation.
  - Engage in self-examination.

TABLE 15.2 Cancer Screening Schedule

Breast	Mammogram start at age 40
	Breast exam every 3 yr for women in twenties or thirties
	Breast exam every year for women 40+
	Women at risk (family history, genetic tendency, past breast cancer) start tests early
Colon/rectum	Over 40 and at age 50 yr
	Fecal occult blood (FOBI) every year
	Sigmoidoscopy (FSIG) every 5 yr
	Double contrast barium enema every 5 to 10 yr
	Colonoscopy every 10 years
Prostate	Prostate specific antigen (PSA) and digital exam every year at age 50
	High risk (African-American men, men with benign testing, first-degree relation having it) start at age 45 yr
Uterus	Cervix: All who have been sexually active or are aged 18 or older, annual Papanicolaou (Pap) test and pelvic exam. After three successfully test then do not need to test as often.
	Endometrium: Report unexpected bleeding and spotting. Test at age 35.
General	Cancer related checkup every 3 yr between 20 and 39 and every year 40+
Oral	Self-examination
	Annual exam of mouth and teeth
Testicular self-exam (TSE)	Most common cancer at 15 to 34 yr
	Perform monthly after a warm shower or bath when skin of the scrotum is relaxed
	Stand in front of the mirror. Gently roll each testicle between thumb and fingers of both hands; should be smooth, oval-shaped, and rather firm.
	Warning signs: Painless swelling, feeling heavy, hard lump size of a pea, sudden collection of fluid in scrotum, dull ache in lower abdomen or groin, pain in testicle or scrotum, enlargement or tenderness of breasts

Seven Warning Signs of Cancer

- C = Change in bowel or bladder habits
- A = A sore that does not heal

- U = Unusual bleeding or discharge from any body orifice
- T = Thickening or a lump in the breast or elsewhere
- I = Indigestion or difficulty in swallowing (dysphagia)
- O = Obvious changes in wart or mole
- N = Nagging cough or hoarseness

15.11 Biopsy

- Remove a portion of or the entire tumor
- Used to diagnose cancer
- Determines:
  - Whether it is benign or malignant
  - Origins of tumor
  - Degree of cellular differentiation

Type of Biopsy

- *Needle biopsy*: Aspiration using large-bore needle
- *Incisional biopsy*: Scalpel or dermal punch
- *Excisional biopsy*: Remove entire tumor if tumor <2 cm, intestinal polyps, breast mass
- *Endoscopic*: Use endoscopy scope to perform biopsy on gastrointestinal, respiratory, and genitourinary systems

Tissue Examination

- A frozen section or a permanent paraffin section is prepared using the biopsy sample.
- Frozen section: Takes minutes before a diagnosis is made. Provides fewer details of the section when compared with the permanent paraffin section.
- Permanent paraffin section: Takes 24 hours before a diagnosis is made. Provides clearer details of the sample.

15.12 Treatment Goals

- Cure: The patient is free of disease.
- Control: The disease exists. The patient resumes activities of normal living.
- Palliation: The disease exists. Minimize pain and discomfort.
- Adjuvant therapy: Supplemental therapy

Factors That Determine Treatment

- Cell type
- Tumor location
- Tumor size

15.13 Surgical Therapy

- The tumor is surrounded by normal tissue.
- The tumor grows at a slow rate.
- Remove the least amount of tissue possible followed by adjuvant therapy.
- Tissues where cancer normal spreads are surgically removed.
- Debulking procedure: Remove as much of the tumor as possible followed by chemotherapy or radiation therapy. This is used when a tumor is attached to an organ.

15.14 Radiation Therapy

- Radiation: A relatively high emission of energy that is absorbed into cells, destroying the cell's ability to reproduce.
- Radiation therapy destroys cancer cells and normal cells.
- Goal of radiation therapy:
  - Cure: Remove tumor in basal cell carcinoma of skin, tumor on vocal cords, and stage I or IIa Hodgkin's disease
  - Control: Inoperable tumor
  - Palliation: Reduce the size of the tumor to relieve symptoms, pain, and obstruction
- External radiation: An external beam radiation provides therapy.
- Internal radiation (brachytherapy): Temporary implant of radioactive material is placed in the tumor. Used for tumors of head, neck, gynecologic. In the prostate may be permanent.
  - Sealed implants: The implant is enclosed in a container, so it does not circulate in the body.
  - Unsealed implants: The implant is not encased in a container and circulates in the body.

Types of Radiation

- Alpha: Cannot pass through skin (rarely used)
- Beta: Cannot pass through skin. Emitted from radioactive isotopes. Used for internal implants
- Gamma rays (X-rays): Passes through skin. Used for external radiotherapy.

Care for the Patient with Radiation Therapy

- Wear a film badge that measures exposure to radiation.
- Do not share the film badge.
- Limit the time that is spent with the patient to 30 minutes per care provider per shift.
- Limit visitors to 30 minutes per day, and visitors must stand 6 feet from the patient.
- Dispose of bed linens and dressings in the normal manner once the radiation source is removed.
- Female patients may resume intercourse after 10 days if the radiation implant was cervical or vaginal.

Side Effects of Radiation Therapy

- Fatigue:
  - Rest when fatigued

- Difficult eating, swallowing, talking:
  - Xerostomia: Decreased salivary flow caused by dry mouth.
  - Use artificial saliva so patient can taste food and clean teeth.
  - Patient may report having a lump in his or her throat and feeling of food getting stuck.
  - No tobacco.
  - No alcohol.
  - Assess for dental carries.
  - Use a saline solution (1 L of water and 1 tsp of salt) to clean teeth.
- Nausea and vomiting:
  - Eat and drink small, frequent high-protein/high-calorie meals when not nauseated.
  - Serve food in a pleasant environment.
  - Administer antiemetics before meals.
  - Use diversional activities.
  - Monitor weight.
- Diarrhea:
  - Administer antidiarrheal agent.
  - Eat low-residue, bland, high-protein meals.
  - Provide good perineal care.
  - Monitor electrolytes, particularly sodium, potassium, chloride.
- Constipation:
  - Administer stool softener.
  - Eat high-fiber food.
  - Monitor liver tests.
- Anemia:
  - Schedule rest periods.
  - Eat high-protein diet.
  - Increase iron (diet of red meats, organ meats, whole wheat products, spinach, and carrots).
  - Increase folic acid (diet of green vegetables, liver, citrus fruits).
  - Increase vitamin B_{12} (diet of glandular meats, yeast, green leafy vegetables, milk, cheese).
- Leukopenia and thrombocytopenia:
  - Avoid groups and crowded places to prevent infection
  - Wash hands
- Thrombocytopenia:
  - Assess for bleeding.
  - Use electric razor.
  - Use soft toothbrush.
  - Avoid injury.
- Alopecia:
  - Avoid excess brushing and shampooing.
  - Do not use electric hair dryer or curlers.
  - Prepare the patient for hair loss.
  - Use a wig.

- Skin reaction (redness, itching, burning):
  - Lubricate dry skin.
  - Use no soaps.
  - Keep skin clean by washing with plain water and pat dry.
  - Use no medication, powder, or ointments that contain heavy metals.
  - Avoid injury to skin.
  - Itching: Use olive oil, cornstarch. No talcum powder.
  - Avoid exposure of skin to heat and cold.
  - Do not wear constricting clothing.
  - Do not use deodorants.
  - Rinse with saline.
  - Expose area to air.
  - Wear no wool and corduroy.
  - Wear lightweight cotton clothes.
  - Use gentle detergent when washing clothes.
  - Do not swim in salt water or chlorinated pool.
- Anorexia:
  - Tumor necrosis factor (TNF) and interleukin are released by macrophages when tumor dies, and these have an appetite-suppressing effect.
  - Weigh twice a week.
  - Eat small, frequent, high-protein/high-calorie meals.
  - Meals should not be immediately before or after therapy.
  - Give nutritional supplements.
- Bone marrow suppression:
  - Week 1 of radiation therapy: white blood cell (WBC) count decreases.
  - Week 2 of radiation therapy: Platelets decrease.
  - Month 2 of radiation therapy: Red blood cells decrease.
  - Nonirradiated bone marrow becomes more active.
  - Immunosuppression is not significant.
  - Infection/bleeding is rare.

Care for the Patient with Radiation Implants

- Only the implant is radioactive, not the patient.
- Assign the patient to a private room.
- Place a "radioactive material" sign on the patient's door.
- No pregnant women are to enter the room.
- No small children should visit.
- The patient should remain in bed with little movement so as not to jar the implant.
- Keep a lead-lined container in the room to dispose of the implant should the implant become dislodged.
- Wear latex gloves when handling contaminated secretions.

- Assume that all of the patient's secretions are radioactive.
- Stand the greatest distance as possible from the patient.
- Minimize bedside care by keeping supplies and equipment within the patient's reach, and check on the patient from the patient's door.
- Wear a radiation badge.
- Do not wear the radiation badge outdoors.

15.15 Chemotherapy

- Chemical agents that destroy rapidly dividing cells by disrupting different stages of cell growth
- Does not differentiate between cancer cells and normal cells
- Chemotherapy drugs are categorized by their effect on the cell growth cycle.
- Two major categories:
    - Cell-cycle nonspecific: Effect cells that are replicating and cells in resting stage (G0)
    - Cell-cycle phase specific: Effect cells in process of replication (G1, S1, G2, M)

Factors Determining Chemotherapy Treatment

- Miotic rate of the tissues from which the tumor arises:
    - More rapid rate, better the response
- Size of tumor:
    - Smaller the number of cells, better response
- Age of tumor:
    - The younger, the better the response
- Location of tumor:
    - Sites in the brain not affected because few chemotherapy drugs cross the blood-brain barrier
- Presence of resistant tumor cells:
    - Mutation of cancer cells can result in resistance to chemotherapy.

Classification of Chemotherapy Drugs

- Alkylating agents:
    - Cell-cycle nonspecific
    - Damages DNA and prevents cell division
- Antimetabolites:
    - Cell-cycle phase specific
    - Interferes with making DNA and cell metabolic process
- Antitumor antibiotics:
    - Cell-cycle nonspecific
    - Modifies DNA and RNA
- Plant alkaloids (miotic inhibitors):
    - Cell-cycle specific
    - Stop metaphage
    - Makes the host's body less favorable environment for growth of cancer cells

- Nitrosoureas:
  - Nonspecific
  - Block enzymes
- Corticosteroids:
  - Nonspecific
  - Disrupt cell membrane
- Hormone therapy:
  - Nonspecific
  - Steroids and sex hormones
  - Alters the endocrine environment

Chemotherapy Preparation and Administration

- Chemotherapy is toxic to cancer cells of normal cells of both the patient and health care provider.
- Wear gloves.
- Health care provider can absorb chemotherapy through inhalation and skin contact.
- Take precautions while handling patient's excretions.
- Do not administer chemotherapy if patient is pregnant.
- Check placement of intravenous (IV) line frequently by aspirating blood.
- Stay with patient throughout the administration of chemotherapy.
- Dispose of IV equipment in appropriate waste receptacle.
- Chemotherapy drugs can cause necrosis in skin if accidentally infiltrated (extravastration).
- Signs of extravastration:
  - Pain
  - Swelling
  - Redness
  - Ulceration
  - Necrosis

Chemotherapy Administration Methods

- Oral
- Intramuscular (IM): Antineoplastic drugs irritate vessel wall
- Central line
- Regional administration: Involves delivery of chemotherapy drugs directly into tumor
- Intra-arterial chemotherapy: Chemotherapy drugs directly given in arterial vessels that supply the tumor
- Intraperitoneal chemotherapy: Chemotherapy drugs into the peritoneal cavity
- Intrathecal or intraventricular: Chemotherapy drugs inject drug into the lumbar to allow drug to cross the blood-brain barrier
- Intravesical bladder chemotherapy: Chemotherapy drugs into bladder

Side Effects of Chemotherapy

- Fatigue:
  - Rest when fatigued.

- Mouth sores (stomatitis):
  - Rinse with viscous lidocaine before meals.
  - Rinse with plain water or hydrogen peroxide after meals.
  - Apply K-Y jelly to lubricate cracked lips.
  - Suck on a popsicle.
- Nausea and vomiting:
  - Eat bland foods in small amounts after chemotherapy.
  - Administer an antiemetic every 4 to 6 hours and before chemotherapy begins.
  - No foods or fluids 6 hours before chemotherapy begins.
- Diarrhea:
  - Administer an antidiarrheal agent.
  - Drink clear liquids.
  - Eat low-residue, bland, high-protein meals.
  - Provide good perineal care.
  - Monitor electrolytes, particularly sodium, potassium, and chloride.
- Anemia (low RBC count):
  - Schedule rest periods.
  - Eat a high-protein diet.
  - Increase iron (red meats, organ meats, whole wheat products, spinach, and carrots).
  - Increase folic acid (green vegetables, liver, and citrus fruits).
  - Increase vitamin B_{12} (glandular meats, yeast, green leafy vegetables, milk, and cheese).
- Leucopenia (low WBC count):
  - Reverse isolation if WBC count <1000.
  - Avoid groups and crowded places to prevent infection.
  - Wash hands.
- Thrombocytopenia (low platelet count):
  - Do not take aspirin.
  - Do not administer IM injections.
  - Assess for bleeding.
  - Use an electric razor.
  - Use a soft toothbrush.
  - Avoid injury.
- Alopecia:
  - Hair loss is not permanent.
  - Avoid excess brushing and shampooing.
  - Do not use an electric hair dryer or curlers.
  - Prepare the patient for hair loss.
  - Use a wig.
- Renal damage:
  - Administer Zyloprim (allopurinol) to prevent the formation of uric acid.
  - Increase fluids.
  - Increase voiding to excrete chemotherapy drugs.

- Anorexia:
  - TNF and interleukin are released by macrophages when a tumor dies that have an appetite-suppressing effect.
  - Weigh twice a week.
  - Eat small, frequent, high-protein/high-calorie meals.
  - Meals should not be eaten immediately before or after therapy.
  - Give nutritional supplements.
- Late side effects:
  - Occur months and years after treatment stops
  - Hypoplasia of stem cells
  - Alterations of connective tissues
  - Risk for leukemia
  - Might cause secondary malignancy

15.16 Biological Therapy

- Treat the patient's immune system to help it destroy cancer cells.
- Biological therapy is used as the primary or secondary treatment for cancer.
- It slows or stops the growth of cancer cells.
- It prevents cancer cells from spreading.
- It enhances the immune system.

Interventions

- Monitor the vital signs.
- Schedule rest periods.
- Administer:
  - Acetaminophen before treatment and every 4 hours after treatment
  - IV Demerol for chills

Interferon (Cytokines)

- Types:
  - Alpha
  - Beta
  - Gamma
- Protects cells from being infected by a virus by inhibiting the virus from replicating DNA
- Slows down tumor cell division
- Stimulates proliferation
- Causes cancer cells to differentiate into nonproliferative forms
- Prevents cancer cells from proliferating
- Administer:
  - IV
  - IM
  - Subcutaneous
  - Not orally

- Side effects:
  - Flulike symptoms
  - Fever
  - Chills
  - Headache
  - Myalgias (muscle pain)

Interleukins (Cytokines)

- Increase production of T lymphocytes (tumor-killing cells)
- Help differentiate immune system cells to recognize and destroy abnormal body cells
- Side effects:
  - Capillary leak syndrome
  - Fluids shift from intravascular to extravascular

Monoclonal Antibiotics

- Bind to specific cells including tumor cells
- Prevent proliferation of cancer cells

Hematopoietic Growth Factor

- Increases the proliferation of blood cells

Colony-Stimulating Factor (CSF)

- Increases recovery from bone marrow depression
- Stimulates granulocyte WBCs to prevent infection as a result of chemotherapy

Erythropoietin (EPO)

- Stimulates growth of erythroid cells (RBCs)

Oprelvekin

- Stimulates growth of platelets

15.17   Bone Marrow Transplant (BMT)

- Types:
  - Allogeneic:
    - From donor
    - Human leukocyte antigen (HLA) matches test WBC
  - Autologous:
    - Patient receives his or her own bone marrow, which is removed before treatment.
  - Syngeneic:
    - Patient receives stem cells from identical twin.

- Treatment for:
    - Malignancies
    - Blood disorders
    - Solid tumors such as breast cancer and brain tumors

Method

- 1- to 2-hour procedure
- Aspirated from iliac crest or sternum
- 500 to 1000 mL of marrow aspirated
- Marrow filtered to remove cancer cells and cells that may cause graft-versus-host disease
- Pain at site treated with pain medication
- Bone marrow replaced in a few weeks
- Bone marrow administered through the patient's central line
- Marrow is infused:
    - During a 30-minute period
    - By IV push directly into the central line
- Success occurs when the WBC, erythrocyte, and platelet counts rise.
- Takes 6 weeks before success occurs.

Pretransplant Care

- Recipient becomes immunosuppressed by total body irradiation (TBI).
- Space is created in host marrow to allow transplanted cells to grow.
- Strict reverse isolation is enforced.
- Place patient in a laminar airflow room.
- Surveillance cultures are taken twice a week
- Objects must be sterilized before being brought into the room
- Monitor central lines frequently.
- Prepare patient and family that the patient will become very ill.
- 2 or 3 months of hospitalization are required.

Posttransplant Care

- Maintain reverse isolation.
- Administer antibiotics.
- Assess for infection.
- Monitor vital signs.
- Rinse mouth with viscous lidocaine, and antibiotic rinses.
- Do not use lemon or glycerin swabs.
- Monitor for bleeding.
- Assess for occult blood in emesis and stools.
- Assess for bruising, petechiae on skin, mucus membranes.
- Conduct daily platelet count.

- Measure intake and output.
- Increase fluid, protein, and caloric intake.
- Weigh daily.
- Monitor hydration stats.
- Assess urine for glucose, ketones, protein.
- Instruction the patient:
  - To keep the home clean
  - Not to have pets
  - To limit visitors who are not infected
  - To schedule rest periods
  - To avoid crowds

15.18 Complications from Cancer

Malnutrition

- Fat and muscle become depleted.
- At 10 lb loss, it is difficult to maintain without supplements.
- Administer nutritional supplement at loss of 5% of weight.

Altered Taste

- Bitter taste buds are stimulated.
- Sweet, sour, salty taste is affected.
- Avoid foods the patient dislikes.
- Use spices and seasoning to enhance taste.
- Use lemon juice, onion, mint, basil, fruit juice marinade to enhance taste of meat and fish.
- Use bacon bits, onion, pieces of ham to enhance taste of vegetables.

Infection

- Tumor compresses vital organs, resulting in ulceration and necrosis.
- Immune system is depressed, resulting in immune compromise.
- Infection can cause death.

15.19 Oncological Emergencies

Sepsis and Disseminated Intravascular Coagulation (DIC)

- Increased risk for infection
- DIC resulting in decreased clotting capability and risk of bleeding
- Interventions:
  - Strict aseptic technique
  - Monitor for infection

- o Administer:
  - IV antibiotics
  - Anticoagulants
  - Cryoprecipitated clotting factors

Syndrome of Inappropriate Antidiuretic Hormone (SIADH)

- Tumors stimulate the brain to synthesize antidiuretic hormone
- Symptoms:
  - o Weakness
  - o Muscle cramps
  - o Loss of appetite
  - o Fatigue
  - o Serum sodium levels 115 to 120
  - o Water intoxication
  - o Weight gain
  - o Personality changes
  - o Confusion
  - o Extreme muscle weakness
  - o Seizures
  - o Coma
- Interventions:
  - o Fluid restriction
  - o Increased sodium intake
  - o Administer:
    - Demeclocycline (Declomycin)
    - Monitor serum sodium levels

Spinal Cord Compression

- Tumor enters the spinal cord and vertebral column collapses.
- Symptoms:
  - o Back pain: Usually before neurologic deficits
  - o Numbness
  - o Tingling
  - o Loss of sensation in the urethra, vagina, and rectum
  - o Muscle weakness
- Interventions:
  - o Assess for back pain.
  - o Assess for neurologic deficits.
  - o Radiation and chemotherapy can be used to reduce tumor and relieve compression.
  - o Surgery to remove the tumor
  - o Use of neck or back braces to reduce movement

Hypercalcemia

- Increased calcium
- Late manifestation of malignancy
- Occurs with bone metastasis
- Decreased physical mobility increases hypercalcemia
- Symptoms:
  - Fatigue
  - Anorexia
  - Nausea
  - Vomiting
  - Constipation
  - Polyuria
  - Severe muscle weakness
  - Diminished deep tendon reflexes
  - Paralytic ileus
  - Dehydration
- Interventions:
  - Monitor serum calcium level
  - Dialysis if renal impairment occurs

Superior Vena Cava Syndrome

- Superior vena cava is compressed or obstructed by tumor growth.
- Blood flow is blocked to the head, neck, and upper trunk.
- Symptoms:
  - Edema of the face, especially around the eyes
  - Stokes' sign: Tightness of shirt or blouse collar
  - Edema in the arms and hands
  - Dyspnea erythema of the upper body
  - Epistaxis (nosebleed)
  - Hemorrhage
  - Cyanosis
  - Mental status changes
  - Decreased cardiac output
  - Hypotension
- Interventions:
  - Radiation therapy

Tumor Lysis Syndrome

- Large numbers of tumor cells are destroyed rapidly.
- Destroyed tumor cells are released into the bloodstream faster than the body can remove them.

- Can cause:
  - Severe tissue damage and death
  - Hyperkalemia
  - Hyperuricemia, leading to acute renal failure
- Interventions:
  - Increase fluids
  - Administer:
    - Diuretics to increase urine flow through kidneys
    - Allopurinol (Zyloprim) to increase excretion of purines
    - IV glucose and insulin to treat hyperkalemia
    - Dialysis if hyperkalemia and hyperuricemia persist

15.20 Oncological Obstructive Emergencies

Superior Vena Cava

- Signs:
  - Facial edema
  - Periorbital edema
  - Distention of veins of the neck and chest
  - Headache
  - Seizure
- Common in:
  - Hodgkin's disease
  - non-Hodgkin's disease
  - Lung cancer

Spinal Cord Compression

- Signs:
  - Back pain aggravated by Valsalva maneuver
  - Motor weakness
  - Dysfunction
  - Sensory parenthesis
  - Change in blow and bladder function
- Common in:
  - Breast cancer
  - Lung cancer
  - Prostate cancer
  - Gastrointestinal cancer
  - Melanoma
  - Renal cancer

Third-Space Syndrome

- Shifting fluid from vacuolar space to interstitial space
- Signs:
  - Hypovolemia
  - Hypotension
  - Tachycardia
  - Decreased urine output
- Secondary to extensive surgery
- Interventions:
  - Replace fluids
  - Replace electrolytes
  - Replace plasma protein

15.21 Oncological Metabolic Emergencies

Syndrome of Inappropriate Antidiuretic Hormone (SIADH)

Hypercalcemia

- Signs:
  - Apathy
  - Depression
  - Fatigue
  - Muscle weakness
  - Polyuria
  - Nocturia
  - Anorexia
  - Nausea
  - Vomiting
- Tumor lysis syndrome (TLS)
- Septic shock

15.22 Oncological Infiltrative Emergencies

Cardiac Tamponade
- Signs:
  - Heavy feeling over chest
  - Shortness of breath
  - Tachycardia
  - Cough
  - Dysphagia
  - Nausea
  - Vomiting

Carotid Artery Rupture

Solved Problems

15.1 What is normal cell proliferation?

Normal cell proliferation is:

- Normal cells undergo the cell cycle where the new cell is produced, grows, degenerates, and dies.
- New cells are generated when existing cells die.
- New cells are considered immature and undifferentiated, which means the new cells can become any type of cell. These are known as *stem cells*.
- New cells become differentiated when the new cell matures, which means the new cells have become a specific type of cell.
- Proto-oncogenes regulate cell growth.
- New cells continue to grow until the boundary of other cells is contacted, causing the new cells to stop growing. The new cell is then considered in the mature state.

15.2 What is cancer cell proliferation?

Cancer cell proliferation is:

- Cancer cells are abnormal cells where growth is unregulated.
- They do not stop growing when in contact with other cells
- They will grow on top of and between normal cells.
- They divide indiscriminately, sometimes producing two cells at the same time.
- They proliferate at the rate of normal cells from the same tissue where it originated, which is why some cancer cells proliferate slower or faster than other cancer cells.
- An abnormal growth of cells is called a *neoplasia*, commonly called a *tumor*.

15.3 What is neoplasia?

Neoplasia is both benign and malignant tumors.

15.4 What causes unregulated growth of abnormal cells?

It is not clear what causes the unregulated growth of abnormal cells, which is why it is difficult to develop a cure for cancer.

15.5 What is an oncogenic virus?

- Oncogenic virus: A virus either disables the proto-oncogenes or introduces the oncogenes.

15.6 What is cell differentiation?

Cell differentiation occurs when a stem cell matures into a specific type of cell.

15.7 How do cancer cells cause large tumors?

Cancer cells cause large tumors by growing on top of each other.

15.8 What is anaplastic?

Anaplastic means the cell is undifferentiated.

15.9 Why do cancer cells metastasize?

Cancer cells metastasize because normal cells bind together, cancer cells lack adhesion to bind together, and a lack of adhesion enables cancer cells to spread to other locations in the body.

15.10 What are the common sites of breast cancer metastases?

Common sites of breast cancer metastases are bones and lungs.

15.11 What is the common site of lung cancer metastasis?

The common site of lung cancer metastasis is the brain.

15.12 What are the common sites of prostate cancer metastasis?

The common sites of prostate cancer metastasis are bone, spine, and legs.

15.13 What is the common site of prostate cancer metastasis?

The common site of prostate cancer metastasis is the liver.

15.14 How do cancer cells spread?

Cancer cells spread by:

- Local seeding: Distribution occurs in the local are of the primary tumor
- Blood-borne: Distribution by blood
- Lymphatic spread: Primary sites rich in lymphatics

15.15 What is a benign tumor?

A benign tumor:

- Is encapsulated
- Does not metastasize
- Does not recur
- Has normal cells
- Grows by expansion
- Differentiated: reaches its specialized cell form
- Vascularity (blood supply): Does not have its own blood supply

15.16 What is a malignant tumor?

A malignant tumor:

- Is cancer
- Is not encapsulated
- Does metastasize
- Does recur
- Has abnormal cells
- Grows by infiltration
- Is undifferentiated: Does not reach its specialized cell form
- Vascularity (blood supply): Has its own blood supply

15.17 How does the immune system kill cancer cells?

The immune system kills cancer cells through the following mechanisms:

- Every cell contains antigens on its surface used to identify the cell.
- Normal cells have antigens that identify the cell as a friendly cell.
- The immune system destroys cells that have "nonfriendly" antigens.
- The first lines of defense are cytotoxic T cells, natural killer cells, macrophages, and B lymphocytes that kill cells that have "nonfriendly" antigens.
- The second lines of defense are antibodies that develop once the immune system is sensitized to the "nonfriendly" antigen.

- When a normal cell becomes a cancer cell, the "friendly antigen" is changed to the tumor TAA and is destroyed by the immune system.
- Some cancer cells evades the immune system by:
  - Maintaining the "friendly antigen"
  - Suppressing T-cell production. T cells kill tumor cells.
  - Suppressing the immune system

15.18 What is staging of cancer?

Staging is a process of measuring the status and growth of cancer cells.

15.19 What is histological grading of cancer cells?

- Dysplasia: Abnormality of growth
- Anaplasia: Loss of cellular differentiation and function
- Grade 1 = Cells differ slightly from normal cells (mild dysplasia); well differentiated
- Grade 2 = Cells are more abnormal (moderate dysplasia); moderately differentiated
- Grade 3 = Cells very abnormal (severe dysplasia); poorly differentiated
- Grade 4 = Cells immature and primitive (anaplasia); undifferentiated

15.20 What is the clinical staging of cancer?

The clinical staging of cancer is carcinoma in situ; a lesion with all histological characteristics of cancer except invasion. If left untreated, it will become invasive

- Stage 0 = Cancer in situ
- Stage 1 = Tumor limited to the tissue of origin—localized tumor growth
- Stage 2 = Limited local spread
- Stage 3 = Extensive local and regional spread
- Stage 4 = Metastasis

15.21 What is the TNM classification staging?

TNM classification staging is the standard international used after biopsy.

- Primary tumor (T) = Tumor size
  - T_0 = No evidence of primary tumor
  - T_{is} = Carcinoma in situ
  - T_{1-4} = Ascending degrees of increase in tumor size and involvement (T_2 is between 2 and 5 cm)
- Regional lymph nodes (N) = Degree of spread
  - N_0 = No evidence of disease in lymph nodes
  - N_1 = Spread to an ipsilateral (same side of body) movable node
  - N_2 = Metastasis to an ipsilateral axillary node (armpit) fixed to another node or structure
  - N_{1-4} = Ascending degree of nodal involvement
  - N_x = Regional lymph nodes unable to be assessed clinically
- Distant metastases (M)
  - M_0 = No evidence of distant metastases
  - M_{1-4} = Ascending degrees of metastatic involvement of the host, including distant nodes
  - Mx = Metastasis cannot be assessed

15.22 What is the Karnofsky Functional Performance Scale?

The Karnofsky functional performance scale describes the status of the patient with cancer.

- 100 = Normal; no complaint no evidence of cancer
- 90 = Ability to carry out normal activities; minor signs of disease
- 80 = Normal activity with effort
- 70 = Ability to carry out self-care; unable to carry out work and normal activities
- 60 = Occasional assistance necessary; able to care for most needs
- 50 = Considerable assistance; medical care necessary
- 40 = Disabled special care and assistance needed
- 30 = Severely disabled; needs hospitalization; death not imminent
- 20 = Very sick; hospitalization; active support treatment
- 10 = Morbid fatal process progressing rapidly
- 0 = Dead

15.23 What are the seven warning signs of cancer?

- C = Change in bowel or bladder habits
- A = A sore that does not heal
- U = Unusual bleeding or discharge from any body orifice
- T = Thickening or a lump in the breast or elsewhere
- I = Indigestion or difficulty in swallowing (dysphagia)
- O = Obvious changes in wart or mole
- N = Nagging cough or hoarseness

15.24 What are oncological infiltrative emergencies?

Oncological infiltrative emergencies are cardiac tamponade and carotid artery rupture. The signs of cardiac tamponade are heavy feeling over chest, shortness of breath, tachycardia, cough, dysphagia, nausea, and vomiting.

15.25 What are oncological obstructive emergencies?

Oncological obstructive emergencies are superior vena cava signs, spinal cord compression, third-space syndrome, and intestinal obstruction. The signs of superior vena cava are facial edema, periorbital edema, distention of veins of the neck and chest, headache, and seizure. These are most common in Hodgkin's, non-Hodgkin's, and lung cancer. The signs of spinal cord compression are back pain aggravated by Valsalva maneuver, motor weakness, dysfunction, sensory parenthesis, and change in bowel and bladder function. These are most common in breast cancer, lung cancer, prostate cancer, gastrointestinal cancer, melanoma, and renal cancer. Third-space syndrome is the shifting of fluid from vacuolar space to interstitial space. The signs are hypovolemiaa, hypotension, tachycardia, and decreased urine output. Intervention is extensive surgery. Secondary intervention is replacement of fluids, electrolytes, and plasma protein.

INDEX

Acquired immunodeficiency syndrome (AIDS), 12–13
Acromegaly. *See* Hyperpituitarism
Acute glomerulonephritis
    interventions for, 207
    medical tests for, 206
    signs and symptoms of, 206
    treatment of, 206
Acute leukemia, 34
Acute respiratory disease (ARDS)
    interventions for, 81
    medical tests for, 81
    signs and symptoms of, 80
    treatment of, 81
Acute respiratory failure
    interventions for, 97–98
    medical tests for, 97
    signs and symptoms of, 96
    treatment of, 97
Addison's disease, 139–140
AI. *See* Aortic insufficiency
AIDS. *See* Acquired immunodeficiency syndrome
Amyotrophic lateral sclerosis (ALS)
    interventions for, 108
    medical tests for, 108
    signs and symptoms of, 107
    treatment of, 108
Anaphylaxis, 13–14
Anemia
    aplastic, 29–30
    interventions for, 29
    iron deficiency, 30–31
    medical tests for, 28–29
    pernicious, 31–32
    sickle cell, 39–40
    signs and symptoms of, 28
    treatment of, 29
Angina (Angina pectoris)
    interventions for, 49–50
    medical tests for, 49
    signs and symptoms of, 48
    treatment of, 49
    types of, 48
Ankylosing spondylitis (AS), 14–15
Anorexia nervosa
    interventions for, 254
    medical tests for, 253–254
    signs and symptoms of, 253
    treatment of, 254
Anxiety
    interventions for, 249
    medical tests for, 248
    signs and symptoms of, 248
    treatment of, 248
Aortic aneurysm, 47–48
Aortic insufficiency (AI), 72
Aplastic anemia (Pancytopenia)

    interventions for, 30
    medical tests for, 29–30
    signs and symptoms of, 29
    treatment of, 30
Appendicitis
    interventions for, 155
    medical tests for, 154
    signs and symptoms of, 154
    treatment of, 154–155
ARDS. *See* Acute respiratory disease
AS. *See* Ankylosing spondylitis
Asbestosis, 81–82
Asthma
    interventions for, 83–84
    medical tests for, 83
    signs and symptoms of, 82–83
    treatment of, 83
Asystole
    interventions for, 70
    medical tests for, 70
    signs and symptoms of, 69–70
    treatment of, 70
Atelectasis, 84
Atrial fibrillation
    interventions for, 69
    medical tests for, 69
    signs and symptoms of, 68–69
    treatment for, 69

Basal cell skin cancer, 197
Bell's Palsy, 108–109
Benign prostatic hypertrophy (BPH)
    interventions for, 205
    medical tests for, 205
    signs and symptoms of, 204
    treatment of, 205
Biological therapy, 273–274
Bipolar disorder
    classification of, 251
    interventions for, 252
    medical tests for, 251
    signs and symptoms of, 251
    treatment of, 252
Bladder cancer
    interventions for, 206
    medical tests for, 205
    signs and symptoms of, 205
    treatment of, 206
Bone marrow transplant (BMT)
    method of, 275
    posttransplant care and, 275–276
    pretransplant care and, 275
    types of, 274–275
BPH. *See* Benign prostatic hypertrophy
Brain
    abscess of, 109–110

Brain *(Cont.)*
  cerebellum of, 104
  cerebral cortex of, 103–104
  glands of, 105
  lobes of, 104–105
  tumors of, 110–112
Brain abscess, 109–110
Brain tumor
  interventions for, 111–112
  medical tests for, 111
  signs and symptoms of, 110–111
  treatment of, 111
  types of, 110
Breast cancer
  interventions for, 180
  medical tests for, 179
  signs and symptoms of, 179
  treatment of, 179
  types of, 179
Bronchiectasis, 85
Bronchitis, 86–87
Bulimia nervosa
  interventions for, 255
  medical tests for, 254–255
  signs and symptoms of, 254
  treatment of, 255
Burns, 195–196

CABG. *See* Coronary artery bypass graph
CAD. *See* Coronary artery disease
Cancer
  basal cell skin, 197
  bladder, 205–206
  breast, 179–180
  causes of, 260
  cell proliferation and, 259
  cervical, 180–181
  classification of, 261–262
    anatomic site, 262
  complications from, 276
  DIC and, 276–277
  emergencies from, 276–280
  endometrial, 182–183
  hypercalcemia and, 278
  immune system and, 263
  kidney, 207
  lung, 90–91
  ovarian, 185–186
  prevention and detection of, 265
  prostate, 208–209
  screening schedule for, 265
  SIADH and, 277–278
  skin, 197
  squamous cell skin, 197
  stages of, 262–263
    clinical grading of, 264
    histological grading of, 263
    Karnofsky functional performance scale, 264
    TNM classification of, 264
  superior vena cava syndrome and, 278
  testicular, 211–212
  therapies for, 267–276
  tumor lysis syndrome and, 278–279
  warning signs of, 265–266
Carcinogenesis, 260
Cardiac tamponade, 280
  interventions for, 55
  medical tests for, 54
  signs and symptoms of, 54
  treatment of, 54–55

Cardiogenic shock
  interventions for, 56
  medical tests for, 55
  signs and symptoms of, 55
  treatment of, 55–56
Cardiomyopathy
  interventions for, 57
  medical tests for, 56–57
  signs and symptoms of, 56
  treatment of, 57
  types of, 56
Cardiovascular system
  AI and, 72
  angina and, 48–50
  aortic aneurysm and, 47–48
  asystole and, 69–70
  atrial fibrillation and, 68–69
  blood flow and, 47
  CAD and, 51–53
  cardiac tamponade and, 54–55
  cardiogenic shock and, 55–56
  cardiomyopathy and, 56–57
  CHF and, 59–60
  definition of, 46–47
  electrical conduction in, 46
  endocarditis and, 57–58
  heart sounds and, 47
  hypertension and, 60–61
  hypovolemic shock and, 61–62
  MI and, 50–51
  mitral insufficiency and, 73
  mitral stenosis and, 73–74
  mitral valve prolapse and, 74–75
  myocarditis and, 62–63
  pericarditis and, 63–64
  peripheral artery disease and, 53–54
  pulmonary edema and, 65–66
  Raynaud's disease and, 66
  rheumatic heart disease and, 66–67
  surgical complications of, 238–240
  thrombophlebitis and, 67–68
  tricuspid insufficiency and, 75–76
  valves in, 46
  ventricular fibrillation and, 70–71
  ventricular tachycardia and, 71–72
Carpal tunnel syndrome, 2–3
Cell dysfunction
  defective proliferation of, 260
  differentiation of, 260–261
  spread of, 261
Cellulitis
  interventions for, 198
  medical tests for, 198
  signs and symptoms of, 198
  treatment of, 198
Cerebral aneurysm
  interventions for, 112
  medical tests for, 112
  signs and symptoms of, 112
  treatment of, 112
Cerebral hemorrhage
  interventions for, 107
  medical tests for, 106
  signs and symptoms of, 106
  treatment for, 106–107
  types of, 106
Cerebrovascular accident (CVA), 122–124
Cervical cancer
  interventions for, 181
  medical tests for, 180

signs and symptoms of, 180
treatment of, 180
types of, 180
Chemotherapy
administration methods of, 271
categories for, 270
classification for, 270–271
factors determining, 270
preparation for, 271
side effects of, 271–273
CHF. *See* Congestive heart failure
Cholecystitis
interventions for, 156
medical tests for, 155–156
signs and symptoms of, 155
treatment of, 156
Chorea. *See* Huntington's Disease
Chronic fatigue syndrome. *See* Epstein-Barr virus
Chronic leukemia, 34
Cirrhosis
interventions for, 158
medical tests for, 157–158
signs and symptoms of, 156–157
treatment of, 158
Congestive heart failure (CHF)
interventions of, 60
medical tests for, 59
signs and symptoms of, 59
treatment of, 59–60
Conn's syndrome. *See* Primary aldosteronism
Cor pulmonale
interventions for, 88
medical tests for, 88
signs and symptoms of, 87
treatment of, 88
Coronary artery bypass graph (CABG), 49
Coronary artery disease (CAD), 51–53
Crohn's disease
interventions for, 160
medical tests for, 159
signs and symptoms of, 159
treatment of, 159
Cryosurgery, 197
Cushing's syndrome
interventions for, 141
medical tests for, 141
signs and symptoms of, 140
treatment of, 141
CVA. *See* Cerebrovascular accident

Deep vein thrombosis (DVT), 4
interventions for, 41
medical tests for, 41
signs and symptoms of, 40–41
treatment of, 41
Dehydration, 229
Delirium
interventions for, 256
medical tests for, 255
signs and symptoms of, 255
treatment of, 256
Depressive disorder, 250
Dermatitis
interventions for, 196–197
medical tests for, 196
signs and symptoms of, 196
treatment of, 196
Diabetes insipidus, 138–139
Diabetes mellitus
insulin guide for, 147

interventions for, 147
medical tests for, 145–146
oral hypoglycemic agents for, 147–148
signs and symptoms of, 145
treatment of, 146
types of, 145
Diaphragmatic hernia. *See* Hiatal hernia
Disseminated intravascular coagulation (DIC)
cancer and, 276–277
interventions for, 33
medical tests for, 33
signs and symptoms of, 32–33
treatment of, 33
Diverticulitis disease
interventions for, 161
medical tests for, 160
signs and symptoms of, 160
treatment of, 160
DVT. *See* Deep vein thrombosis
Dysmenorrhea, 181
Dysmetabolic syndrome. *See* Metabolic syndrome

Ectopic pregnancy, 182
Electrolytes. *See* Fluids and electrolytes
Emphysema, 88–90
Encephalitis, 113
Endocarditis, 57–58
Endocrine system
Addison's disease and, 139–140
Cushing's syndrome and, 140–141
definition of, 128–132
diabetes insipidus and, 138–139
diabetes mellitus and, 145–148
hyperparathyroidism and, 144–145
hyperpituitarism and, 136
hyperprolactinemia and, 136–138
hyperthyroidism and, 133–134
hypoparathyroidism and, 143–144
hypopituitarism and, 135–136
hypothalamus and, 128–129
hypothyroidism and, 132–133
metabolic syndrome and, 148
ovarian follicle and, 132
parathyroid glands and, 131
pheochromocytoma and, 142–143
pituitary gland and, 129–130
posterior pituitary gland and, 129–130
primary aldosteronism and, 141–142
SIADH and, 139
simple goiter and, 134–135
testes and, 131–132
Endometrial cancer
interventions for, 183
medical tests for, 183
signs and symptoms of, 182
treatment of, 183
Eosinophils, 11, 12, 27
Epstein-Barr virus/chronic fatigue syndrome
interventions for, 21
medical tests for, 20
signs and symptoms of, 20
treatment of, 20–21
viruses causing, 20

Fluids and electrolytes
acid-based balance and, 217
definition of, 216–217
dehydration and, 229
fluid regulation and, 217
hypercalcemia and, 220–221

Fluids and electrolytes *(Cont.)*
  hyperkalemia and, 222–223
  hypermagnesemia and, 224–225
  hypernatremia and, 218–219
  hyperphosphatemia and, 228
  hypocalcemia and, 219–220
  hypokalemia and, 222
  hypomagnesemia and, 223–224
  hyponatremia and, 218
  hypophosphatemia and, 227–228
  metabolic acidosis and, 225–226
  metabolic alkalosis and, 226–227
  osmolarity and, 217
  regulation of, 217
Fractures, 2, 3–4

Gastritis
  interventions for, 165
  medical tests for, 164–165
  signs and symptoms of, 164
  treatment of, 165
Gastroenteritis
  interventions for, 162
  medical tests for, 161
  signs and symptoms of, 161
  treatment of, 162
Gastroesophageal reflux disease (GERD)
  interventions for, 163
  medical tests for, 162
  signs and symptoms of, 162
  treatment of, 163
Gastrointestinal bleeding
  interventions for, 164
  medical tests for, 163–164
  signs and symptoms of, 163
  treatment of, 164
Gastrointestinal system
  appendicitis and, 154–155
  cholecystitis and, 155–156
  cirrhosis and, 156–158
  Crohn's disease and, 159–160
  definition of, 152–153
  digestion and, 153
  diverticulitis disease and, 160–161
  gastritis and, 164–165
  gastroenteritis and, 161–162
  gastrointestinal bleeding and, 163–164
  GERD and, 162–163
  hepatitis and, 165–167
  hiatal hernia and, 167–168
  hormonal control of, 153–154
  intestinal obstruction and paralytic ileus and, 168–169
  lower tract of, 152
  pancreatitis and, 169–171
  peritonitis and, 171–172
  PUD and, 172–173
  surgical complications of, 242–243
  ulcerative colitis and, 173–174
  upper tract of, 152
Genitourinary system
  acute glomerulonephritis and, 206–207
  bladder cancer and, 205–206
  BPH and, 204–205
  definition of, 203–204
  kidney cancer and, 207
  kidney stones and, 208
  prostate cancer and, 208–209
  pyelonephritis and, 209–210
  renal failure and, 210–211
  testicular cancer and, 211–212
  urinary tract infection and, 212–213

GERD. *See* Gastroesophageal reflux disease
Gestational diabetes mellitus
  interventions for, 147
  medical tests for, 145
  signs and symptoms of, 145
  treatment of, 146
Gigantism. *See* Hyperpituitarism
Gout, 4–5
Graves' disease. *See* Hyperthyroidism
Guillain Barré syndrome, 114

Hematologic system
  anemia and, 28–29
  definition of, 26–28
  DIC and, 32–33
  DVT and, 40–41
  hemophilia and, 33–34
  iron deficiency anemia and, 30–31
  ITP and, 42
  leukemia and, 34–36
  multiple myeloma and, 36–38
  organs within, 26–28
  pancytopenia and, 29–30
  pernicious anemia and, 31–32
  polycythemia vera and, 38–39
  sickle cell anemia and, 39–40
Hemophilia, 33–34
Hepatitis
  interventions for, 167
  medical tests for, 166
  signs and symptoms of, 166
  treatment of, 167
  types of, 165
Hiatal hernia (Diaphragmatic hernia)
  interventions for, 168
  medical tests for, 168
  signs and symptoms of, 167
  treatment of, 168
  types of, 167
HIV. *See* Human immunodeficiency
Hodgkin's disease, 16
Human immunodeficiency (HIV), 12
Huntington's Disease (Chorea), 115
Hypercalcemia
  interventions for, 221
  medical tests for, 221
  signs and symptoms of, 220–221
  treatment of, 221
Hyperkalemia, 222–223
Hypermagnesemia
  interventions for, 225
  medical tests for, 225
  signs and symptoms of, 224–225
  treatment of, 225
Hypernatremia, 218–219
Hyperparathyroidism
  interventions for, 144–145
  medical tests for, 144
  signs and symptoms of, 144
  treatment of, 144
Hyperphosphatemia, 228
Hyperpituitarism (Acromegaly and Gigantism), 136
Hyperprolactinemia, 136–138
Hypertension
  classifications of, 60
  interventions for, 61
  medical tests for, 60
  signs and symptoms of, 60
  treatment of, 61
Hyperthyroidism (Graves' disease)
  interventions for, 134

medical tests for, 133
signs and symptoms of, 133
treatment of, 133
Hypocalcemia
interventions for, 220
medical tests for, 220
signs and symptoms of, 219–220
treatment of, 220
Hypokalemia, 222
Hypomagnesemia, 223–224
Hyponatremia, 218
Hypoparathyroidism, 143
Hypophosphatemia
interventions for, 228
medical tests for, 227
signs and symptoms of, 227
treatment for, 228
Hypopituitarism
interventions for, 136
medical tests for, 135
signs and symptoms of, 135
treatment of, 135
Hypothalamus, 128–129
Hypothyroidism (Myxedema)
interventions for, 133
medical tests for, 132
signs and symptoms of, 132
treatment of, 132
Hypovolemic shock, 61–62

IDDM. *See* Insulin-dependent diabetes mellitus
Idiopathic thrombocytopenic purpura (ITP), 42
Immune system
AS and, 14–15
AIDS and, 12–13
anaphylaxis and, 13–14
cancer and, 263
definition of, 11–12
Epstein-Barr virus/chronic fatigue syndrome and, 20–21
KS and, 15–16
lyme disease and, 21–22
lymphoma and, 16–17
mononucleosis and, 19–20
rheumatoid arthritis and, 17–18
scleroderma and, 18–19
septic shock and, 22–23
SLE and, 23–24
Infection
intervention for, 242
medical tests for, 241
signs and symptoms of, 241
treatment of, 241
Infertility
causes of, 184
intervention for, 185
medical tests for, 184–185
signs and symptoms of, 184
treatment of, 185
Influenza, 99–100
Insulin guide, 147
Insulin-dependent diabetes mellitus (IDDM)
interventions for, 147
medical tests for, 145–146
signs and symptoms of, 145
treatment of, 146
Integumentary system
burns and, 195–196
cellulitis and, 198
definition of, 194–195
dermatitis and, 196–197
pressure ulcers and, 198–199

skin cancers and, 197
wounds and, 199–200
Intestinal obstruction and paralytic ileus
interventions for, 169
medical tests for, 169
signs and symptoms of, 168
treatment of, 169
Intraoperative period
anesthesia and, 237
attire during, 236
closure and, 237
risk during, 237
surgical routine for, 237
surgical team for, 236–237
Iron deficiency anemia
interventions for, 31
medical tests for, 31
signs and symptoms of, 30
treatment of, 31
ITP. *See* Idiopathic thrombocytopenic purpura

Joints, 1–2

Kaposi's sarcoma (KS), 15–16
Karnofsky functional performance scale, 264
Kidney cancer, 207
Kidney stones, 208
KS. *See* Kaposi's sarcoma

Leiomyomas. *See* Uterine fibroids
Leukemia
acute, 34
chronic, 34
interventions for, 36
lymphocytic, 34
medical tests for, 35
myelocytic, 34
signs and symptoms of, 34–35
treatment of, 35–36
types of, 34
Lung cancer
categories of, 90
interventions for, 91
medical tests for, 90–91
signs and symptoms of, 90
treatment of, 91
Lyme disease
interventions for, 22
medical tests for, 21
signs and symptoms of, 21
treatment of, 21
Lymphocytic leukemia, 34
Lymphoma, 16–17

Melanoma, 197
Meningitis, 115–117
Menstruation cycle
follicular phase of, 178
luteal phase of, 179
ovulatory phase of, 178
Mental health
anorexia nervosa and, 253–254
anxiety and, 248–249
bipolar disorder and, 251–252
bulimia nervosa and, 254–255
definition of, 247–248
delirium and, 255–256
depressive disorder and, 250–251
initial disorder signs of, 247
neurotransmitters and, 248
panic disorder and, 249–250

Mental health *(Cont.)*
   schizophrenia and, 252–253
Metabolic acidosis
   interventions for, 226
   medical tests for, 226
   signs and symptoms of, 225
   treatment of, 226
Metabolic alkalosis
   interventions for, 227
   medical tests for, 226
   signs and symptoms of, 226
   treatment of, 227
Metabolic syndrome (Syndrome X/Dysmetabolic syndrome), 148
Metastases, 261
MI. *See* Myocardial infarction
Mitral insufficiency, 73
Mitral stenosis
   interventions for, 74
   medical tests for, 74
   signs and symptoms of, 73–74
   treatment of, 74
Mitral valve prolapse
   interventions for, 75
   medical tests for, 74
   signs and symptoms of, 74
   treatment of, 75
Mohs' surgery, 197
Mononucleosis, 19–20
MS. *See* Multiple sclerosis
Multiple myeloma, 36–38
Multiple sclerosis (MS)
   interventions for, 118
   medical tests for, 117
   signs and symptoms of, 117
   treatment of, 117–118
Musculoskeletal system, 1–10
   bone classification of, 1
   carpal tunnel syndrome and, 2–3
   fractures and, 2, 3–4
   gout and, 4–5
   joints and, 1–2
   muscles and, 2
   osteoarthritis and, 5–6
   osteomyelitis and, 6–7
   osteoporosis and, 7–8
Myasthenia gravis
   interventions for, 119–120
   medical tests for, 119
   signs and symptoms of, 118–119
   treatment of, 119
Myelocytic leukemia, 34
Myocardial infarction (MI)
   interventions for, 51
   medical tests for, 50
   signs and symptoms of, 50
   treatment of, 51
Myocarditis, 62–63
Myxedema. *See* Hypothyroidism

Nervous system
   ALS and, 107–108
   Bell's Palsy and, 108–109
   brain abscess and, 109–110
   brain tumor and, 110–112
   cerebral aneurysm and, 112
   cerebral hemorrhage and, 106–107
   Chorea and, 115
   CVA and, 122–124
   definition of, 103–105
   divisions of, 103–105

   encephalitis and, 113
   Guillain Barré syndrome and, 114
   meningitis and, 115–117
   MS and, 117–118
   myasthenia gravis and, 118–120
   Parkinson's disease and, 120–121
   seizure disorder and, 124–125
   spinal cord injury and, 121–122
NIDDM. *See* Non–insulin-dependent mellitus
Non-Hodgkin's lymphoma, 16
Non–insulin-dependent mellitus (NIDDM)
   interventions for, 147
   medical tests for, 145–146
   signs and symptoms of, 145
   treatment of, 146

OB-GYN
   breast cancer and, 179–180
   cervical cancer and, 180–181
   definition of, 178–179
   dysmenorrhea and, 181
   ectopic pregnancy and, 182
   endometrial cancer and, 182–183
   infertility and, 184–185
   ovarian cancer and, 185–186
   ovarian cysts and, 186–187
   pelvic inflammatory disease and, 187–188
   preeclampsia and eclampsia and, 190–191
   Rh incompatibility and, 189
   trophoblastic disease and, 188–189
   uterine fibroids and, 183–184
OGTT. *See* Oral glucose tolerance test
Oncology. *See also* Cancer
   biological therapy for, 273–274
   biopsy and, 266
   BMT for, 274–275
   cancer cell proliferation and, 259
   carcinogenesis of, 260
   cell dysfunctions of, 260–261
   chemotherapy for, 270–273
   classification of, 261–262
   definition of, 259
   emergencies from, 276–279
   infiltrative emergencies from, 280
   metabolic emergencies from, 280
   metastases and, 261
   normal cell proliferation and, 259
   obstructive emergencies from, 279–280
   radiation therapy for, 267–270
   surgical therapy for, 267
   treatment goals for, 266
Oral glucose tolerance test (OGTT), 145
Oral hypoglycemic agents, 147–148
Osteoarthritis, 5–6
Osteomyelitis
   intervention for, 7
   medical tests for, 7
   signs and symptoms of, 6–7
   treatment of, 7
Osteoporosis
   interventions for, 8
   medical tests for, 8
   signs and symptoms for, 7–8
   treatment of, 8
Ovarian cancer
   intervention for, 186
   medical tests for, 185
   signs and symptoms of, 185
   treatment of, 186
   types of, 185

Ovarian cysts
  interventions for, 187
  medical tests for, 186
  signs and symptoms of, 186
  treatment of, 187
  types of, 186

PACU. *See* Postanesthesia care unit
Pancreatitis
  interventions for, 170–171
  medical tests for, 170
  signs and symptoms of, 169–170
  treatment of, 170
  types of, 169
Pancytopenia. *See* Aplastic anemia
Panic disorder, 249–250
Parathyroid glands, 131
Parkinson's disease
  interventions for, 121
  medical tests for, 120
  signs and symptoms of, 120
  treatment of, 120–121
Pelvic inflammatory disease
  causes of, 187
  interventions for, 188
  medical tests for, 187
  signs and symptoms of, 187
  treatment of, 188
Peptic ulcer disease (PUD)
  interventions for, 173
  medical tests for, 172
  signs and symptoms of, 172
  treatment of, 173
Pericarditis
  interventions for, 64
  medical tests for, 64
  signs and symptoms of, 63–64
  treatment of, 64
Perioperative period
  cardiovascular complications in, 238–240
    intervention for, 239–240
    medical tests for, 239
    signs and symptoms of, 239
    treatment of, 239
  classification of, 233
  definition of, 233
  gastrointestinal complications in
    intervention for, 242–243
    medical tests for, 242
    signs and symptoms of, 242
    treatment of, 242
  infection in, 241–242
  intraoperative period in, 236–237
  postoperative period in, 237–238
  preoperative period and, 234–236
  respiratory complications in
    intervention for, 241
    medical tests for, 240
    signs and symptoms of, 240
    treatment of, 240–241
Peripheral artery disease
  interventions for, 54
  medical tests for, 53
  signs and symptoms of, 53
  treatment of, 53–54
Peritonitis
  interventions for, 171–172
  medical tests for, 171
  signs and symptoms of, 171
  treatment of, 171

Pernicious anemia
  interventions for, 32
  medical tests for, 32
  signs and symptoms of, 31–32
  treatment of, 32
Pheochromocytoma
  interventions for, 143
  medical tests for, 142
  signs and symptoms of, 142
  treatment of, 142–143
Pituitary gland, 129–130
Pleural effusion, 91–92
Pneumonia
  interventions for, 93
  medical tests for, 93
  signs and symptoms of, 92
  treatment of, 93
Pneumothorax
  interventions for, 94
  medical tests for, 94
  signs and symptoms of, 93–94
  treatment of, 94
  types of, 93
Polycythemia vera
  interventions for, 39
  medical tests for, 38
  signs and symptoms of, 38
  treatment of, 38–39
Postanesthesia care unit (PACU), 237
Posterior pituitary gland, 130–131
Postoperative period
  assessment during, 237–238
  consciousness return progression during, 238
  pain management during, 238
Preeclampsia, 190–191
Preoperative period, 233–234
  clearance for, 234
  informed consent for, 234
  teaching in, 234–235
  transfer in, 235
Pressure ulcers
  interventions for, 199
  medical tests for, 199
  signs and symptoms of, 198–199
  stages of, 198–199
  treatment of, 199
Primary aldosteronism (Conn's syndrome)
  interventions for, 142
  medical tests for, 141
  signs and symptoms of, 141
  treatment of, 142
Prostate cancer, 208–209
PUD. *See* Peptic ulcer disease
Pulmonary edema
  interventions for, 65–66
  medical tests for, 65
  signs and symptoms of, 65
  treatment of, 65
Pulmonary embolism
  interventions for, 99
  medical tests for, 98
  signs and symptoms of, 98
  treatment of, 98
Pyelonephritis, 209–210

Radiation therapy
  implants and, 269–279
  patient care and, 267
  side effects of, 267–268
  types of, 267

Raynaud's disease, 66
Renal failure, 210–211
Respiratory acidosis
    interventions for, 95
    medical tests for, 95
    signs and symptoms of, 94
    treatment of, 95
Respiratory system
    acute respiratory failure and, 96–98
    ARDS and, 80–81
    asbestosis and, 81–82
    asthma and, 82–84
    atelectasis and, 84
    bronchiectasis and, 85
    bronchitis and, 86–87
    cor pulmonale and, 87–88
    definition of, 79
    emphysema and, 88–90
    function of, 79–80
    influenza and, 99–100
    lung cancer and, 90–91
    pleural effusion and, 91–92
    pneumonia and, 92–93
    pneumothorax and, 93–94
    pulmonary embolism and, 98–99
    respiratory acidosis and, 94–95
    surgical complications of, 240–241
    tuberculosis and, 95–96
Rh incompatibility, 189
Rheumatic heart disease, 66–67
Rheumatoid arthritis
    interventions for, 18
    medical tests for, 18
    signs and symptoms of, 17
    treatment of, 18
Rule of nines, 195

Schizophrenia, 252
Scleroderma, 18–19
Seizure disorder
    interventions for, 125
    medical tests for, 124
    signs and symptoms of, 124
    treatment of, 124
Septic shock
    interventions for, 23
    medical tests for, 22
    signs and symptoms of, 22
    treatment of, 22
SIADH. *See* Syndrome of inappropriate antidiuretic hormone
        secretion
Sickle cell anemia
    interventions for, 40
    medical tests for, 40
    signs and symptoms of, 39–40
    treatment of, 40
Simple goiter
    interventions for, 135
    medical tests for, 134
    signs and symptoms of, 134
    treatment of, 134–135
Skin cancer, 197
SLE. *See* Systemic lupus erythematosus
Spinal cord compression, 277, 279
Spinal cord injury
    interventions for, 122
    medical tests for, 121
    signs and symptoms of, 121
    treatment of, 122
Squamous cell skin cancer, 197
Superior vena cava syndrome, 278, 279
Syndrome of inappropriate antidiuretic hormone secretion
        (SIADH), 280
    cancer and, 277–278
    interventions for, 139
    medical tests for, 139
    signs and symptoms of, 139
    treatment of, 139
Syndrome X. *See* Metabolic syndrome
Systemic lupus erythematosus (SLE)
    interventions for, 23–24
    medical tests for, 23
    signs and symptoms of, 23
    treatment of, 23

Testicular cancer, 211–212
Third-space syndrome, 280
Thrombophlebitis
    interventions for, 68
    medical tests for, 68
    signs and symptoms of, 67–68
    treatment of, 68
TIA. *See* Transient ischemic attack
Tissue plasminogen activator (TPA), 123
TNM. *See* Tumor, lymph nodes, metastases classification
TPA. *See* Tissue plasminogen activator
Transient ischemic attack (TIA), 122
Tricuspid insufficiency
    interventions for, 76
    medical tests for, 75
    signs and symptoms of, 75
    treatment of, 75
Trophoblastic disease
    interventions for, 189
    medical tests for, 188
    signs and symptoms of, 188
    treatment of, 189
    types of, 188
Tuberculosis, 95–96
Tumor, lymph nodes, metastases (TNM) classification,
        264

Ulcerative colitis
    interventions for, 174
    medical tests for, 174
    signs and symptoms of, 173
    treatment of, 174
Urinary tract infections, 212–213
Uterine fibroids (Leiomyomas)
    interventions for, 184
    medical tests for, 184
    signs and symptoms of, 183
    treatment of, 184

Ventricular fibrillation
    interventions for, 71
    medical tests for, 70
    signs and symptoms of, 70
    treatment of, 70–71
Ventricular tachycardia
    interventions for, 72
    medical tests for, 71
    signs and symptoms of, 71
    treatment of, 71–72

Wounds, 199–200